Mr Hilhouse of Bristol
Shipbuilder for the Navy
1749–1822

This book is dedicated to my wife, Zena. Without her help, enthusiasm and encouragement it would not have been written.

Adrian & Dee

Mr Hilhouse of Bristol
Shipbuilder for the Navy
1749–1822

Andrew Whitefield

Drew.

16/12/10.

Author.

redcliffe

First published in 2010 by Redcliffe Press Ltd.,
81g Pembroke Road, Bristol BS8 3EA
www.redcliffepress.co.uk
info@redcliffepress.co.uk

ISBN 978-1-906593-68-1

British Library Cataloguing-in-Publication Data
A catalogue record for this book is available from the British Library

Design and typesetting by Stephen Morris www.stephen-morris.co.uk
Printed by HSW Print, Tonypandy, Rhondda

Contents

Foreword

FROM 1756 TO 1815 BRITAIN WAS IN COMPETITION OR OPEN CONFLICT WITH FRANCE, A FAR LARGER state both in territory and population. When the final act was played out, the French Emperor Napoleon was a prisoner, the economy of France was in ruins and Britain commanded a navy which had more battleships than the rest of the world put together. This final and complete victory has left British hindsight tinged with complacency and the feeling that this result was inevitable. But this was not so. At times the country was losing badly and in great danger from invasion, particularly during the French Revolutionary and Napoleonic Wars, when there were periods when the continuance of the country as an independent state was in doubt.

The government had therefore to harness every part of the economy to fight these wars, to produce ships, ordnance, uniforms, munitions, provisions and fresh food, horses and animal fodder, which were needed in ever-increasing quantities for the hundreds of thousands of men who were under arms. Although government dockyards, gunpowder factories, ordnance and victualling yards were extensive, hundreds of merchants and manufacturers of every sort were needed to contract with government. Private capital for war loans came from the institutions and individuals in the City of London. Indeed, a critical advantage over France was the close relations between the government and the City in mobilising capital and specie.

The difficulty in seeing this complex commercial and industrial picture as a whole is that while the state archives in the National Archives at Kew are voluminous and continuous, the business and personal records of government contractors have generally not survived. None were more important than shipbuilders, a business which was very susceptible to business failure because of the size and value of the ships and length of time required to complete them. These men are slowly being rescued from the shadows of history. Modern historians have written on several: Henry Adams of Bucklers Hard and others in the Solent, the Barnards of Ipswich and London, and we have recently learnt about the successful businesses run by two widows, Mary Ross and Frances Barnard. Andrew Whitefield now provides a valuable picture of one of the most important shipbuilders in the second half of the eighteenth century.

James Martin Hilhouse learnt how to build a warship from oak during a seven-year apprenticeship to a naval shipwright in a naval dockyard, unusual for a merchant shipbuilder. From his teenage years and his very young entry into managing his own yard in Bristol, he always maintained a very close relationship with influential people in the Navy, unusual for the time. He built up his business through orders for small merchant ships and from shrewd investments in privateers in the Seven Years War. His most prosperous shipbuilding years were during the American Revolutionary War, but some of the most interesting pages in this book cover the lean years of the late 1780s and 1790s, when government orders dried up, effectively transferring risk to the private sector. Hilhouse sold some of his yards and retrenched, but recovered after the Peace of Amiens, and the business survived into very recent times. The author has not neglected a detailed portrait of the social and domestic life of a successful man, intelligent and artistic, the friend of artists such as Nicholas Pocock and Philip de Loutherbourg. But most importantly, Hilhouse produced well-built and successful ships.

Roger Knight
Greenwich Maritime Institute
University of Greenwich

Introduction

WRITING THIS BOOK HAS BEEN NOT SO MUCH THE FULFILMENT OF A LIFETIME AMBITION BUT MORE a combative response to a challenge that crept up on me as I did research for my recently acquired MA at Bristol University. I should explain that as I collected the available information about James Martin Hilhouse, I became more and more impressed by what this man achieved and more and more dismayed by how this has been overlooked by historians writing about Bristol's famous and sometimes infamous maritime past. He made a seriously significant contribution for which Bristol has to be thankful and he deserves greater recognition for this and some permanent memorial.

In the last quarter of the eighteenth century Bristol's position in overseas trade was in decline partly because of the frequent wars but mainly because of the difficulties and expense of navigating the Severn and the Avon Gorge. Hilhouse created a reputation for shipbuilding and repairing at the port which brought skills and employment that gave prosperity for the city for many generations to come. This was a valuable achievement and I hope that my endeavours will stimulate interest and that more information will be collected about the importance of shipbuilding and repairing and the place of James Martin Hilhouse in Bristol's maritime past.

For my dissertation I had at first intended to write about my family's modest ship trading adventures on the north coast of Devon and Cornwall but Bristol and shipbuilding for the Navy soon seemed the obvious subject, a fact that was put to me clearly and emphatically by Professor Roger Knight who was at the National Maritime Museum when the Hilhouse collection was deposited there and knew the contribution a study could make to the sometimes controversial subject of merchants building for the Navy at this period in our history when the Navy and merchant shipwrights and seamen played such a vital part in securing our future. I am most grateful to Roger Knight for his guidance at the outset and the Foreword he has now written.

I have to say that a personal connection has been a factor and looking back I realise that the late John Hill's inscription in his book *Ship Shape and Bristol Fashion* that he gave to me recognising my involvement with the Charles Hill Company for many years as their legal advisor has played a part in this endeavour. I now regret that during that time I had no idea that I would become so interested in maritime history and so we did not take time to discuss the past. I am sure there is much more that I would have learned from him had we done so. I have however been helped by members of the Charles Hill family in researching this distant and not related founder of the Company and am particularly grateful to Michael Hill for his knowledge of the significance of the paintings, plans and models donated by the Company and for his support and enthusiasm.

I would have liked to give space to explain how the many contributions that I have received came to happen and give greater acknowledgement to the people who have helped me in different ways during my researches but hope they will accept that this is not practicable.

So grateful thanks to the Hill family, John, Richard and Michael for their encouragement and to the many members of the Charles Hill Company with whom I had some memorable experiences, especially Alec Foulds, Ron Thomas and John Luckwell.

I would like to acknowledge the help that I have received from the Bristol University Maritime Archaeology Department staff and students, particularly Kimberly Monk, Mark Horton, Roger Morriss, John MacMillan, Phil Cooper; David Williams, Nigel Sommerville and the staff at the Bristol Records Office; Pat Denny, former Society of Merchant Venturers archivist; Andy King and staff at the former Bristol Industrial Museum (now subsumed into M Shed); Sheena Stoddard and the staff at the Bristol Museum and Art Gallery; John Loosely, secretary of the Bristol and Gloucestershire Archaeological Society; the Bristol City Council Central Library staff and the City Archaeologist, Bob Jones and Michael Handford, author. Further afield, thanks to the National Maritime Museum and staff at the Caird Library and Plans Department; the Devon Record Office at Exeter and the Glasgow Record Office, with particular thanks to Eileen Macgilveray for her research into the Hilhouse Scottish roots; Dr Ann Coats of the Dockyard Society; Rory Cook at the Science Museum, London and David Moore of Sotherby's. Thanks are also due to Victoria Arrowsmith-Brown, publishing advisor, Madge Dresser, historian and editor, Mark Myers, collector and artist, Francis Greenacre, author and curator and Alex Bevan of Bevans Solicitors for facilitating secretarial help when needed.

Andrew Whitefield
Bristol, November 2010

The Hilhouse Family Tree

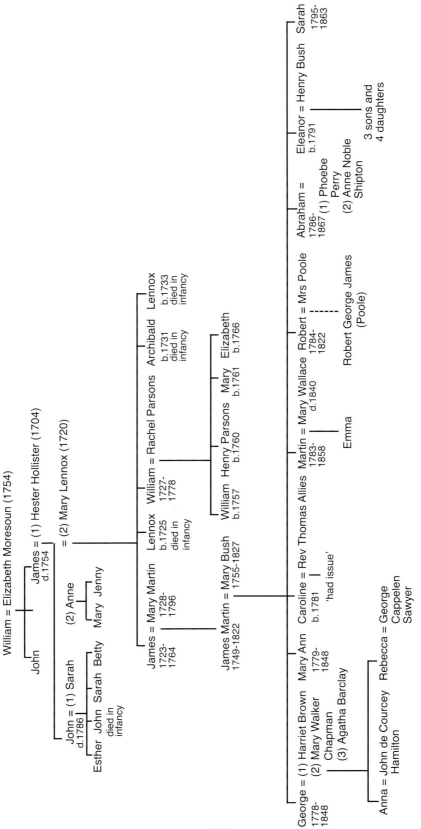

CHAPTER ONE

❦

The Rise of the Hilhouse Family

JAMES MARTIN HILHOUSE WAS BORN IN 1749 INTO A FAMILY OF MERCHANTS WHO HAD BEEN established in Bristol for two generations. He was to become not only the city's foremost shipwright and shipbuilder but a figure of national importance, with technical skills that equalled those of the Naval architects of the royal dockyards and a shrewd business brain that led him to found the shipping company of worldwide repute that became Charles Hill and Sons of Bristol.

His grandfather was a Scot who became a successful Bristol merchant and laid the foundation for James Martin's father to build upon his success; both were determinedly ambitious and bold opportunists with a strong sense of public duty as well as a flair for making money. Their careers in Bristol spanned the years between 1704 and 1764, a time of great change, opportunity and expansion of trade in the city. A period of prosperity, then, but not one of peace: the Hilhouses had to survive the vicissitudes and disruptions to trade caused by four periods of war,[1] with their resultant losses at sea and threats of invasion. Nevertheless, they prospered, creating the wealth and network of relations, friends and contacts which paved the way for James Martin's outstanding career.

The story begins not in Bristol but in Glasgow, which in the 17th century was an important trading port and the centre of Britain's tobacco trade with America. On 26 June 1674 James Martin's great-grandfather William Hilhouse married Elizabeth, the oldest daughter of Thomas Moresoun, a merchant and member of the burgess and guild brethren of Glasgow; a good career move, it might be said, since marriage to a burgess's daughter automatically elevated William to that status. The couple had two sons; John, the first, born in about 1678, became a mariner and master of the 200-ton privateer *Dragon*, obtaining a letter of marque during Queen Anne's War in July 1703. John remains a somewhat shadowy figure, but this link with seafaring and privateering is of note considering the later career of the Hilhouse family in Bristol.

William and Elizabeth's second son, James Martin's grandfather, was named James. A very robust, enterprising and influential character in his later life, he left Glasgow for Bristol at around the turn of the 18th century, and took a leaf out of his father's book when, soon after arriving in the city and setting up in trade, he became a burgess by marrying the daughter of one. He was enrolled on 5 July 1704,[2] 'James Hilhowse merchant', taking an oath of obedience and paying 4s 6d which he must have seen as money well spent. His new wife was Hester, the daughter of John Hollister, a well-to-do linen draper, and his

Broad Quay in the early eighteenth century during James Senior's time, showing merchants on the quay and ships tied up along St Augustine's Reach, with the Cathedral and Brandon Hill in the background. Society of Merchant Venturers

wife Jane, who in 1696 were recorded as living at Castle Precincts in Bristol with their children John, William, Charles, James, Mary and Hester.[3] In fact there might well have been a trade connection between the Hilhouses in Glasgow and the Hollisters in Bristol: the heads of both families were prominent burgesses in their cities, and it was common for merchants in large trading ports to foster links between one another. After all, building up suitable family connections was an excellent way of expanding the network.

James's move to Bristol was not a piece of opportunism by a man of humble origin[4] but a carefully planned operation by an established and far-sighted operator, and he made rapid progress down south. He and Hester had one son, named John after Hester's father, but no other children survived and Hester died young. James did not remain a widower; the burgess books for the brethren in Glasgow record that on 30 September 1719 Mr James Hilhouse, 'Merchant in Bristol', was admitted to the burgess and guild brethren of Glasgow 'gratis'.[5] It is likely that the honour was bestowed on him on his second marriage, for which he returned to his home city. His new wife Mary was connected to the Lennox family, prominent merchants in Glasgow, so again it was a marriage that made shrewd business sense.

The couple returned to Bristol and their first son was born on 3 April 1721. This was James, who became known as James junior and was the father of James Martin. James and Mary had a second son whom they named Lennox, who died, and their next son, named William after his grandfather, was born on 14 July 1727; two later sons, Archibald and another Lennox, again did not survive childhood. James's three surviving sons all married at least once, and had children. John married Sarah and had four children, though their only son, also John, died in childhood. His second wife, Anne, gave him more daughters but again no sons, so John left no male successor. It is said he proved a disappointment to his successful and ambitious father in more than this respect.

James's second son, however, proved to be all his father could have wished for. James junior grew up to be an able and shrewd businessman, and father and son worked shoulder-to-shoulder in building up their business in Bristol. The third son, William, though six years his brother's junior, was close to him as they grew into adulthood, and worked with him and their father in many different ventures, as well as with other merchants. In brief, William built the family reputation alongside James junior; and importantly, he took on a fatherly role for his nephew James Martin when James junior died at the age of 43 in 1764.

The two James Hilhouses built up a respected reputation and feeling of trust among their fellow merchants, as well as the fortune that enabled James Martin to launch his new shipbuilding business in 1772, and to discover how they achieved this calls for a little historical background. The end of the 17th century was a time of great change, particularly in Scotland. The Glorious Revolution of 1688, followed by the Act of Toleration in 1690, made the position of the Protestant Dissenters in Scotland somewhat easier than it had been under the Stuart kings. Congregations of Dissenters grew up throughout the kingdom and by the beginning of the 18th century Bristol had a significant population of them. Coming south from a Dissenting family in Glasgow, it was natural for James to gravitate to like-minded people in Bristol, and he quickly joined the Society of Presbyterian Dissenters at their Meeting House at Lewins Mead. This was the wealthiest and most important of the Dissenting congregations in Bristol, and it gave him immediate entry to a close-knit circle of contacts. His signature first appears on the minutes of the society's annual general meeting on 22 December 1705,[6] and regularly in the years after that.

The Lewins Mead congregation had been formed in the early 1690s, after the Act of Toleration. While Dissenters no longer had to meet in private and were able to keep some records, they were still barred from certain public offices. They were an independent-minded, determined and forthright group of prominent citizens, however, who believed that they would eventually be accepted in the established church but in the meantime would work hard and exert influence outside it. They set great store by the importance of education: the Lewins Mead congregation opened a young men's meeting room in 1706, followed by a school for boys in Stokes Croft in 1722.[7] James served as treasurer for the meeting house, a tribute to his financial prudence, and one of his regular tasks was to allocate its numbered seats to members of the congregation; who sat where and in particular, who sat in the gallery, appears to have been a matter of importance. Special attention was given to the position allotted to the widow of a member, as the congregation took great care of its own, and this was another sensitive task with which James was entrusted.

The Lewins Mead community had among its members people who took their religion and social responsibility very seriously. They came from many parts of Bristol and outside; a lawyer from Clifton attended with his family for many years, as did a clergyman from North Somerset. The majority of the congregation, however, were merchants, who gained knowledge of and confidence in one another by meeting regularly, and names that recur throughout the Hilhouse story are the Nobles, the Farrs, the Eltons, the Munckleys and the Garlicks. The last, like the Hilhouses, were first-generation Bristol, and they also conspicuously used the Lewins Mead connection to help in their business. As the years passed by, the group played an increasingly prominent part in the life of the city, and it was said that at one time all but one of the aldermanic bench were members of this meeting house.[8]

Having established himself in the Society of Presbyterian Dissenters, James lost no time in becoming involved in another influential group in Bristol commerce, the Society of Merchant Venturers. Membership of the society, which controlled the port of Bristol, ensured access to the city's most lucrative trading ventures, contacts and status, and was restricted only to merchants, with mere retailers barred. The family involvement with the brethren in Glasgow had made James all too aware of the advantages of this kind of cachet, and by November 1707 he was a member, by payment of a 'fine'.[9] In the early 18th century only about 100 Bristol merchants were members, but the 'fine' system enabled non-Bristolians to join the society. It was also used by the Miles family, originally from Ledbury, and another Herefordshire family, the Brights. The 'fine' was £30 (equivalent of £2,550 at current values),[10] but this investment was to prove invaluable in enhancing James Hilhouse's standing and the business careers of future generations of his family. His three sons and his grandson, James Martin, were all Merchant Venturers, as were James Martin's four sons. This tradition of family succession was seen as part of the society's strength, and it was regularly reinforced by intermarriage between Merchant families.

James came to Bristol to develop a business importing sugar, and it did not take him long to do that. By the 1720s he was a leading member of the trade in the city and on 27 October 1724 was one of only 100 signatories nationwide to an agreement to fix the 'tares' for sugar imported from Jamaica, the Barbadoes and Leeward Islands.[11] 'Tares' was the weight to be attributed to the casks in which the sugar was contained, and while these were usually hogsheads, they varied in size and weight from island to island and plantation to plantation. The names on this document were those of prominent Bristolians, mayors, sheriffs and masters and wardens of the Society of Merchant Venturers.

Sugar was the most profitable trade in the city at the time and those with any chance of participating in it made every effort to do so. James Hilhouse was not alone in coming to Bristol with that aim. The Garlicks,[12] fellow members of the Lewins Mead Meeting House, as we have noted, stemmed from a family member who had migrated from Worcestershire and became apprenticed to an apothecary in 1692 in order to use his scientific skills to get into the lucrative sugar trade. When the Lewins Mead Meeting House made an appeal for funds in 1722, Garlick made a donation of £2 10s, in contrast with the £200 donated by the established leader of the congregation, Abraham Elton, and the substantial £130[13] contributed by the rapidly up-and-coming James Hilhouse. Five years later Garlick's rapport with Hilhouse and Elton was such that he could persuade them to invest in shares in his Welsh Iron Foundry Company,[14] which proved to be a very profitable venture for them all. James's central business might have been in sugar, but he was always alert to other opportunities and, along with other merchants, had interests in several fields. The rise of the Garlicks in Bristol was not as rapid as that of Hilhouse, possibly because Garlick was not a Merchant Venturer, but the family enjoyed support from the influential Eltons and became established sugar refiners.

By 1728 James was a well-known trader in the commodity, with a sugar baking house next to the Lewins Mead Meeting House. He traded with Britain's West Indian colonies, taking a share in the cargo of merchant ships outward bound from Bristol, above all to Jamaica, with stores and supplies for the plantations. On arrival, these goods were disposed of and Hilhouse's agent would negotiate with the plantation owners for raw sugar for the return voyage. If any other profitable trading opportunities arose, his agent had discretion to take them up, and one of them demonstrates Hilhouse's nose for a good deal. A Jamaican cotton planter, Edmond Pruett, had died, and when his affairs were being wound up, James's man stepped in to buy a quantity of cotton costing £60 7s 7d from the estate.[15] What it sold for in England is not known, but we can be sure it made a significant profit. In addition to Pruett's goods there were slaves on the estate, two of whom were imported by another Bristol merchant, a 'negro boy' for £5 5s and a 'negro wench' for £10 10s.

Unlike several of his fellow sugar merchants, Hilhouse had no financial stake in the West Indies sugar plantations. One who did was William Miles, another incomer to Bristol, who as an apprentice knew James senior but whose close links were with his son James. Miles's correspondence with his factor, Tharp, on his extensive plantations in Jamaica, gives a vivid picture of the pattern and conduct of the trade between Bristol and the West Indies.[16] The Pinney family from Bristol also had large sugar plantations, in their case on the island of Nevis, and their records are equally illuminating on the problems as well as profits of running the business successfully.[17] Another family with whom the Hilhouses were to have family links was the Brights, who had extensive holdings in Jamaica and whose correspondence casts yet more light on the Bristol sugar trade.[18]

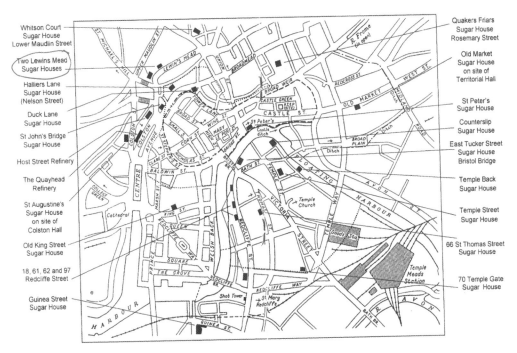

Location of Bristol's sugar refineries in the eighteenth century.

James Hilhouse's sugar house at Lewins Mead.

Given James's ambitions and success in the Bristol sugar trade, his entrepreneurial instincts inevitably led him to have some involvement in the slave trade with which it was often closely linked. Bristol merchants had been pressing for the abolition of the monopoly that had been granted to The Royal Africa Company in London and in 1698 they succeeded. This trade began slowly to increase at Bristol and by 1759, when the Company of Merchants Trading to Africa was formed, Bristol had 237 members, London 147 and Liverpool 89. During the second half of the century this trade dramatically declined at Bristol. John Hill asserts that there is no evidence of the Hilhouse family having taken any interest in this 'nefarious trade' and while this may be true as far as James Martin is concerned, there is evidence of some early involvement by James and later by his son William. It is tempting to avoid delving in to this sensitive subject but for the sake of completeness the evidence should be looked at, keeping in mind that in early days even Quaker merchants were engaged in this trade and there was a widely-held notion that transporting slaves from the West African jungle and the barbarities of tribal warfare was a humanitarian act.[19]

The Bristol Port Books have been researched for details of the ships trading to Africa, their onward passage and return voyage and the results recorded in four volumes published by the Bristol Record Society. An entry in Volume 1 states that in 1709 James Hilhouse was the Agent in Bristol for the *Union Sloop* owned by Christopher Stephenson (the Agent was usually a merchant with a share in the venture). The *Union Sloop* carried an outward cargo on which duty of 10% – amounting to £38 7s 9d – was paid and she was destined for Guinea where she was intended to acquire 140 slaves for transport to Jamaica. She arrived there on 13 June 1710 with 113 slaves. She was mistakenly reported as having been taken but arrived back in Bristol on 24 November 1710. She made a similar voyage in March 1711 but this time William Langdon was the Bristol agent.

In 1713 James Hilhouse & Co were the owners of the *Duke of Cambridge*, 120 tons and 14 guns. Her outward cargo is not recorded but she was bound for Madeira and Barbados where on 31 Dec 1714 she delivered 100 slaves and then returned to London on 26 April 1715. There are no further records in the Bristol Port Books of the *Duke of Cambridge* being engaged in the Africa trade. Likewise, there is no further mention of James, but he could have been a shareholder in the many ventures that were taking place involving ships owned by friends at the Lewins Mead Meeting House; for example Samuel Munckley & Co in 1747 owned the *Iris*, which was intended to take 250 slaves to Jamaica but delivered only 161.

James's son William had a number of different partnerships for different ventures and was frequently involved with Samuel Sedgely who was heavily engaged in slave trading. In 1753 the partnership of Cheston, Sedgely and Hilhouse owned the *Eugenie* and on 22 February 1754 she delivered 250 slaves to Kingston Jamaica and on 13 December 1755, in partnership with Berry and not Cheston, they delivered a further 223. This seems to be the extent of the family's involvement with the transport of slaves from Africa to America. It was a slight involvement and generally not as profitable to them as sugar

The Sugar Cane and the Art of Sugar Making. Engraving for the *Universal Magazine.*
Courtesy Bristol Record Office AC/WO/16/58.

trading and privateering.[20] James Martin's position in the matter is considered later when a committee of Bristol merchants, including his main customers, was formed in 1789 to oppose the abolition of slavery.

From the time of his arrival in Bristol James worked hard at his numerous businesses and within the Society of Merchant Venturers, rising to become its master in 1730. By this time he was aged about 50 and James junior had not yet joined him in partnership. He appears to have entered his year in office with enthusiasm and it is recorded that, unusually, he made a contribution of ten guineas towards the cost of his inaugural dinner and that a year later, in 1731, he imported 56 gallons of French wine from Bordeaux for his personal consumption.[21] No doubt he needed to replenish his depleted cellar after his year in office.

Documentary evidence of James senior's business affairs is sadly sparse. In January 1731 he imported six tons and 17 gallons of Spanish wine to trade and a further three tons in the next month; during the 1730s he also leased a dock and a crane from the Merchant Venturers.[22] It must have been a substantial business as the rent he was paying, if it was similar to that paid by the merchant who later took on the lease, was in the order of £160 a year (£13,000-plus today). By 1740 James had given up the lease and was concentrating on his sugar baking business at Lewins Mead, where he was joined by James junior, who had been admitted to the Merchant Venturers 'for that he be the son of James Hilhouse'.[23]

As well as being successful sugar traders and merchants with interests in several fields, the Hilhouses were like many other Bristol merchants in having another profitable string to their bow: privateering in time of war. Privateers were a great benefit to the Royal Navy, providing, as they did, additional ships to come to the country's defence at a time when Britain's enemies had larger and more powerful armies but could mount a successful invasion only if they could transport them to our shores. Privateering was also valuable in helping the Navy protect the country's trade and shipping, on which its life depended, and it also benefited the Bristol merchants by enabling them to continue to trade during the frequent wars, preserving and sometimes expanding their commercial links and bringing prosperity to the port and its hinterland as well as to themselves. Successes in wars created new markets which the merchants could exploit in peacetime. To fit out and man a private man-of-war, however, was a major business expense and carried a high risk. The cost of insurance was frequently prohibitive: it has been estimated that converting a merchant ship to enable it to obtain a letter of marque cost about £8,000. As a result, the risks and expenses were shared among the merchant community in many different partnerships, and the mutual trust and friendships formed by them continued during the periods of peace and prosperity that followed.

The unusually long period of peace since the end of the War of the Quadruple Alliance in 1721, during which Bristol's trade had thrived and the Hilhouse sugar and other businesses with it, came to an end in 1739. Much indignation was aroused in the city by the account given by the captain of the *Sarah*, a Bristol ship that had been seized by a Spanish man-of-war under dubious pretext and towed ignominiously into Havana in the West Indies. The captain, Robert Jenkins, said his ear had been cut off by the Spaniards and on his return to England he even produced it in the House of Commons to demonstrate his indignation at the treatment he had received. *The London Country Journal* reported that 'the breast of every Bristol citizen was fired with martial ardour and an ambition of plucking off as many Spanish ears as would serve to nail to every gate throughout Great Britain'.[24]

The resulting hostilities became known as the War of Jenkins' Ear, and the cause was embraced wholeheartedly in the *Sarah*'s home port of Bristol. Merchants sprang into action. At their first meeting in October 1739 they subscribed £5,000 for fitting out privateers to avenge the insult to their ship and her captain and expected to raise the same amount at their next gathering. A similar measure of determination was shown by the city magistrates: they sat until 3 a.m. on consecutive days to clear the local prisons of inmates awaiting trial by sentencing them to serve on Naval and privateering ships sailing against the Spanish.

A number of vessels quickly set sail from Bristol and one of them, the *Vernon*, was soon successful, capturing a prize valued at £18,000. More triumphs swiftly followed: in February 1741 the *Princess Augusta*, a Bristol privateer with only 14 guns, attacked and sank a significantly larger Spanish privateer of 24 guns off the Isles of Scilly. Soon after that the *Boyd*, with 60 men under Captain Colt, took two privateers off Jamaica. When the Spanish men-of-war approached her, Captain Colt put 48 of his crew on board the two ships they had taken and ordered them to sail them out of danger, while staying on board the *Boyd* with his few remaining men to fight the enemy. Inevitably in such an unequal fight, they were taken prisoner and sent to Cathegena in the rich Spanish Central American colony, but before long they broke out, seized a yawl and did a little plundering before sailing to Jamaica to retake their two captured privateers, earning themselves a glorious reputation back home.

Bristol was often the port of return for ships from the West Indies, and perhaps the most sensational arrival was that of Admiral Vernon on the 6 January 1743, fresh from the famous campaign in which he had captured Portobello from the Spanish. His ship, HMS *Boyd*, docked in the city laden with a vast fortune taken from the Spanish including 30 chests of silver bullion containing 'nine thousand million' pieces of eight, for onward transport to London. The admiral went on to enjoy the hospitality of the mayor, Abraham Elton, a tavern was named after him on the corner of Princess Street and at least three Bristol ships later bore his name.

It was during the War of Jenkins' Ear that the Hilhouses began a profitable association with a redoubtable privateering captain, John Read, which was to last for many years. He began as an employee of their consortium but progressed to become a partner with James Hilhouse and Company in their privateering ventures, becoming a local hero in the process. He was a formidable commander in both the War of Jenkins' Ear, which evolved into the War of the Austrian Succession and lasted from 1739 to 1748, and the Seven Years' War that followed, from 1756 to 1763. He certainly proved a loyal and faithful captain for the Hilhouses in both wars. In the former, James senior was the primary investor and moving force, but in the Seven Years' War his son James junior took on the role. The ship in which the Hilhouses had an interest at the beginning of these wars was the *Constantine*, a galley of 300 tons with 18 guns owned by James Hilhouse's friend and colleague at the Meeting House, Isaac Elton; a fine vessel, but her success in privateering was due to the bravery and skill of her captain, John Read.

A letter of marque[25] for the *Constantine* had to be obtained for her to take part in privateering, a document which authorised a ship to attack, capture or sink any vessel belonging to a nation with which Britain was at war. The legal processes for issuing a letter of marque were internationally recognised and had to be scrupulously followed, with the owners obliged to provide a bond put up by two independent sources to ensure compliance: £3,000 for a ship with a crew of 150 men or more and £1,500 if fewer. Because of its prominent involvement in privateering, Bristol had its own court to give this authority, which made it easier for investors such as the Hilhouses to set up their ventures.

Privateering was a highly organised and regulated activity, as the merchants who

Nicholas Pocock, *The Southwell Frigate, and Tradeing on Ye Coast of Africa* c.1760. © Bristol's Museums, Galleries & Archives. The two scenes, included as part of the engraving of the *Southwell*, illustrate the importance of the African slave trade to the prosperity of Bristol's sugar industry.

invested in these ships risked a lot of money but stood to gain substantial profits. The captain of a letter of marque ship had to be given precise instructions on meeting all eventualities, so owners were careful in their contracts with them, to ensure that the exact terms were clear to both sides. Detailed instructions on the management of the ship were spelled out, with a strategy for cruising and seeking prizes, and above all for the safe-keeping of valuables seized and their safe delivery to Bristol. The term 'cruising' covered the situation when a ship, whether it was a private man-of-war or a letter of marque vessel, was off a direct trading route and actively seeking to intercept enemy ships wherever they were most likely to be. This was the sole purpose of the private man-of-war. She carried no cargo and crew members were usually not paid wages but promised a share of the prizes taken. James Hilhouse junior took part in this sort of venture, but on the whole the Hilhouses' vessels were letter of marque ships, doing some trading and also cruising whenever the captain saw a likely opportunity.

The letter of instruction written for Captain John Engeldue of the Bristol privateer *Southwell*, dated 23 May 1746,[26] is typical of the care taken by owners to encourage and warn their captains. Captain Read's letter of instructions from the Hilhouses would have been similar, as the documents were in a standard form and varied little through the century. One that has been preserved, written by James Martin Hilhouse's friend and well-known Bristol sugar merchant and banker William Miles, is almost identical, as are the letters from the Brights to their captains, written decades later but in the same explicit terms.

The letter to the *Southwell* captain begins encouragingly: 'From our great opinion of your courage and conduct, together with the recommendations of your former owners, we are cheerfully and unanimously agreed to give you the command of our ship...' The reputation of the commander was of prime importance to the investors, who followed ships' captains' fortunes closely; they were reported upon enthusiastically and respectfully by the press and hero-worshipped by the public. The Hilhouses were particularly careful in their choice of commanders, and it generally paid off for them.

The *Southwell* letter continues:

> We herewith deliver you a letter of marque, also instructions from the Lords of the Admiralty, to which you must strictly conform, and they must be read frequently to the ship's company, that they may be careful in a due regard to them. We also deliver to you a book of martial affairs and a copy of the marine treaty between us and the Dutch...

It was important not to transgress in any of these matters if a prize was to be claimed and loss and expense avoided, so 'frequent perusal' of the documents was recommended. Tips on managing the crew were included – for example, to be careful to ensure there was 'no familiarity between (officers) and the seaman, as it may be of very dangerous consequence'. Given that many of the men would have been hardened criminals released from jail expressly to crew the ships, and that mutinies were frequent, this was not a point that needed much emphasising. The crew needed to be trained in the use of firearms and regularly 'exercised with the great guns so that they may not be at a loss when they come to engage with an enemy'. Great stress was laid upon a 'constant and strict watch over your powder room' and the prohibition of 'candles, lanthorns and use of metal implements' when opening casks. Shoes had to be removed on entry to the powder room, while when it came to provisions, there had to be 'frugality that there be neither waste nor want'.

The area in which the *Southwell* was to cruise was defined by latitude, and there were suggestions from the owners on how the captain might improve his probability of taking prizes and regaining prizes taken by the enemy. The matter of getting the prize home without ceasing to cruise was also treated in detail in the instructions. Records had to be compiled and duplicated and sent home to the owners, and it was necessary to have a clerk on board, since so much was at stake. Jewels, plate and other such valuables had to be listed and consigned with a bill of lading, and it was necessary for prizes condemned (sold) in a neutral port to be recorded by the clerk in a book that kept 'a just and regular account of all transactions on board the privateer'. Sending in a taken ship called for a number of decisions by the commander. He had to select one or more officers to sail her into a selected port and enough crew to prevent her from being seized back, and the letter gives some guidance: 'There must be a sufficient number of her men kept on board in order to obtain a condem-nation, and you are to send them as hereunder directed in giving the charge of such to one or more of your officers that are good navigators, and put on board as many of your own people as may be thought necessary to navigate them, observing always to send as many as can secure the prisoners in irons close in the hold or between decks if no room below.'

The captain was advised that small prizes should when possible be ransomed rather than sent in, as the risk of depleting the ship's complement in order to take such a vessel into port was out of proportion to its value. Valuable prizes, on the other hand, were to go to a specified port where there were known agents to deal with them. Very valuable prizes should be conveyed to a safe distance from Falmouth, Kinsale or Bristol 'as winds may offer'.

A cruise was defined as 'four months from the time of taking your departure from the Island of Londie', and the successor to the commander 'in case of your mortality (which God forbid)' was specified. The letter also contained a request that the commander should join another privateer if one was met at sea, as long as it was 'of equal or superior (not less) force than ours'; in these circumstances, prizes taken would be shared equally, but permission was given to make more flexible arrangements if appropriate. The letter concluded in a congenial way:

> We most heartily wish you health and success in this your cruise. We now commit you to the protection of the Almighty in whom we trust for your safety and happy return to Bristol. Your friends and owners of the Southwell privateer.

The difference between being a private man-of-war on a cruise to find prizes and a merchant ship armed with a letter of marque to legitimise aggression could be quite subtle, but at least notionally, the letter of marque ship was engaged in trade. The Hilhouses' *Constantine* was a spectacularly successful version of the latter, making a lot of money for James senior's consortium and later for James Hilhouse and Company and for Captain John Read. She took three prizes in the first three weeks of the war against France, among them a vessel valued at £14,000 and a Martinicoman with a cargo of 173 hogsheads of sugar and 80 pounds of coffee worth £6,000. A little while later, in 1747, Captain Read's vessel arrived at the port of Mahon, Menorca, having taken a French ship laden with 95 bales of cloth worth £5,000, said to be the fifth prize she had seized since the beginning of the war. Apparently all this was on the *Constantine*'s normal trading route in the Mediterranean, without cruising.

These feats were reported by many authorities to be a remarkable example of what an ordinary, well-equipped merchantman with a daring captain could do in collecting prizes as the opportunity arose.[27] On the other hand, the cost of fitting out the *Constantine* and privateers like her would have been considerable, so taking valuable prizes was absolutely necessary if the venture was to be profitable. Many were not, and privateering was a trading venture strictly for wealthy merchants like the Hilhouses, who were prepared to take the risk of capturing no prizes and possibly losing their ship. For James Hilhouse, however, the gamble paid a handsome reward, more than compensating for the disruption to his trade in time of war.

The *Constantine* continued to be successful, as a later report reflects:

On the 2nd January 1748, when bound for Venice on his passage through the Malta Channel, Captain Read fell in with six merchantmen from the Levant for Marseilles.

He took three of them, the *Jean Baptiste*, 12 guns, 58 men, the *St Blaize*, ten guns, 33 men and a polacca. The two larger ships were laden with silk and linen and were valued at £30,000. All three were left in Malta, and the safe arrival of the *Constantine* in Venice was considered important enough to be announced in the *London Gazette*: more success and profit for the Hilhouse venture, acquired again while trading in the Mediterranean.

The effects of these privateering ventures in Bristol are vividly described in accounts of the celebrations of the newly-rich crews once they arrived back home: 'Our sailors are in the highest spirits, full of money, and spend their whole time carousing.' Many hundreds of French prisoners from captured ships were thrust into Bedminster Bridewell prison, and the dashing deeds of the *Queen of Hungary*, *Prince Charles*, *King William*, *Vulture* and *Tryall* kept the people of Bristol abuzz throughout 1744. In the following year the excitement continued when two London privateers, the *Prince Frederick* and the *Duke*, both fitted out at Bristol, towed across the Atlantic and brought up the Avon two French merchantmen valued at upwards of £175,000. They carried 1,093 chests of silver bullion, weighing 2,644,922 ounces, as well as gold and silver wrought plate. Twenty-two wagons were needed to carry away the booty. Regrettably, the crews of the ships were begrudged their share of this fabulous prize, and some years later they took proceedings in the Chancery Court to wrest some reward from the owners.

With the possibility of riches like this, it is hardly surprising that the Hilhouses and their merchant friends took to privateering so eagerly. Indeed, it was a time of great activity and profit for both the city and James Hilhouse. Friendships his family made through these privateering partnerships lasted through generations, most notably with John Noble, whose son married James junior's sister-in-law Anne Martin and who was to play a major part in guiding James Martin in his career and in setting up his new business. Noble was the owner of the *Lion*, which was said to have taken the most valuable prize in the war, the French vessel *Prophet Elias*, and there survives a lengthy written account by that ship's captain about the way in which he and his crew had been dealt with by the Englishmen: 'They treated us like brethren. We are at a loss to express (their) goodness to us; never did prisoners-of-war meet with so much kindness with their enemies.' This testimony shows that there was at times discipline and honour in this lucrative trade, but this was not always so. The boarding and capture of enemy ships called for courage and daring, and many Bristol sailors were killed, many more maimed. A list of the city's privateers showing those that had been captured and recaptured makes plain the risks involved for the crews as well as the investors.

In the course of this hectic period of war James junior entered into partnership with his father in the family business, now named James Hilhouse and Company. In a brief period of peace in 1748, at the age of 28, he married Mary, daughter of Thomas Martin, who had been a tobacco merchant in Swan Lane, Castle Green. Before they wed, James executed a deed of settlement for his wife should he die before her, naming as one of the trustees William Martin, 'merchant of Bristol'. This was her uncle, the younger brother of her father, who had already died; William Martin was a well-respected merchant, sheriff in 1740 and mayor in 1757, and he was assiduous in looking after his brother's daughters and ensuring their good marriages, Mary to James Hilhouse and her sister Anne to Hilhouse's friend John Noble junior. However, no record of the marriage between James and Mary has been found, and an element of mystery is created by a curious affidavit sworn by George, James Martin's eldest son, on 19 January 1830. This simply asserts that his grandparents were married but does not say when or where; married they were, however, and their only son, James Martin Hilhouse, was born a year later, in 1749. He was christened at Lewins Mead Meeting House on Christmas Day that year.

James junior was by now a respected figure in Bristol society. In 1751 he was the treasurer of the Society of Presbyterian Dissenters at Lewins Mead and in the same year a warden of the Society of Merchant Venturers. James senior was beginning to hand over the business to him, while his younger brother, William, was in partnership with Samuel Sedgely. Their trade to Maryland and the Chesapeke for many years included transporting indentured servants and convicts from the Exeter Assizes[28] to the North American colonies, while importing tobacco and pig iron. In another partnership, as Sedgely, Cheston and Hilhouse, they transported slaves between Jamaica, where they dealt with the Bristol Bright family, and Maryland, where they again loaded pig iron and tobacco.

In 1751 came another event that was to influence the future happiness and prosperity of the Hilhouse family, the marriage of George Bush, a cooper and one of Bristol's leading West India merchants, and Mary Bright. She was the daughter of Henry Bright, like James Hilhouse an immigrant to Bristol and a prominent Dissenter, who had prospered both as a merchant at home and through his family's extensive plantations and other business concerns in Jamaica. He had five sons, all involved in the family business, and his daughter Mary was his youngest child. George and Mary's daughter, also Mary, was to marry James Martin Hilhouse in yet another example of the inter-relationships between merchant families which underpinned their commercial life.

At the start of the 1750s the Hilhouse family was doing well in its various trading and privateering ventures, but despite his prosperity James senior, unlike many of his fellow merchants, showed no desire to raise his status by moving home to a more highly regarded area of the city. He remained living in the parish of St Stephens near the port, resisting the temptation to take one of the elegant houses in Queen Square, favoured by several merchants involved in the sugar trade, or up the hill to College Green, to which James junior moved after his marriage. Surprisingly, however, in 1753, the year before his death, he bought a house in Walcot Street, Bath, seeing the investment potential of the then fashionable spa resort. In fact the property was at first seen solely as an investment, and several years passed before any of the family lived there.[29]

Also in 1753 James senior made his will, a document that reveals much about him. In it he makes precise provisions for his eldest son, John, and his children, but the bulk of his estate is left to James junior after providing generously for his youngest son, William. The will begins by giving a legacy of £200 to John plus an annuity of £70 a year, but it then goes on to recite at length the son's indebtedness to his father for bills paid, totalling £4,120. He forgives him the debt but spells out very carefully that the provision to John in the will is in full satisfaction of any claims he might have or 'pretend' to have, either in his own right or arising from his deceased mother Hester's marriage settlement or any other agreements. It appears that John had already received money under this marriage settlement on Hester's death, in addition to the money he had borrowed from his father. There was clearly an element of mistrust of John by James senior, further reflected in the way in which he gave legacies to his son's children. He clearly dealt robustly with John, who must have been a disappointment to him. The eldest son did not share his father's and brothers' business acumen, and indeed went bankrupt – but also unlike his younger brothers he lived to a ripe old age, apparently dependent on charity; the Merchant Venturers' records contain an entry dated 14 March 1786: 'Mr John Hilhouse Pensioner of this Society is lately dead'.

To John's family, however, James senior was quite generous, while making a distinction between the children by his son's first wife, Sarah, and of his second wife, Anne. A number of John's children known to have been baptised are not named in the will, in particular a son called John, but it is likely that these had died in childhood, rather than being discriminated against by their grandfather. In fact all John's offspring named in the will were girls; the legacies came into effect when they were 21, and if they did not reach that age the money reverted to James junior, not their father. James senior expected his legacies to set his grand-daughters up in a trade or business, a significant stipulation: to expect the young women to have to go into trade to support themselves shows a cool appreciation of the reality they faced through their father's financial straits. If they received any of this money in advance, it was to be deducted from their legacy, while he also gave each of the grand-children annual payments of £15 or £13 for their support and maintenance before they reached 21.

While not prepared to pay out John, he showed through his provision for his grand-daughters that he had not abandoned them entirely; and while seeing them as ultimately his son's responsibility, he felt the need to help them in a shrewd way that did not amount to throwing good money after bad. In addition to these family legacies, James senior left £100 to his servant and £50 to the Bristol Infirmary in Maudlin Lane. On his death, James's estate comprised various properties in Bristol and interests in a number of businesses. He specifically referred to the sugar baking business at Lewins Mead in which his son James junior was a partner with him, and to his premises in Baldwin Street, let to soap boilers. In all, his estate was worth £30,000, the equivalent of £1.2 million today.[30]

It is a tribute to his acumen and Protestant principles that he divided the bulk of his estate between his two younger sons, leaving four-sevenths of it to James junior, out of which he had to pay all expenses, and three-sevenths to William. This division, while favouring the elder, was more equal than might have been expected at the time, gave freedom of enterprise to each and so maintained the close relationship that existed between them. Had there been envy or enmity between his father and uncle, James Martin would not have had the support and encouragement he received from William after James's early death. During his life as a merchant James senior had proved himself a determined man of business who could see the opportunities on offer, seize them and make his money work for him. Through the often turbulent years of Bristol's boom as the second trading city in the kingdom he had established a business, a reputation and a fortune for his sons to build on.

Following his father's death James junior, now head of the family, was also busy in civic affairs, becoming sheriff of Bristol in 1755. Insight into his serious personal character, the result of his Dissenting upbringing, can be gleaned from some of the publications he bought for his own pleasure – for example, the sermons of John Conybeare, paraphrases on the books of Job, Psalms, Proverbs and Ecclesiastes, selected sermons on practical subjects by the 17th-century Nonconformist Edward Reyner and interestingly, *A View of Sir Isaac Newton's Philosophy*. His would appear to be a model 18th-century mind, serious and inquiring, and it might well be that his son's wide interests and openness to new ideas, as well as his strict probity, sprang in part from the example of his father.

James junior continued to run the family sugar business and branch out into other ventures, still trading as James Hilhouse and Company. While his father had been successful in privateering ventures in the War of Austrian Succession, James junior had his opportunity to follow this course when the Seven Years' War began in 1756, and also made good money from his ships. In this war against France and Spain the number of commissions for privateers in Bristol again increased, with 344 issued, covering 256 ships averaging 187 tons each.[31] On the declaration of war: 'Immediate measures were taken by the leading merchants and ship owners (of Bristol) for the fitting out of privateers. The zeal displayed on this occasion produced a fleet of cruisers far exceeding anything attempted in the previous wars: for within little more than 12 months nearly 40 Bristol ships had been equipped and sent to sea, over 20 being added in the two subsequent years.'

This initial level of activity fell away through the law of diminishing returns: the number of English privateers cruising was so great that the French did not put to sea. Unemployed sailors became a source of trouble around Bristol docks, particularly those of the free-spirited type recruited for privateering. James junior, following his father's example, ensured that the *Constantine* was engaged very early, while the pickings were good. In December 1756 she took a large ship bound for St Domingo and a French snow or snaw, a type of brig; but in April 1757 she herself was captured and taken by the *Hippopotame* into Marseilles, news that was a serious financial blow to James junior.

Luckily, he had more strings to his bow. He had a share in the *Britannia* and the *Drake* with John Noble, who had an interest in far more privateers than any other Bristol merchant during this war. Apart from Noble and Hilhouse, the *Britannia* consortium included the familiar names of Isaac Elton, Thomas Harford, William Reeve and John James. Captain Charles Davids made a declaration for a letter of marque on 7 July 1756, and during the consortium's ownership, which lasted until 1762, there were two more captains, Fowler and Olive. Several significant prizes were taken but at considerable cost in life and limb. Casualty figures are not entirely reliable, but it appears that more than 100 of her crew were killed in her various engagements and 50-plus wounded. In addition, when she put in to Corunna in 1758, ten men were said to be dead and 80 sick; a high price was being paid by those at sea.

James Hilhouse and Company obtained a letter of marque for the *Fortune* in July 1757, and while the *Constantine* might have been captured, the irrepressible Captain John Read soon reappears as part-owner of the *Phoenix*, jointly with James Hilhouse and Company.

Like Captain Colt of the *Boyd* some ten or more years earlier, he escaped from prison. The foreign gaols could not confine these doughty privateers. In 1758 he took the French privateers *Groignard* and *Bellone*, and the newspapers quoted a letter from the *Phoenix*'s second captain which gives an insight into the fearsome reputation earned by another Bristol privateer, the *Tartar*: 'I told Captain Read that I would board the Frenchmen with the boat, and did so with five men and myself: and by making use of the name of the Tartar man-of-war and presenting my pistol to the captain's breast, struck them with such a panic that they could not stand. My men backed me bravely and we drove them with our cutlasses like a flock of sheep when all on board the *Phoenix* thought we were cut to pieces.' It is a good story but told with tongue in cheek, since there is no way that Captain Read would have stood by and allowed his second-in-command to be killed in this way.

It was on 25 May 1758 that James junior formed a partnership with John Noble and others to obtain a letter of marque for the *Drake*, which very quickly took the 600-ton *Nuestra Senora del Buen Viage* and sent her into Dartmouth. As a very good friend and brother-in-law – he had married Mary Hilhouse's sister, Anne Martin – John Noble was ever active and forthright, and together with another merchant, Robert Gordon, whose family were early supporters of James Martin, he wrote a letter to their MP, Robert Nugent, to highlight the political and other difficulties faced by privateers.

Dated 22 May 1758 and further signed by other eminent Bristol merchants, it called for the protection of the Government in 'our deplorable case of the Dutch captures'. The matter of concern was that of neutral ships' status in time of war. Bristol privateers had captured some Dutch ships, officially neutral but trading with the enemy, France. This led to problems over prize money, and a petition drawn up for presentation to Parliament accompanied the letter. The petitioners alleged that 'at an expense of three hundred thousand pounds they had equipped and sent out a great number of privateers, which had been instrumental in preserving the commerce of the country and annoying the enemy', and they went on to say:

> Many French privateers had been captured, as well as ships laden with provisions, ammunitions and goods for the enemy, and more would have been caught but for the wiliness of the French in shipping their imports in neutral bottoms.

The petitioners, encouraged by the King's declaration that he would not suffer French trade to be carried under foreign flags, had seized vessels flying the Dutch and other colours trading with the French colonies. This had encouraged the petitioners to send out more privateers 'at great expense', and these in turn had captured more neutral ships. Now, they argued, if these were to be returned, as was demanded by neutral governments, many of the petitioners, who had 'adventured all or a large part of their property on the faith of the King's declaration, if not totally ruined, will be greatly injured, and many thousand brave

Cornwallis House, Clifton. James Hilhouse Jnr bought the leasehold as soon as the house was built and lived there until his death. The portico was added in 1813.

seamen, whose sole dependence is upon their prize money, would be reduced to the uttermost distress'. The matter nearly occasioned a war with the Dutch, but eventually one ship was given up to them, and the privateers' owners were ordered to be more careful in their treatment of neutrals in future.

James junior, however, had other matters on his mind. Having accumulated a further fortune through his privateering ventures, he decided to use the money to take another step up the property ladder. In 1758 he and his family moved from College Green up the hill to Clifton, and into one of the most prestigious houses newly-built there; since he had recently been sheriff of Bristol, he felt this magnificent dwelling would suit his enhanced status. In the late 1750s the Society of Merchant Venturers had seen the development potential of Clifton, then a village outside the city, and bought land there. Indeed, one of the most valuable acquisitions made by the society during the century was the manor of Clifton. It granted building leases on its land and one was granted to a Mrs Hibbs, to build two houses on Cornwallis Grove. She kept one for herself and the other was leased to James junior – the splendid Cornwallis House, with its tall, spacious rooms, clean air and wide views across the city and out to the countryside beyond the Avon. The society gave him a 'free gift' of ten pounds to build a roadway to the house.

The move to Cornwallis House clearly indicated the wealth James had acquired, and marked his rise in Bristol society. This impression was reinforced three years later, we learn from the 19th-century Bristol historian John Latimer, who recorded an account of the Duke of York's visit to Bristol on 28 December 1761. As he was the brother of George III and the heir to the throne, the corporation made elaborate plans to impress him by bestowing upon him the freedoms of the city and the Merchants Hall, followed by a magnificent dinner. There would be 400 dishes and a special chef was recruited from Bath. The tableware had to be equally impressive, and was to be provided by 'the wealthier Aldermen and Councillors'. These were listed as: 'Thomas Deane and James Hilhouse, three dozen each; John Durbin and Alderman Smith, two dozen each; Alderman Laroche and Alderman Abraham Elton, Isaac Baugh, Henry Bright, Daniel Harson, Charles Hotchkin and M Mease, one dozen'. As we see, James junior was at the forefront of these wealthy dignitaries, who included two Members of Parliament.

Such a lifestyle, of course, had to be paid for, and James Hilhouse returned to privateering. This time he formed a consortium with John Noble, Isaac Elton and Abraham Watson, all members of the Lewins Mead Meeting House, who invested in the *King George*, a large private man-of-war of 500 tons with a crew of 180; her captain, of course, was the dependable John Read. All started well, and on a cruise early in May 1761 she took a brigantine from Bordeaux and sent her into King Road, off Avonmouth. Soon after this, however, came a serious and unusual setback in the form of a mutiny.

The facts are well recorded, as the ringleaders were prosecuted at the Old Bailey, and the Bristol newspaper *Felix Farley's Journal* contained a full report:

On 5th May when off Cape Ortegal, a general mutiny occurred (on the *King George*). They overpowered the Captain and other Officers whom they secured in a cabin and proposed to massacre by stapling them down on the deck and firing at them with a nine-pounder loaded with round shot, whereby they were to be torn to pieces. They were dissuaded by Mr Gardner, the sailing master, and he was the only person able to carry the ship into any port, would feign have brought to their party by offering him their command, declaring they intended to hoist the Jolly Robin and the Crossbones at the mast and go a-pirating in the East Indies, but he refusing they confined him and took command of the ship themselves. Thomas Smith took the command and running her before the wind and sea towards the Quarnes Bay, which the confined Master seeing and representing the danger of going into that place they again gave him the command and he steered her to Carmarinas in Spain where they took to boats and up to one hundred escaped. Captain Read had his nose almost cut off in the action, one Murphy a ringleader was shot dead and Maine who was also convicted was shot in the back. They had little to say in defence, but complained, though they appeared without occasion, of shortness of allowance and other hardships and each insisted upon his own innocence.

Four of those captured were convicted and two hanged, but while this was obviously not a successful venture for the Hilhouse consortium, it continued to back Captain Read and he was ready for action when war was next declared against Spain in January 1762, and the usual preparations for harrying the enemy's merchantmen fell into place. During 1762 he had several notable encounters with the foe, especially an 'obstinate engagement' with the French *Tiger*, commanded by Captain de Fabry. By this time, however, the Seven Years' War was nearing its close, and 1763 marked the end of James junior's privateering ventures with Captain Read.

Newspapers love colourful heroes, however, and the old sea dog continued to attract their attention, even when he was on land:

> On the 19th June 1758, Captain John Read, late of the *Phoenix* privateer, when near Uphill, was attacked about 3 a.m. by two highwaymen, dressed like farmers, armed with large clubs: but on Captain Read declaring that he would not be robbed by anyone and that he would knock down the first one (who) should oppose him, they gave a signal and made off.

He was clearly a man who commanded respect and at sea he did well both for himself and for the Hilhouses, a wise choice by them as captain of their ships.

In retirement he lived in Frenchay and years after the end of the war was still making news, as the *Bristol Journal* reported in May 1768:

> Certain ill-disposed persons in and about Frenchay have propagated a report that Captain John Read of that place had murdered a negro servant and that Thomas Mountjoy of Whiteshill, surgeon, had dissected the body.

A £10 reward was offered for the exposure of the rumour-mongers, and the report added that: 'in order to clear his character', Captain Read had been to the expense of returning to Frenchay from London and bringing the negro with him, 'not withstanding he had made him the property of another person by sale'. He died a dozen years later in Frenchay, on 10 December 1780, and was given a fitting epitaph:

> A man no less esteemed for his loyalty than his intrepidity, of which he gave eminent proofs in the two proceeding wars with the French and the Spaniards. He commanded several private ships of war out of this port.

Back in 1764, however, the year after the end of the Seven Years' War, came a passing that shook the world of Bristol merchants to its roots. Only six years after moving into Cornwallis House, James junior died at the height of his success, at the age of 43. It was all so unexpected that while he had made his will much earlier, in 1752, he had never revised it, though his wife Mary shrewdly went about compensating for that. The will confirmed the marriage agreement made in July 1748 with William Martin, Mary's uncle, Samuel Brice and John Wraxall, [32] all said to be city of Bristol merchants, in which they would pay to his trustees, in the event of his wife surviving him for a month, the sum of £3,000 – £2,000 to go to Mary for her own use and the other £1,000 to be invested to pay her an income for life. If there had been a child or children, however, she would receive only £1,000, with £2,000 invested for her and the money going to any child or children equally when they were 21. If there were no surviving beneficiaries his brother William should inherit; his wife and trustees should be responsible for the education of any children until they reached 21; and for James Martin and any other sons, the substantial sum of £300 should be available to place them as apprentice 'in such trade or business as judged proper'.

The trustees were his brother William and his friend Samuel Brice, inevitably another prominent Bristol merchant; the papers to enable the trustees to prove the will had been drawn up for signature by the two of them and Mary, but their names were lined through and those of John Noble and Thomas Evans written above. This document, with its significant alterations, was then signed by Mary, Evans and Noble, who accepted a bond of £500 which would be forfeited to the Bishop of Bristol if they failed to provide a full inventory of every item in the estate to the registry of the Episcopal Court of Bristol, and administer the estate in accordance with the law and terms of the will. Of course this inventory would enlighten us greatly on the extent of James junior's estate, but unfortunately searches of the Episcopal Court records have not yet discovered it.

It is apparent that despite the shock of her husband's sudden death and with few close members of her own family to advise her, Mary Hilhouse showed herself a thoroughly competent and decisive woman, able to take control of her own affairs. A document dated 1 September 1764 records:

> Administration of the goods of the above named James Hilhouse deceased with his last will and testament annexed was granted to Mary Hilhouse widow of the deceased and lawful guardian of James Martin Hilhouse, a minor... (Samuel Brice and William Hilhouse joint fiduciary executors named in the will having first renounced).

It was Mary who arranged for these two executors to be superseded. The will had, after all, been made 12 years previously, in different circumstances. The reasons for this major change are not given, but she and James would have discussed the future of their only son and decided on the provisions they wanted to make for him. His unexpected death meant that he had not made the changes to his will before he died, so Mary carried out his wishes, knowing his high regard for John Noble, who as his brother-in-law as well as his friend was particularly suited to guiding their son. She and William knew that James and John Noble had had many discussions during their privateering ventures in which they had looked into the future of the port of Bristol, seen what was lacking and identified the opportunities that shipbuilding presented. William was happy to renounce the obligation in favour of Noble, knowing that he himself would be readily accepted as a father figure by James Martin, and Mary would be confident that he would be a reliable support for her in the immediate future.

This, then, provides a rational explanation for what might at first seem to have been an uncharacteristically spontaneous change in arrangements, but Mary, as we have seen, was not a woman to shy away from important issues. Another early decision she took after James's death was for her and her son to leave Cornwallis House[33] and go to live with William Hilhouse, his wife and their lively young family in their spacious house at 12, St James Square. At this time William and Rachel had three young children – William, who was seven, his brother Henry Parsons, four, and Mary, three; their last child, Elizabeth would be born two years later.[34] In making this decision, Mary had her son's welfare in mind as much as her own, and it is testament to the close family bond that the arrangement was a happy one.

With the sudden death of his father, James Martin's childhood effectively came to an end, and he was faced with deciding on the course of his own future. He had much going for him: the people James junior had entrusted with his only son's welfare and guidance; the substantial fortune he was able to bequeath him; and the best legacy of all that James Martin Hilhouse could have received – the traits of character and example he inherited from his father and grandfather. Now his future was up to him.

CHAPTER TWO

☙ ❧

1765-1772: Apprentice to a True Master

JAMES HILHOUSE'S DEATH IN 1764 BROUGHT SUDDEN AND UNEXPECTED CHANGES FOR HIS SON. James Martin was 15 years old, an only child. For the first nine years of his life, from his birth in 1749, he had lived with his parents in their first house on College Green, above but not far from the teeming river, docks and harbour amid warehouses and trading premises clustered in the tight-knit streets at the hub of commercial life in Bristol. He would have been aware, if only as the background to his life, of the businesses in which his father, grandfather and uncles were engaged, and the excitement in the city when the privateering ships came back to port with news of their successes during the Seven Years' War, which started when he was seven. Then, when he was nine, the family had moved up the hill to the elegance of Cornwallis House in the fashionable village of Clifton. Now, with his father's death, all this came to an abrupt end; his mother was a 36-year-old widow with a 15-year-old son whose future career had to be set in motion from his uncle's house.

The most pressing preoccupation in the months after his father's death was discussing the arrangements for his apprenticeship. Much as James junior enjoyed the fruits of his success, he had no intention of allowing his son to take them for granted, and he expected him to work hard, as he and his father had. He felt the most important legacy he could leave the boy was to buy him a suitable apprenticeship. As we have seen, in his will he ordered that a sum not exceeding £300 should be laid out to secure him an apprentice 'to such trade or business as shall be judged proper'. This might at first seem surprising, certainly as far as joining the Society of Merchant Venturers was concerned; completion of an apprenticeship was indeed one qualification for membership, but the Hilhouses themselves had demonstrated that there were other ways in. After all, the family had first joined the society through the payment of a 'fine' and James junior had attained burgess status and entry to the Merchant Venturers as the son of his father; this course would equally be open to James Martin, but an apprenticeship was clearly a matter upon which the father placed great importance.

He did not specify the field in which James Martin should be apprenticed – after all, back in 1752 he had had no way of knowing what talents his toddler son would show as he grew up, and he was also quite shrewd enough to realise that the pattern of Bristol trading would continue to evolve in the future. It is certain that in the years since he had written his will he had come to have definite ideas in mind, but he saw no need to put them in writing. It had become clear to him that shipbuilding and ship repairing were of central

Joseph Farington, *Chatham Dockyard*, 1785-1794, oil on canvas © National Maritime Museum, Greenwich, London. BHC1782. The layout of the dockyard had not changed since Hilhouse's time.

importance to merchants in Bristol in their trade overseas, and even more so in time of war; war, after all, had been almost continuously the background to James junior's working lifetime and he had observed that unlike merchant traders who might suffer in times of hostility, shipbuilders prospered, particularly if they could win Royal Navy contracts.

In shipbuilding an apprenticeship was of course essential, and there were many advantages in being trained by the Navy in their dockyards. James junior's thoughts on this were known to the men he chose as his son's trustees as well as to his brother, and he talked about the matter in depth with James Martin himself. Any doubt over whether this boy who was the heir to a considerable fortune would have the grit and determination to branch out and start up a business in a new direction, rather than follow the easier route of coasting in the family trade, was allayed as he grew up and his character and talents became obvious. John Noble was eminently suited to mentor the young James Martin: he was engaged in discussions with William Champion and the Farr brothers to launch a shipbuilding business at Farr's Dock in Hotwells.

As leading Bristol privateers, the Noble family was well known in the royal dockyards, the nearest of which to Bristol was at Plymouth. The Nobles' reputation and that of James junior as enthusiastic privateers whose deeds helped the Navy as well as themselves was well known to the Plymouth dockyard officers, and it was this connection that secured for James Martin an apprentice master there. Many merchant shipbuilders would have been willing to take him on and take the £300, but John Noble saw the advantages of the training the young man would be given in the Navy's specialised and disciplined environment. He was also far-sighted, assertive and confident enough to think further ahead, and believe that James Martin would be capable of impressing the Navy and winning orders to build its ships. After all, this was the John Noble who·when he became mayor of Bristol in 1791, travelled to London in his regalia and surprised the judges in the High Court of Justice Admiralty Division by claiming his right to a seat on their bench, by ancient statute or custom. His strong influence at this point and later in acquiring the dock at Hotwells was crucial in guiding Hilhouse's career. He must be seen as an eminence grise, the most important person in the young man's story following the death of his father.

His plans would of course have come to nothing if James Martin had not had the aptitude, enthusiasm and determination to follow his advice; but he had, and over and above that he was intelligent, artistically talented and well educated in the skills he would need to become a competent shipwright. There is no record of where he was educated, but his family would have ensured that he received the best schooling in the city, with a view to his continuing their upward rise in society. Maybe he attended the school founded by his grandfather and other early Presbyterian Dissenters at Stokes Croft in 1722. The Lewins Mead Meeting House started the school, and it seems probable that his father was educated there in the 1720s and early 1730s. By the 1750s and early 1760s, however, there were other opportunities at expanding education establishments near both College Green and Cornwallis House. No surviving attendance records for Bristol schools show his name; his cousin Richard Bright, a few years younger than him, was sent away to the Reverend Mr Seddon's Nonconformist Academy in Warrington, where he received an outstanding education from some of the foremost scientific men of the time, but there is no evidence that James and Mary opted for that option. What is certain is that by the time he embarked on the next stage of his education at the Navy dockyard at Woolwich he showed himself to be a capable and confident youth with a sound grasp of mathematics and special draughtsmanship skills. He was used to discussions with serious and intelligent people and was well able to cope when he encountered the highest-ranking dockyard officers.

Once the decision on an apprenticeship in a Naval dockyard had been reached, it remained to find him an apprentice master – and it was here that John Noble's contacts again came into play. From 1750 and into the Seven Years' War Joseph Harris had been the assistant master shipwright at Plymouth, outstanding in his work and a rising man. In 1765 he moved to Woolwich royal dockyard with promotion to master shipwright at a salary of £150[35] a year, along with extra payments. On 29 June 1765, at the age of 16, James Martin became one of four 'servants' or apprentices training under him, and he soon reaped the benefit. After two years at Woolwich Harris moved on and up again, this time to Chatham, the Navy's most important shipyard, and his 'servants' went with him. His salary rose to £200 a year, and he remained at Chatham until he retired in 1777. In reality, he stayed in the yard even after that, dispensing advice when it was needed, such was the esteem in which he was held; indeed, his name is recorded as the builder of some of the Navy ships in the yard, a recognition not usually accorded to Royal dockyard shipwrights.[36] In brief, Hilhouse simply could not have trained under a more accomplished master.

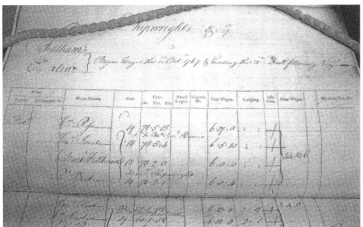

Entry in the Chatham Dock Yard Ordinary Pay Book, October 1767. Hilhouse's name is third from the top, grouped with his fellow apprentices. © National Maritime Museum, Greenwich, London. HIL/1.

The transition from the comfortable, familiar surroundings of his uncle's house in Bristol to the unknown environment of a bustling Naval dockyard outside London was a big step, but he took it in his stride. On his arrival at Woolwich he moved into Harris's home, along with the three other apprentices. For practically all his seven years' apprenticeship, William Ross, Francis Jones and Richard Bechinhoe were Hilhouse's colleagues and fellow 'servants'. They had to pay some contribution towards their board and lodging in addition to the initial payment of £300, but being together in this way they must have formed a close relationship. We know nothing of the background of the other three, or what they went on to do in their careers, but for Hilhouse, an only child whose father had just recently died, the company of three other young men with similar interests to his was most welcome, and their shared experiences made a lasting impression upon him.

Life as Harris's apprentice was hard and demanding. The records show that from the start of his apprenticeship Hilhouse worked long hours. There were 78 or 79 'working days' each quarter, and a working day was from 6 a.m. to 6 p.m. Hilhouse did not work any 'Nts' (nights) until he had been at Woolwich for nine months, which was probably the usual practice for new apprentices. 'Nights', involving five-and-a-half-hour shifts, were regarded as the equivalent of a 'day', so one can imagine that they were not altogether unwelcomed. 'Tides' of one-and-a-half hours were the usual form of overtime, and Hilhouse is recorded as working many of them; indeed, in his last three years he did what seems an amazing amount of overtime, as did his three colleagues. In the final year of his apprenticeship, 1771 to 1772, he worked 313 days, 30 nights and 70 tides; in the previous year he had worked similar days and nights but also a staggering 414 tides.[37]

Joseph Harris certainly got the most possible out of his apprentices, and the early training stuck, for Hilhouse continued this work ethic ingrained in him during his time at Woolwich and Chatham when he came to set up his own yard. The amount he and his colleagues did is particularly surprising since his apprenticeship coincided with a rare period of peace, when the pace in royal dockyards traditionally slowed down; but at least he had the satisfaction of being paid for all his long hours of work, seeing his earnings progress steadily as he became more skilled. His final rate of 2s 4d a day was significantly more than he paid his apprentices when they were on top rate four years later at his Hotwells dockyard.

Hilhouse's apprenticeship took place during a period when the traditional designs and methods of building ships for the Navy were under review. Britain's encounters with the French in recent wars had led to comparisons being made and serious questions being raised about the Navy's vessels. At Chatham, Hilhouse was able to study the latest theories and practices in ship design and building through access to the intelligence gained from the capture of French vessels, and their close examination in the dockyard. Their construction was carefully examined as, rightly or wrongly, French ships were generally regarded at that time as superior to their British counterparts. In fact this was a contentious issue, hotly debated, but their lines, technical details and sailing qualities were sometimes adopted or adapted. Frigates came under particular scrutiny because of their important role as ships of speedy communication in home waters, as well as in service off the Caribbean and the North American eastern seaboard. It was now accepted that in the many parts of the world the Navy had to patrol, frigates were the eyes of the fleet, able to sail independently of the convoys, gathering intelligence of enemy movements and capable of taking on all but the large ships of the line.

During his time at Woolwich and Chatham Hilhouse gathered first-hand knowledge of a variety of ships built in both yards, some new and revolutionary, others based on updated older designs. Among the latter was the *Barfleur*, an 80-gun three-decker launched at Chatham the year after Hilhouse arrived there, based by Thomas Slade, a name forever associated with the design of HMS *Victory*, on a venerable 1719 pattern. Her construction took from 1762, when her keel was laid, to 1768, the leisurely pace perhaps reflecting the lack of urgency felt in the Navy after hostilities ceased in 1763. Despite her vintage design, the *Barfleur* enjoyed a distinguished and long career, achieving fame as Admiral Hood's ship at the Battle of the Saintes in 1782.[38] The keel of the *Formidable*, her sister ship which served as the flagship of Hood's superior, Admiral Sir George Rodney, at the same famous battle, was laid at Chatham in 1769, and Hilhouse was also involved in her building during his last years at the dockyard. This was not, of course, the size of vessel he had in mind to build himself, but these massive ships of the line were the pride of the Navy and the largest built in the Royal dockyards.

The *Raisonable*, 64 guns, was more modern in style, being a Slade design in the new Ardent class, built at Chatham between 1765 and 1768; her later fame was as the first ship Nelson served on as a midshipman. Without doubt, Hilhouse's work on her at Chatham was useful when he came to build her sister ship in his own dockyard. Another Slade design of 1769, encapsulating the latest in Navy thinking, was the *Roebuck*, whose keel was laid in 1770. The first in the class that bore her name, she was an elegant 44-gun two-decker

Envelope of Noble's letter to Hilhouse at Chatham which provided the
first clue to Hilhouse's important apprenticeship to Joseph Harris.
Courtesy Bristol Record Office.

with a distinctive stern, and Hilhouse saw her lines again when he built the *Serapis* in the
same class. It was perhaps the Enterprise class of 36-gun frigate, however, a 1770 design
produced by John Williams, the chief navy surveyor, that most captured Hilhouse's imagi-
nation; the *Siren* in this new class was built at Chatham between 1771 and 1773, so she was
unfinished when he completed his apprenticeship. Her lines made a profound impression
on him, however, as he saw them appearing on the stocks, and it was no coincidence that
four years later he laid another Enterprise class frigate's keel in Bristol.

Hilhouse felt well prepared on his return to Bristol to set up his own shipbuilding
business. He had seen first-hand and worked on many vessels built to the latest specifica-
tions, and as well as his good fortune in serving his apprenticeship under the foremost
shipwright in the royal dockyards, he formed another important relationship that was to
have a major influence on his career. Working as assistant to Joseph Harris at Woolwich
was a surveyor and ship designer named Edward Hunt, upon whom the young Hilhouse
made a very good impression. The younger man in turn appreciated the quality of Hunt's
work, and the two became friends. As was so often the case in the Hilhouses' world,
friendship could carry with it commercial advantages, and in later years an informal
business relationship developed between the two of them when Hilhouse began building
ships for the Navy. Edward Hunt progressed to become at first joint navy surveyor with
Sir John Williams and then, after the latter's retirement through ill health, the main ship
designer and overseer of shipbuilding for the Navy in both the royal dockyards and
merchant yards. This clearly was excellent news for Hilhouse.

During his seven years' apprenticeship he had extensive experience of every aspect of
the work carried out in two of the foremost Naval dockyards in the country and single-
mindedly made the most of his opportunities. He worked on every stage of building Navy

ships of all sizes, from laying the keel to the final fitting out of the rigging; he learned the importance of the choice of timber and how to work with it; he saw the imperative of correctly costing the various components, and the need to keep strict account of all expenditure; he studied ships' drawings and plans, learned the necessity for good design by studying the details of captured French ships and observing the work of his superiors; he was involved in handling a large work force in a way that used it most efficiently; and he understood the value of treating apprentices well and fairly and training them correctly.

Above all, perhaps, he observed the workings of the all-important Navy Board in its dealings with the dockyards, and understood how its systems worked. He learned what the Navy wanted and how it obtained it. His time was well spent, and he was sure that his future was on course and would be successful. During his training at Chatham he proved to have a real aptitude and the requisite skills for his chosen profession. His name appears at the top of Harris's list of apprentices – in recognition of his abilities, since he was by no means the most senior in terms of length of service.

Hilhouse completed his seven years on 30 June 1772 and went back to Bristol immediately, bringing with him a combination of his inbred self-discipline, determination and capacity for hard work and a thorough technical knowledge of ship design and building and the workings of a large dockyard. Very early on he had been convinced of the need to create a dockyard capable of building ships not only for merchant clients but for the Navy, and influential contacts made at Chatham and Woolwich bolstered his confidence that he could build ships for the Naval fleet to designs not previously built anywhere else in Britain. The self-belief that had already impressed those he met at Chatham, not least Edward Hunt, does much to explain the apparent ease with which he moved on to the next stage of his career. Even before his apprenticeship had come to an end he had planned his next move, and with the help of his mentor John Noble he had started negotiations to lease a shipyard at Hotwells. He lost no time in making a smooth and rapid transition from apprentice to shipyard owner and shipbuilder – a journey eased not only by his own ability but by the substantial wealth previous generations of Hilhouses had passed down to him.

CHAPTER THREE

૭૪૪૭

1770-1776: 'The Finest Docks on the Avon'

James Martin Hilhouse celebrated his 21st birthday in 1770 – a landmark event in that not only did he attain his majority, but he took charge of his fortune. He interested himself in his inheritance immediately, and took time off from Chatham to come home to Bristol to execute some documents and make changes to the lease he now owned on the premises in Baldwin Street occupied by a soap maker. He also gave serious thought to his future career. Two years earlier John Noble had himself entered the ship repairing and building business. In 1768, together with William Champion, he had gone into partnership with Thomas Farr at Farr's Dock at Hotwells. The Farrs were shipwrights and since Noble and Champion were ship owners and merchant investors, the joint venture made good sense. Indeed, four years earlier, William Champion had embarked upon an ambitious project to build a large floating dock and two dry docks close by at Hotwells. Hilhouse was very much aware of this, and listened intently to what Noble had to say about it in 1770. With the realisation of his inheritance and the freedom it brought, Hilhouse began to think seriously about his future plans; at that time he had two years of his apprenticeship to complete, but any idea he might have had of pursuing a career in the royal dockyards was now firmly supplanted by an ambition to achieve success independently, backing his judgement with his own venture in Bristol.

Business was not going well for Champion. He had been very successful in manufacturing fine porcelain and traded with America in this and the copper and brass his family also produced in this country. The business thrived and he employed as one of his captains Nicholas Pocock – but then his porcelain interests were dealt a serious blow by Josiah Wedgwood, who challenged his patent and enjoyed strong political support in doing so. As a consequence Champion's fortunes were severely damaged, despite his strong family trading connections in America, and by 1770 he was forced to sell his Hotwells dock project in a still-uncompleted state. The auction took place on 24 June, but it was not well attended and a rope maker, John Fowler, was quietly able to buy the incomplete floating dock for £2,615 and pay an extra £1,420 for the house, land and dry docks next to it.

These disappointingly small sums caused some raised eyebrows, and the Bristol diarist William Dyer[39] was not alone in seeing the sale as at 'a low price'. There appears to have been no interest from the Society of Merchant Venturers at this time, but a year later, having done nothing with the dock, Fowler agreed to sell it to the society for what he had paid for it. In fact he was himself a Merchant Venturer, and the deal might simply have been a ruse to acquire this valuable facility with the minimum of attention and thus at 'a low price'. What is certain is that the Merchants wasted no time in setting about adding to it; they extended the two dockyards by buying adjoining land from a Mr Glover so that it could be used for 'ripping up ships and building small vessels', and also acquired further land for a saw pit. The society extended the unfinished floating dock, which had become known as Champion's Dock, and renamed it Merchants Dock.

But all these were prohibitively expensive exercises, and after the work was done it dawned on the society that it could not afford to complete the whole dock scheme and manage it profitably, even though it controlled the Port of Bristol. Early in 1772 it was forced to the conclusion that it would have to dispose of a substantial part of what it had purchased, and at a meeting in April 1772 it decided to try to lease out all the adjacent property it had acquired, apart from the still-to-be-completed Merchants Dock.

The owners of the new business nearby, Noble, Champion and Farr, watched all this with considerable interest. Not only were they well able to assess the potential of what their shrewd partner Champion had begun to create; they developed a plan to realise its true value, and young Hilhouse had the money and expertise to complete the project, the ideal person with whom to share facilities and from whom to take a lease of the smaller of the two dry docks. There would be great benefits for all of them; they just had to make sure that Hilhouse could do the best deal possible with the society when reclaiming Champion's Dock, and in this respect they had a considerable advantage. At that time the master of the Society of Merchant Venturers was none other than Thomas Farr.

There was an immediate need for Hilhouse to put forward a proposal that would take advantage of the Merchant Venturers' predicament and pre-empt further interest; he would offer to take all the property on offer, and after a respectable lapse of time, give a lease on the smaller dry dock to Noble, Champion and Farr. Hilhouse could use his knowledge to complete the floating dock for the society and negotiate special arrangements for them all to use it. The terms of his offer were agreed upon and John Noble put it forward. Surprisingly, he was not a member of the society, and neither was his father; he became a radical supporter of the controversial statesman and philosopher Edmund Burke and the leader of the local Whig party, so he would have found several aspects of the Merchant Venturers not to his liking. Be that as it may, he certainly managed to keep his personal involvement out of the discussions, and was keen to drive as hard a bargain as he could, and so it came about that on 9 June 1772 Noble attended a meeting at the society's hall to put forward Hilhouse's proposal to the master and his committee. Whether the master, Thomas Farr, expressed surprise or merely cool interest is not known, but the outcome was that the proposal was favourably received, pending further discussions. Noble reported back to Hilhouse on the same day, in a letter that later found its way into the society's archives.

'Mr Hilhouse, Sir,' he wrote:

Portrait of John Noble by Bird.
Mayor's Collection, Bristol.
Courtesy Bristol Record Office.

This morning and not before I attended the Committee of the Merchants Hall, and after your proposal had been conveyed, I was call'd in, and the following Resolutions were agreed to, to accept of your proposal of £175 per Annum for seven years, and if after ye term you chuse to continue it 7 years longer You are to pay £200 per Annum. Every Repairation is to be made that is necessary, and for Storehouses etc you are allowed £200, and if a further sum should be wanted, You are to have it at the rate of 5 per cent per Annum. These are the Conditions as nearly as I can recollect, and as it is so far determined. I think it necessary you come down here as soon as possible when everything may be properly settled. These matters however you are to keep to yourself until we meet wch I hope will be soon...[40]

There is a whiff of conspiracy about these proceedings, but they resulted in a plan that proved to be the foundation for the future of shipbuilding at Bristol. Hilhouse was a sensible and cautious young man, well aware of the risks involved in the trade and the all-too-frequent bankruptcies among shipyard owners, but this was a unique opportunity to acquire what were said to be 'the finest Docks on the Avon at a place called Hotwells'.[41] He had no hesitation in going for it: a better chance to start a business to build the ships he aspired to in Bristol was very unlikely to arise. He had the capital to invest, but was nevertheless intent on spending as little of it as he could in the ensuing negotiations. All in all, he was confident of his future, and the way in which Noble concludes his letter throws light on the easy relationship between the two men. 'Mr Champion and myself,' he writes, 'may be in London Thursday evening and may be heard of at the Hum Mums Covent Garden but may not stay more than one day. I sincerely wish you Health and success and I remain Really yours affectionately, John Noble.'[42] They were at ease with each other and familiar with the entertainments London provided.

Hilhouse and Noble worked out the detail so that in early July the latter, on the former's behalf, offered 'to take for seven years certain from March next or 14 years uncertain at his option the whole of the premises advertised (excluding the capital dwelling house) at a rent of £175 p.a. The Smithy being added thereto and the following alterations and additions being made viz: the gates of the Little Dock to be fitted with a capstan and a snatch and croin made across the gates, a house for boiled pitch and a drawing cabin for the Moulding Loft'.[43] How much Hilhouse was advised in his negotiations by Noble is open to speculation, but from the wording of the offer it is clear that the knowledge of the technical requirements for building large ships he gained in the Royal Docks was crucial in informing his proposal. He had a firm idea of the scale of operation he wanted, he knew what he would need in order to build the ships he had in mind and in his offer he concentrated on getting what he would need and on having it provided by the Merchant Venturers as part of the deal.

Hilhouse's offer was not the only one the society received. There was another offer for the Little Dock only for which a Mr R Bond offered a rent of £25 p.a., rising to £50 when improvements had been made. With these two offers before it, the society's committee met on 11 July and had no difficulty in deciding to deal with Noble on behalf of Hilhouse. They generously agreed that they would 'lay out £200 for improvements and expenditure above that would attract additional rent of 5 per cent on the expenditure'. Negotiations went ahead smoothly and by January 1773 the terms of the lease had been agreed. Hilhouse had also negotiated facilities for access, day and night, to ships in the adjacent floating dock – Merchants Dock – which was owned by the society, and this was to prove of great value for fitting out ships once they were launched.[44]

With typical energy Hilhouse set about the task of getting the dockyards completed to his satisfaction. As expected, because of his knowledge and experience of dockyard matters, he was engaged by the society to carry out the enlargement of Merchants Dock and complete this project for them – a contract which immediately generated income for him while his own dockyard was being improved. He assigned the lease of the Little Dock to Noble, Champion and Farr in September 1773, as had been agreed, and at the end of the following month this arrangement was fully accepted by the society, granting the company a lease on the agreed terms. This meant that Hilhouse was in the very satisfactory situation of having the £200 capital expenditure for improvements to the Great Dock paid for by the Merchant Venturers, while any further work he needed to be carried out would be subject to only a small increase in rent. Furthermore, in Noble, Champion and Farr – who had acquired what they wanted quietly and without loud allegations of insider dealing or conflict of interest – he had influential allies to bring pressure on the society to complete their obligations to him speedily.

Hilhouse continued to be demanding and authoritarian in his requirements for his own docks, as the new master of the Merchant Venturers, James Daltera, was to learn in a letter of 9 June 1773:

> Sir, the Storehouses and Saw pits which was erecting for the use of the yard being stopp'd and as my business is at a stand for want of them I beg that you would please to give proper Directions, agreeable to the covenant in my Lease. I am Sir Yr most obedient, James M Hilhouse.[45]

Daltera replied immediately, but his request for plans, estimates and other details was at odds with Hilhouse's sense of urgency:

> ...I await your determination about the building erecting for storehouses and a sawpit, which stopp'd by Order of the Committee. As the 2 walls are erected, the roof nearly finished, and the pit dug, I shall be oblig'd to you for it, as I much want conveniences of that kind...

He concludes by requiring 'Tradesmen' to attend 'as speedily as your convenience will admit. I am with Respect Sir, Yr most humble Serv't, James M Hilhouse'. Not very humble, it seems, but well-mannered and very confident for a young man just starting his career. He was obviously not to be baulked.

Thanks to his determination in pressing the society to carry out its obligations, Hilhouse's planned improvements to his docks went ahead fast, and a month or so later he was in a position to begin shipbuilding and repairing at Hotwells. On 12 February 1774 a general meeting of the Merchant Venturers admitted James Martin Hilhouse, aged 26, to 'the Hall and to the freedom' of the society, 'for that he is the son of James Hilhouse late a member hereof'. He immediately began to contribute energetically on the society's committees dealing with shipping and dock matters, while ensuring his own interests were served in relation to his dock. As for the Merchant Venturers, it is fair to assume that they acted swiftly to make him a member, being aware that his representative John Noble was not.

By October 1774, with the yard taking shape to his liking and orders in his books, Hilhouse's confidence was such that he offered to take a lease on the dock for 21 years, so long as certain further improvements were made. He stipulated that three launching slips should be created, believing this would free the dry dock to be used for repairs and enable him to build as many as three new ships at a time.

The extent and appearance of the Hotwells dock at this stage of Hilhouse's career is best illustrated by the assessment of the respected architect and surveyor James Paty in the 1776 survey commissioned by the Merchant Venturers. Facilities there continued to evolve during this period of intense activity and are described in the particulars for the auction of the premises after Hilhouse gave notice to quit some years later, on 28 January, 1787:

> The dock is 265 foot in length at the bottom and 44 foot upwards in width at the gates and is capable of receiving a fifty gun ship. The yard is very spacious and there are three slips for launching. A crane for landing timber. Moulding lofts, Sheds. Saw pits. A steam kiln. Smiths shop. A ground for melting pitch and tar. Two small tenements for a foreman or workman.[46]

From the start, his family's connections were of great value in attracting business, though his own reputation was already earning him respect. One of his first customers was Samuel Munckley, who had come to Bristol from Exeter as a fatherless child, had been adopted and brought up by the Farr family[47] and was a fellow member of the Lewins Mead Meeting House. Munckley had become a very successful sugar merchant, taking over the Whitson Court sugar house, and was so well respected in the community that he was referred to, presumably deferentially, as 'the Chancellor'. Named after his home city, the *Exeter*, at 270 tons, was the first vessel Hilhouse built for him. She traded successfully to Savannah La Mar in Jamaica and in 1776 Munckley placed a further order with Hilhouse for another ship for the West India trade, 'of 300 tons burthen', this time named after that Jamaican seaport. In addition to providing ships for clients, Hilhouse appears to have built speculatively, even at this early time in his career, since *Felix Farley's Journal* for 7 May 1774 contains an advertisement for 'the auction of the ship *Perkins* lying at Mr Hilhouse's dock gates'. It was brave for a newly established shipbuilder to operate in this way, but ample evidence of Hilhouse's confidence. The notice went on to say 'she may be sent to sea at little expense'.[48]

As well as winning orders for ships to build and repair, a priority for Hilhouse was the recruitment of a skilled workforce. Labourers would not be hard to recruit: the traditional business of Bristol's port, where there were already several other shipbuilding firms, meant a ready supply of men familiar with ships and shipbuilding. He took the decision early on to employ his own apprentices and train them to his high standards, but this was a long-term strategy. His immediate priority was to recruit skilled shipwrights to work with and train the novices and labourers, and how he set about this is illustrated by his wages book for 1775,[49] which records in meticulous detail the names of all his workforce, when they worked, what they were paid and the tasks they were employed upon.

Starting his own business from scratch and needing to build a quick reputation for his yard both in Bristol and the wider shipbuilding community, Hilhouse might have been

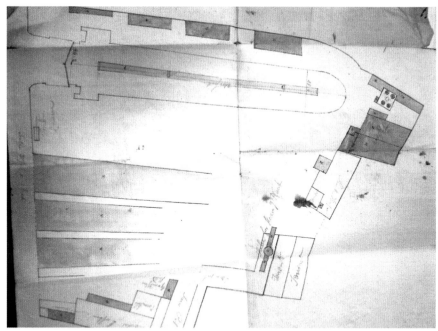

Plan attached to Hilhouse's lease of the Great Dock from the Society of Merchant Venturers in 1774, showing the layout he stipulated for three slips in the key wall, two saw pits, moulding loft, the Great Dock, etc. Courtesy Bristol Record Office.

Paty's 1776 Plan showing the Floating Dock and the layout of the Great Dock and Little Dock, in the early years of Hilhouse's tenure of the Merchants Dock site. Courtesy Bristol Record Office.

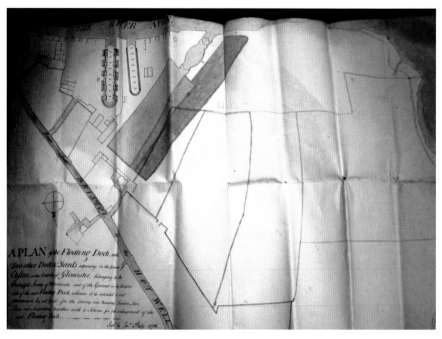

expected to try to persuade some shipwrights he had worked alongside in the Navy dockyards to join him; the shipbuilder Henry Adams at Bucklers Hard, for example, attracted skilled men away from the Navy yard at Portsmouth by offering them a higher wage. This was not Hilhouse's way, and the wages book makes it clear that his key workers came not from Chatham or Woolwich but from nearer home; one or two might have come from Plymouth, the nearest Navy dockyard to Bristol, but there is no proof. A good number came from South Wales;[50] all the men in the merchant yards of the Bristol Channel, and especially those at Newport, Cardiff and Swansea, would have known there was a new young shipwright at Bristol who had a well equipped dockyard, money and influence, and some of the more ambitious ones would have been prepared to join him in the hope of success and steady employment.

While needing to attract good workers, Hilhouse knew his wage bill was a significant component of his overall expenditure. He needed to employ the best he could, yet he would not have been prepared to overpay his men and upset the local economy. It is said that wages paid in merchant yards were higher than at the royal docks, but while this was markedly so on the Thames, there is little evidence of it elsewhere. What is certain is that job security was not as great: in a merchant yard, where the profit motive was imperative, employment could be short-lived, with workers laid off when orders dried up. The norm was for men to be hired to work on a particular ship, rather than being kept on regardless of what else was on the books, as was usual in the Navy yards.

As for wages, a comparison of the Chatham books with the Hilhouse wages book reveals that the average shipwright at the former was receiving 2s 6d a day in 1772, paid quarterly in arrears – or sometimes not; at Plymouth, for instance, the payment for the Christmas quarter for 1774 was not paid until May 1775.[51] While 2s 6d a day was the same rate Hilhouse paid his shipwrights, they received it weekly rather than quarterly in arrears, which was obviously a great improvement. Set against this, however, was the fact that they were not entitled to a pension, unlike Naval workers. Hilhouse's three top shipwrights, some of his sawyers[52] and his main boat builder had wages ranging from 17s 6d to £1 10s per week, equating to 2s 11d to 3s 6d a day, and while a six-day week was the norm, Sundays might have been worked in merchant yards if it was needed to complete a contract.

It seems Hilhouse was paying his workers at about the average rate in merchant yards; for instance, we read that 'Hampshire shipwrights were paid 3s 6d (a day) and on the Thames the rates were 6d higher',[53] and elsewhere that 'a shipwright received on average the sum of 2s 1d as a daily wage'. It must also be remembered that, as Hilhouse discovered when he was an apprentice, overtime of 'tides' and 'nights' commonly increased the pay workers took home; the wages book tells us that some workers on *Medea* were given extra pay at critical times to ensure that work progressed on schedule, and from all we know of Hilhouse's business acumen, it is likely that he paid his men fairly and in return expected them to work hard; in 1770 the average daily wage for a labourer was 1s 4d, while a skilled craftsman like a mason or plumber could earn 2s 6d in Bristol. There was some dissatisfaction among Bristol shipwrights but no indication that Hilhouse had any serious problems at a time when unemployment was high. What made a merchant yard successful, as he was to demonstrate, was good organisation.

When recruiting labour he included almost from the start an unusually high proportion of apprentices – a few, like himself, from wealthy or influential dynasties, but the large majority from local labouring families. He knew what he had reaped from his own apprenticeship with Joseph Harris and believed he could pass on this benefit to others. Taking apprentices into the business had several advantages: they were easy to recruit quickly to meet the sudden and increasing need to fulfil orders, especially when, in the face of the urgent need for ships to fight the American War, he started to receive orders from the Navy, with its strict timetable. Also, in return for their training, Hilhouse believed his apprentices would work hard and acquire burgess status. Having been trained to his own high standards, if well treated they would remain part of a loyal and increasingly skilled and proud workforce capable of building to the latest designs in a rapidly developing maritime world. In brief, their recruitment was part of a long-term strategy for his business, with the added benefit of an economic contribution to the local community.

Apprentices were relatively inexpensive to employ but they had to be fed and lodged as well as responsibly trained. The standard contract was for seven years and stipulated that 'friends' should provide the young man with clothing and washing facilities and the 'master' should provide 'good and sufficient meat and drink'. The Bristol Record Office holds details of numerous Hilhouse apprentices, which give a clear picture of how the system worked in his dockyard. The indenture of Charles Stewart is a good example: it is in a standard form and as well as all the conditions to do with the apprentice's work includes an express prohibition of both fornication and matrimony during the term of the contract.[54] The records show that Stewart did well and went on to become a burgess. At the time he completed the *Medea*, his first ship for the Navy, Hilhouse had a total of 24 apprentices, of whom 18 came from Bristol and the local area. From further afield he took on one from Ireland, one from Dunster, one from Gloucester and one from the West Indies, whose father was a 'planter' and maybe a connection of Hilhouse's family or friends. The occupations of other fathers include two shipwrights, one from 'the Hilhouse dock' and one from 'Bristol', three were mariners, including the father of the apprentice from Dunster, one was a customs officer from Portishead and then there came a weaver, a confectioner, a baker, two shoemakers (one from Ireland), two gardeners and nine labourers. Hilhouse's extensive use of apprentices might well have been exceptional; Henry Adams[55] of Bucklers Hard did not employ any, as he believed they got in the way of the skilled shipwrights he recruited from Portsmouth royal dockyard. In fact he was in a different situation generally, working exclusively for the Navy without having to meet the competing demands of contracts for merchants.

In tracing how Hilhouse developed his new business and organised his workforce, the wages book for 1775-1776 is the most comprehensive and in many ways most valuable surviving record of his business. There are no records for the previous years, many of them destroyed in a fire in 1922. At its simplest, the book records the work Hilhouse had in progress each week and what his wage bill amounted to, but beyond this it shows how each trade was deployed throughout the progress of a ship, from laying the keel to launching. In his first years at Hotwells the wages book shows that Hilhouse was mainly concerned with work on his docks and for his local connections. For example, during the latter part of 1775 the yard was working on Robert Gordon's West Indiaman. In February 1776 Hilhouse and his men began work on new ships for Gordon and Richard Bright. On 13 April work began upon a 'new ship for Mr Meyler' (a business partner of the Brights) and a few months later the well-known privateer John Chilcott also ordered a new vessel. All the while there was a steady flow of repair and refitting work on Bristol merchant ships. To sum up, there was no lack of work for the new yard, and Hilhouse's venture was off to a good start.

In 1776, in the midst of this hectic period for his fledgling business, Hilhouse took another important step. He had been back in Bristol for four years, during which time he had successfully launched his business; he was 27, a Merchant Venturer, accepted into the ranks of Bristol's commercial elite and a man of ample financial security, and he sensed that this was the time to embark on the considerable new venture of marriage. The wife he chose was Mary Bush, the 21-year-old daughter of George Bush, a large, convivial man, a successful merchant and cooper who traded in the partnership of Bush, Elton and Bush, with interests in many fields. Hilhouse proposed marriage to Mary, was accepted and the couple were married on 27 November 1776, by special licence in her parish church of St Thomas. There is every reason to believe that the match met with much approval on both sides: the two families knew each other well and both were connected to the Bright family. George Bush and James and William Hilhouse had long-standing business links and while the Bushes were not Dissenters and were anti-abolitionists, they were a wealthy family of large, congenial people. The marriage proved long-lasting, weathered some difficult times and produced a large family, and there is every reason to believe it was a happy partnership.

On his return to Bristol Hilhouse first moved back into his uncle William's house in St James Square, where his mother continued to live; in 1774 his name is recorded on the poll register[56] as resident in the parish of St James. He is recorded as having voted for Edmund Burke, the prominent politician and benefactor whose national and local fame is commemorated by a statue now in Bristol's Centre, and of whom more later. The newly-married Hilhouses might perhaps have moved into the Dock House on the Hotwells Dock complex, but being cautious, sensible and above all a single young man at the time he first took up the lease of the dock, he had declined to take on the house and it was no longer available. He later rectified this, but in all probability he and Mary started married life by renting a house in Hotwells close to the dock, where he spent very long hours practically every day.

It soon became apparent that Mary was excellent for him. She entered enthusiastically and fully into his life, and provided him with a capable, supportive partner and helpmate in his business. Hilhouse's apprentices, as they joined his workforce, were from now on apprenticed jointly to the couple. She took on responsibility for providing them with food and lodging and acting in many ways as a mother to the succession of young men, most of whom would at first have lived in lodgings near the dock; after the eventual move into the Dock House, some doubtless lived with the family there[57] – a growing family, since the Hilhouses had ten children, of whom eight – four boys and four girls – survived. Theirs was a large and busy household, full of babies, children and apprentices, and what a contrast to his own childhood it must have seemed to the head of the family.

CHAPTER FOUR

☾☽

1776-1783: The American War of Independence

DURING THE FIRST YEARS OF HILHOUSE'S SHIPBUILDING VENTURE IN BRISTOL, WHEN HE RELIED largely upon work from merchants in the city, national events were again moving towards war, with its inevitable effect on trade both nationally and locally. This time the conflict was with Britain's American colonies, the Government's policy towards which had put it at loggerheads with many Bristol merchants; some of them, the Crugers and the Champions, for instance, had families living in the colonies, and identified closely with them and their growing aspirations. Of more pressing concern to other merchants was the effect of increased taxation on their trade, and they were increasingly concerned that the inflexibility of the Government's policy towards the colonialists, and the harshness of its taxes on them, would force them to rebel and sever their lucrative trading connections with Bristol. After all, the Boston Tea Party of 1773 had served all-too-graphic notice that this was no idle speculation. The merchants' frustration was all the more intense as the city's representatives in Parliament did not reflect their concerns but supported the Government line; the lodging of a petition[58] had been to no avail, but in the autumn of 1774 those opposed to the British policy saw their chance to challenge it with the dissolution of Parliament.

Latimer's annals become uncharacteristically animated when he records the passions that were aroused in the 'most interesting election that ever took place in Bristol'. The existing MPs were Lord Clare,[59] well connected and popular with the Bristol Council – the newly constructed main thoroughfare had just been named Clare Street – and Matthew Brickdale, both of whom offered themselves for re-election. Henry Cruger, described by the fervent Whig Lowbridge Bright, Robert Bright's cousin, as 'lately returned from his native country full of American patriotism and politicks' and 'the champion of our liberties to endeavour to save a sinking state',[60] deemed Clare 'an obsequious supporter of the King's American policy', and was enthusiastically welcomed when he offered himself to the Whig Party to oppose him.

Brickdale was also in the firing line and two influential Quakers, Joseph Harford and Richard Champion, put forward Edmund Burke to oppose him. In a febrile run-up to the election, Lord Clare was bitterly disappointed by the lack of popular support for him and withdrew his candidacy, while as there was opposition from the Bristol Tories to Burke's late entry into the contest, he had to present himself in the city with some urgency, covering 270 miles in just over 44 hours in order to do so. Only freemen of the city had the right to vote in Parliamentary elections, and during the 23 days that the polls remained open both parties made frenetic efforts to swell their support and spent money creating new freemen. A common way to obtain the right to vote was to marry the daughter of a freeman, and to this end numerous marriages were hastily arranged; the tittle-tattle of the time had it that many of these couples separated for ever immediately on leaving the church.[61] In addition, 400 freemen were brought to Bristol from London, and others from Ireland, Guernsey and America, and when the polls finally closed the result was Cruger, 3,565; Burke, 2,707; Brickdale, 2,456; and Lord Clare, 283. A resounding victory for the anti-Government Whigs in Bristol then, but nationally Lord North's Tories stayed in power and remained so for many years to come.

Hilhouse's uncle by marriage and close associate, John Noble, was the leader of the Whig party in Bristol, and as we have seen, electoral records show that Hilhouse voted for Burke, thus declaring himself against the policy that led to the war with America. To the alarm not only of Bristol but the great Atlantic seaport of Liverpool, the colonial rebels fitted out privateers to prey upon British merchant shipping to such an extent that trade with America and Africa was at a virtual standstill: the price of tobacco, for instance rose rapidly from sevenpence-halfpenny to 2s 6d.

Discontent in the North American colonies broke out into full rebellion in 1775, and England found itself yet again at war. By 1776 the British Army was involved in a series of bitter campaigns in the American colonies, and the Navy found itself struggling to keep the land forces supplied, to blockade the eastern seaboard to prevent the Americans' supporters, France and Spain, from supplying them with aid, and to try to protect the nation's merchant shipping crossing the Atlantic in both directions. All this highlighted an acute shortage of ships for the Navy, and its first decision was to seek help from British merchants in fighting the enemy, as it had in all previous wars in the century. In April 1777 the Admiralty asked private ship owners to apply for commissions against the American rebels – but while the merchants in Bristol took up the invitation to apply for a letter of marque, this time they did not do so as eagerly as they had done in the past. Some wanted to fit out private men-of-war and dispatch them to seek a fortune, but others merely wished to arm their trading ships to enable them to defend themselves. For Hilhouse the implications were dramatic. He fully understood what war with the American colonies meant for the shipbuilding business, and grasped the opportunity it provided for his yard. Beside that, like his father before him, he was also about to become involved in privateering, and adjusted quickly to the new situation.

In Bristol a general atmosphere of anxiety and tension was brought to fever pitch by events on the morning of 16 January 1777, when there was discovered a 'villainous scheme for destroying the shipping in the harbour'. The *Savannah La Mar*, recently built by Hilhouse for Samuel Munckley, was set on fire during the night as she lay in the port loading for Jamaica, and attempts were made to fire two other ships near by. It was low tide, when all the ships in the harbour were grounded on the mud, and damage would have been immense if the blazes had not been promptly suppressed. This event was followed by several other arson attacks on Bristol businesses, and an intense search for the culprit was boosted by a large reward put up by George III, the city council and Edmund Burke. Watch patrols combed the streets and the climate of fear and anti-American feeling was exacerbated by local politicians all blaming one another. Eventually 25-year-old James Aitken, alias Jack the Painter, was arrested and confessed to the Bristol incidents and a previous arson attack at Portsmouth dockyard. Promptly taken to Portsmouth, he was tried, convicted and hanged there from gallows '67 feet high'.

In such conditions, with the war coming right into Bristol's heart, Hilhouse's order book was very soon filled with commissions from his customers to fit out their ships as privateers, and to build and fit out new private men-of-war. Typically, he was even confident enough to build such ships speculatively. Among the first privateers recorded in his wages book is the *Tartar*, built at Hotwells in 1778. We might recall that 20 years earlier, in Hilhouse's father's privateering days, there had been a famous Bristol privateer by that name, the reputation of which was such that the captain of the *Phoenix* had used it to subdue the crew of a ship he was trying to take. It is possible that in this new war her owners hoped this illustrious name would give their ship some of her namesake's success – and it seems the scheme worked. She cruised in that year, 1778, commanded by Captain John Chilcott, and took the French brigantine *Babet*, regained the captured *Santa Maria* and took a Swedish ship and the French *Ferme*; all these prizes were sent into Bristol.

Hilhouse swooped on these triumphs to advertise his next ship, the *Mars*, which he completed in August 1779: 'On a six month cruise, against the united enemies of Great Britain. The new Frigate *Mars*, copper sheathed, John Chilcott, Commander (late of the *Tartar*). Mounting 30 carriage guns, 22 of which are 12-pounders on one deck and intended to carry 150 men. She is built on an approved plan of the famous *Ceres*, esteemed the fastest sailor in the British Navy, has exactly the same accommodations and cover for her people as His Majesty's frigates and is allowed by all judges to be the most complete private ship of war in Great Britain. All Gentlemen Officers and Seamen, as well as able bodied Landmen, willing now at the commencement of a Spanish War, to make their fortunes in this ship where sailing and force are united, will meet with the greatest encouragement, by immediately applying to Captain Chilcott at his house on Kingsdown.' Many well known public houses where men might enlist are then listed, and the advertisement concludes: 'Application may likewise be made to Mr Thomas Easton on the Exchange; or at Messrs Bush, Elton and Bush in Redcliffe Street.'[62]

Also listed are the merchants who invested in the *Mars*, including Hilhouse's father-in-law George Bush, whose partner Thomas Easton is named as the owner in the declaration for letter of marque dated 12 August 1779. The *Mars* was the type of ship Hilhouse longed to build, and it is no surprise that he did so as soon as the opportunity

The privateer *Mars*, print after Pocock. Built on the lines of HMS *Ceres* in 1779 by Hilhouse for a consortium including his father-in-law, George Bush, she was lost in a storm off the Azores on her first voyage.

© Bristol's Museums, Galleries & Archives

Mars model. This model of the *Mars* remained with Charles Hill and Sons, until the firm closed.

© Bristol's Museums, Galleries & Archives

arose. At last he could put into practice the specialised knowledge he had gained at Chatham and Woolwich, where the *Ceres* was built. Hilhouse would have been fully familiar with this iconic ship and her sailing qualities, much admired at the time and still to be admired today through her model and sketches at Bristol City Museum. Hilhouse also built speculatively a similar ship, the *Termagant*, which the Navy could not resist buying on the stocks when they visited the 'new yard at Redclift'. The *Mars* sailed in August 1779 and it was reported in the following month that she had taken a Spanish privateer and the *Maria* from New England, both of which were sent home to King Road, off Avonmouth. There was a heavy price to pay for this proud venture, however, and not long after these triumphs the *Mars* is believed to have been lost with all hands in a violent storm in the Azores. It was a tragedy for many Bristol families, and a bitter disappointment for Hilhouse and his associates.

At the same time as building and equipping privateers for clients, and perhaps seeing the returns on the money their ships' successful cruises were bringing them, Hilhouse decided to take a stake in such a venture himself. In September 1778 a declaration was made on his behalf and that of Andrew Maxse, a merchant for whom he did much work over the years, as owners of the *Jackal*. She was not large, a sloop of 100 tons carrying 14 guns and 12 swivels with a crew of 60, but she was alleged to have taken 23 prizes in her career for the American navy before being captured.[63] How Hilhouse and Maxse acquired the *Jackal* is not known, but the wages book shows she was being worked on at Hotwells on 19 September 1778. As soon as she was fit for sea she sailed across the Atlantic and in February 1779 took the American brigantine *Peace and Harmony*. In the May she was in the Caribbean where she captured a Bermudan sloop and carried her with her cargo into Tortola, and later that month came her most famous exploit.

Along with four other private ships of war the *Jackal* attacked and captured the French Caribbean island of St Bartholomew, a feat that earned her and her companion ships considerable rewards and much publicity. *Felix Farley's Journal's* account gives a flavour of the response in Bristol: 'The *Jackal* is a small privateer belonging to this port. The judicious conduct of that spirited young commander, Captain McDivitt (sic), throughout this cruise, must ensure him the esteem of the owners of that vessel and consequently recommend him to future confidence and favour in this city.' From Admiralty Court records it is apparent that Bernard McDavitt had indeed been rewarded for the *Jackal's* successes; he also had a financial interest in her as one of her four owners, and Richard Brown is named as the employed commander of the sloop. Richard Toombs, another shipbuilder in Bristol, who produced a colourful and detailed plan showing his proposed scheme for creating a floating harbour in 1792, stood as one of the sureties for the bond of £1,500 for the *Jackal*, along with George Watson.[64]

An affidavit sworn on 3 September 1779 for the vessel's second cruise affirmed that she was 'employed in trade for attacking, surprising, seizing and taking the goods belonging to the inhabitants of the rebellious colonies', and it was further stated that she would be carrying a cargo of bricks, bread and bottled liquor for a voyage from Bristol to Gibraltar. In view of her stated aims, this was perhaps a standard form of words for the first stage of a blatantly non-trading exploit. The *Vigilant*, owned by Richard Toombs and Thomas Easton, was said to be carrying exactly the same cargo to the same destination, Gibraltar, in a declaration made a year earlier, and one might legitimately query what kind of a state the bread would have been in by the time they reached port. McDavitt returned to Bristol in July 1779 after this eventful and successful venture and was appointed to the *Hornet*, but again we are reminded of the intense risks involved in these adventurings. It was recorded that Captain Bernard McDavitt died 'on 7 October (1780) at Major Williams's, the Grove, Newfoundland; a truly brave and humane man, esteemed, respected and regretted by all ranks who had the least knowledge of him'.[65]

The *Jackal* was refitted by Hilhouse and set sail again in October 1779, but again it was a cruise that ended in calamity. She was driven ashore in a storm in the Azores, lost with almost all her crew, and a letter to her owners from the second lieutenant, William Jenkes, described the scene:

> I am sorry to have to write to you on so an unfortunate circumstance as the loss of your sloop, the Jackal. She was drove on shore in a most violent gale of wind at a place called Villafranca where she went instantly to pieces and out of her whole crew not a soul but six were saved, among them is Mr Turner, the remainder are foremast people; poor Captain Brown and every other officer are no more...[66]

These two disasters so close together in October 1779 in the Azores – the *Jackal* and the *Mars* possibly lost in the same storm – had a great effect on Hilhouse both emotionally and financially. After this, although he continued to assist Bristol merchants in their privateering ventures with letters of marque, particularly his father-in-law's company Bush, Elton and Bush and Noble, he did not build any more private men-of-war. Clearly, privateering was not as successful for Hilhouse in the American Revolutionary War as it had been for his father and other Bristol merchants earlier in the century, and this was to be the way of the future. As the chronicler Latimer noted in connection with the French Revolutionary War:

> It is remarkable that the ardour for privateering manifested by Bristolians in previous wars was on this occasion entirely lacking. The papers do not record the fitting out of a single cruiser.

In the light of this, the emphasis of Hilhouse's work inevitably changed; one small but interesting commission at this time, for instance, was from the Stroudwater Canal, now nearing completion, for a ceremonial directors' barge for its grand opening in July 1779.[67]

Significantly, this is the only recorded instance of Hilhouse's bill being paid late and not in full. Maybe he saw this small commission as not important, since he was already engaged in building for the Navy and his efforts were concentrated on making a success of this long-held ambition. Both in privateering and in his Naval work his skill and dynamism made a significant contribution to the American War, a conflict not foreseen and badly managed by the Government. In fact it was a disaster for Bristol merchants and their trade not only with America but with the West Indies. On the other hand, it gave considerable impetus to Hilhouse's new business, and created a connection with the Navy which was profitable in the short term and long-lasting in terms of his reputation. As the saying goes. 'Tis an ill wind...'

CHAPTER FIVE

◌◌◌

Achieving the Objective: Building HMS *Medea*

1776 WAS A MOMENTOUS YEAR IN HILHOUSE'S LIFE, BOTH PROFESSIONALLY AND PERSONALLY. IN October he took the big step into matrimony, but before that he was commissioned to build a ship that would establish the course of his career and give lustre to the reputation of shipbuilding in Bristol. On 14 May the Navy Board placed an order with him to build a frigate, to be named HMS *Medea*, and this was the opportunity he had been waiting for. He was the first merchant to receive an order for one of the Enterprise class frigates the Navy needed, and it was a new venture not only for him but for Bristol, where no Navy ship had been built for 100 years.[68] If he managed the contract to the board's satisfaction there was the prospect of further and more lucrative contracts; if there were problems and he failed to deliver, the Navy's long-standing prejudice against merchant builders in general and Bristol in particular would be reinforced, and there would be no second chance. There was a lot at stake, but the Navy Board had seen fit to give an order to a 28-year-old shipbuilder with barely four years' experience of running his own dockyard almost a year before its general request for merchant bids in April 1777, as the war was intensifying. Why would it do this?

In fact the timing of the offer owes more to Hilhouse himself than to the crisis the Navy faced with the War of American Independence, to which it belatedly awoke the following year. It was four years since he completed his time at Chatham, during which he had impressed both Joseph Harris, who was still in charge of shipbuilding there, and Edward Hunt. These two supporters with influence in decision-making at the top level of the Navy not only knew his proven qualities but had discussed with him his ambition to build for the Navy. Hilhouse's understanding with them was that they would award him a frigate to build when he was ready to do so, and they plainly felt the time had come. As a rule the board's preference, if it had to use merchant builders, was for yards on the Thames, the Medway or other locations close to London, where they felt they could easily oversee work in progress.[69] Otherwise, yards given orders were usually close to other Navy dockyards, and with a relatively new dockyard at Plymouth, a long and difficult journey down the Bristol Channel, around Land's End and back up the English Channel, Bristol had been generally ruled out of the Navy's reckoning.

Bearing all this in mind, why did the Navy Board abandon its prejudice against the city? It is plain that all that had changed there was the shipbuilder who now owned the Hotwells yard. As Hilhouse had already shown in his dealings with the Merchant Venturers over the lease and fitting out of his dock, he had a clear idea of what he wanted and was not afraid to be forceful in making sure he got it. This clear vision extended to his desire to build for 'the King', and he used all the resources at his command to bring his vision to fruition. Faced with an able, determined, well-connected and well-financed young shipbuilder who had been trained in its own yards – one who understood the working methods and ethos of the Navy and was being vouched for by two of its own top men – the Navy Board obviously had no reservations about signing a contract with Hilhouse of Bristol.

The rapidly deteriorating situation in the American colonies that caught the Navy so woefully unprepared was not the impetus behind Hilhouse's contract. This is borne out by the fact that having awarded him the *Medea* commission, the Navy Board was quite happy for him to defer building for a year while her timber stood to season, as was normal practice. It was not until the following year that the Navy fully realised the urgency of its need for more vessels, and began in earnest to contract with other merchant yards. If the Navy Board had the confidence to sign a contract with Hilhouse, he himself had supreme confidence in his ability to fulfil it. He had the advantage of his seven years' inside knowledge of Naval yards, what their standards and priorities were and how best he could meet them. He knew what the Navy demanded in terms of quality of material and construction, and the importance of keeping to the costs and time-scale laid down in the contract; he was also well aware that any work he did for the Navy would be closely scrutinised and supervised by its overseer, and he was prepared for this. He had spent the years since his return to Bristol in recruiting and training his own capable workforce and building a network of suppliers, and now felt fully assured that he and his team had the skills necessary to take on a Navy frigate.

From a financial standpoint he knew that the work would pay well, and as long as he worked carefully within the timetable set down in the contract he stood to make a good profit. He was also in the fortunate position of having capital behind him, a useful safety net to cushion him from the unforeseen delays and difficulties centred on cash-flow that so bedevilled the Barnards[70] and other merchants building for the Navy. He knew the contract would bring him prestige, and as long as it went well, others would follow to secure his order book and hopefully lead to orders for larger and even more valuable and profitable ships. Further orders would not only provide work on a scale not seen before in Bristol, it would yield profits to invest in developing a successful future for his company.

No shipbuilding contract for the *Medea* survives; indeed, none can be found in the Admiralty records for any of Hilhouse's Navy ships but there are records, yet to be examined, of Adams at Bucklers Hard and a merchant at Blackwall for this time at the National Maritime Museum. Navy contracts with merchant yards changed only in small details during the eighteenth century, however, so the form it took can be deduced with some certainty from the contract for the building of the sloop *Viper* by Thomas West of Deptford in 1755.[71] In essence, the contract and the ship's draughts gave specific instructions for the construction of the vessel and what was included in the builder's remit. Excluded was responsibility for the masts and yards, furnaces and pumps in the ship, which would be fitted in the Navy's own yards once the hull was complete and delivered. In terms of time scale – and this was often an area where merchants ran into trouble – the date for launching was stipulated in months from the date of the signing of the contract, and there were penalties for exceeding this time. The *Viper* contract recorded the rate of payment per ton, restricting the number of tons to the maximum specified. Payment to the builder was always by instalments, and for the *Viper* there were five; the first, to enable West to buy the timber needed to start building, was made on the signing of the contract; the second was due when the keel was laid; the third when the top timbers were in place; the fourth when the deck was laid; and the fifth and 'perfect' instalment came when the ship was launched or 'delivered safe afloat'.

This system of payment was customary until about the time of the *Medea*, but shortly before Hilhouse's first contract an incident led the Navy Board to change its thinking. This was down to an unhappy experience it had with the builder of the *Fury* at Leith, who used its first payment not on that vessel but to build other ships. This sharp practice only reinforced the board's suspicion of merchant yards, and around 1777 or 1778 it changed the timing of the first instalment to when the keel was laid and the yard had sourced enough timber to build the ship. Not surprisingly, the effect this had on some merchant builders was catastrophic, since without a down payment to buy timber and other supplies they found themselves under considerable financial stress. The Ipswich and Harwich shipwright Barnard and the builders of the *Nemesis* in Liverpool both went bankrupt as a result, and they were not alone. To guard against this, the Navy Board added a further stipulation to its contracts, asserting its right to enter a yard and take over if the builder went bankrupt and failed to deliver the ship. In addition, the board put in place a scale of penalties for not launching on time: 5s per ton at the launch date, rising to 10s per ton after seven months' delay. On the other hand, if the Navy Board was more than seven months late in paying its bills the contractor was entitled to 4 per cent interest, but this is not as generous as it might sound, as the Navy Bills in which he was paid were often discounted by up to 11 per cent by the banks. They did not like them – as Barnard found to his cost.[72]

Hilhouse would have been only too aware of all these risks and pressures, the advantage of having capital behind him, the need to have cash coming in from other work in the yard and the importance of keeping to the timetable for the Navy contract. On the other hand, he was aware that in the case of the *Medea* the Navy seemed to be relaxed in its time scale, and we discover through his wages book that having signed the contract in May 1776 and laid the keel probably late in that year, no further work on her took place until 13 September 1777, some three months after she was originally planned to be launched. The reason for this delay is not known, through the absence of correspondence and the

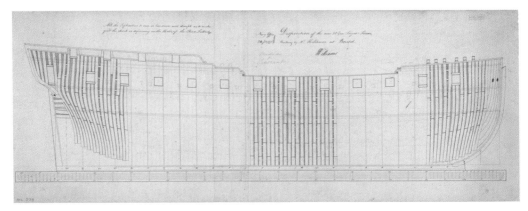

Draught profile plan for HMS *Medea*, partial frames drawing, Navy Board instruction. 'All timbers to run so low down and scarp as to make good the chock or deficiency on the Heads of the Third Futtock'. © National Maritime Museum, Greenwich, London.

contract, but there are clues among the Navy Board minutes. These stated that the rigging and fitting out was as usual to be carried out by a royal dockyard, and on 26 June 1776 the Navy Board wrote to the Plymouth dock to warn it of its requirements:

> Having agreed with Mr James Martin Hilhouse to build in his Yard at Bristol for his Majesty a 28-gun ship burthen 594 tons at £10 13s 0d per ton and to launch her in June 1777. These are to direct and require you to prepare and send us an estimate in due form of the charge of building and fitting her for sea and completely equipping her with masts and yards sails rigging and stores to an eight month proportion and to have the same in readiness against the time of her launching and you are to supply her with an iron fire hearth and a copper double kettle of suitable dimensions for a compliment of 200 men.[73]

The draught for the *Medea*, held at the National Maritime Museum's Brass Foundry in Woolwich, is dated 24 July 1776, two months after the signing of the contract to build, and signed by Edward Hunt's superior as surveyor to the Navy, Sir John Williams; by this time, however, Williams was a sick man shortly to retire, and it is likely that Hunt himself was responsible for it. Despite all these arrangements, however, the work at Hotwells did not proceed. Hilhouse's yard was hard at work on other clients' ships, of course, but he would never have ignored his Navy contract in favour of other jobs unless he had been sure that there was no pressure from the authorities to start work. Indeed, the delay was apparently no cause for concern or even comment, and it certainly incurred no censure or penalty. The probable explanation comes in a letter written at the end of summer in the following year, by which time the Navy had woken up to the urgent need for additional frigates.

On 2 August 1777 the Navy Board ordered: 'Write to Mr Hilhouse to proceed in carrying on works on *Medea* without her standing to season. Acquaint the Overseer.'[74] This is a reminder that while the elm keel was laid in late 1776, it had been acknowledged that the oak timber from which the frame was to be built had to wait to season. The correct seasoning of timber was something Hilhouse spoke passionately about when giving evidence in 1792 to a commission led by Sir Charles Middleton[75] to review timber used by the Navy during the previous 20 years. Contract or no contract, Hilhouse believed that timber should stand for a year to season before he felt it proper to use it, and the fact that the Navy Board was content to allow him to do this demonstrates his confident handling of relations with the authorities as well as their trust in him. The concern about seasoning oak timber remained, but by the time Hilhouse received his second Navy order, for the *Crescent*, the hard-pressed board was prepared to compromise. On 10 March 1778 it ordered: 'Write to Mr Hilhouse's Overseer of *Crescent* not to stand to season but do not approve the plank being brought on till the frame is compleat.'[76]

Two draughts relating to the *Medea* survive: one is the original Williams document, clearly a standard Navy Board form, while the other profile drawing is almost certain to be by Hilhouse himself.[77] He was a skilled draughtsman and this is likely to be one of his earliest surviving drawings. The Navy Board document is unusual in that it is only a partial frames drawing, and as the draughts held in the Brass Foundry archive do not include frames drawings for any Enterprise class frigate, no comparison with the *Medea* can be made. It would seem that this was a special drawing issued by the surveyor to explain a particular detail, and it is inscribed: 'All the timbers to run so low down and scarp as to make good the chock or deficiency on the Heads of the Third Futtock.'

Once work on the *Medea* started in September 1777 it proceeded with brisk efficiency, as we would expect of Hilhouse. Building for the Navy meant he was not entirely in control of the project, however, since his progress was closely scrutinised by the overseer appointed by the critical Navy Board. This was of course a factor Hilhouse had been prepared for, but it still caused him a few additional problems. The overseer regularly reported on progress to the Navy Board in London, which in turn reported to its masters at the Admiralty. Some of these records survive at the National Archive at Kew and at the National Maritime Museum at Greenwich, making it possible partially to track progress on the vessel; but there are many gaps in these records and it is Hilhouse's wages book that records most about the building of the *Medea*, giving an invaluable picture of how he set about this, his first and so most important commission for the Navy.

He arranged his men in teams to work on particular ships, with a leader of each team to supervise and maintain continuity, and it was a system that gave him flexibility to meet demand for skills and manpower at different stages during the building of the *Medea*. While Hilhouse was in charge of organising his workforce, the overseer was instructed to ensure that sufficient men were regularly employed on her. This was normal procedure, but what is not clear is why the authorities were so concerned over manpower that it issued a specific direction to its overseers in Liverpool and Bristol 'to be carefull that more workmen or a greater quantity of materials are not charged for... And to keep a diary'. After all, it was in the shipbuilder's interests to manage the contract as efficiently and effectively as possible. The only exception was the fact that there were a few instances during the course of a contract in which work was specifically charged 'To the King', and the Navy Board was directly responsible for payment; it can be appreciated that in these cases it was incumbent on the overseer to ensure that the charge for that work was correct.

The Hilhouse wages book shows that work started in earnest on the *Medea* in the week ending Saturday 13 September 1777. Each ship at Hotwells was allocated a column which records the number of days or parts of a day she was worked on by each man, and also lists the different categories of workers used. There is a separate double page in the book for each week, Monday to Saturday, detailing exactly who worked on which task and for how long, and from these records we can see that the *Medea* work continued for 37 consecutive weeks after that September start. In the first week Hilhouse was employing a total of 57 shipwrights in his dockyard, an impressive number of skilled men to have assembled. The foreman, J Jones, was paid £1 10s weekly, his assistant J Pinnington, £1 5s. Jones is one of several key men with a Welsh name, and as foreman, he was assigned to the *Medea* along with 20 other shipwrights who were on the standard rate of 15s per week. In September 1777 Hilhouse had 14 sawyers on his workforce, and in the first week on the *Medea* nine of them were allocated to work on her. They were rightly well paid at 18s a week, since theirs was a responsible job, calling for accuracy and stamina as they sawed all the large timbers needed for the ship's frame. The wages book also shows Hilhouse was employing the large number of 47 apprentices at this time, but the skilled nature of the work called for at the beginning of a ship's construction meant that he deemed only seven of them capable of serving on the *Medea* at this stage. He paid his apprentices 3s per week at the start of their training, but this rose each year to the finishing wage of 8s at the end of seven years. As work progressed he used his apprentices extensively on the frigate, and even by week three he had allocated 22 to her. He employed 12 'labourers' at between 8s and 10s a week, and all of these were called in at the start of work on the new ship. In fact the wages paid for work on the *Medea* during the first four weeks totalled £103 11s 3d, the highest monthly wage bill during the whole period of her construction; the average monthly bill was £70.

Intensive activity, then, but we must remember the yard was also working on seven other ships at the time, and Hilhouse was kept busy juggling his workforce to keep all his contracts on schedule. His life became even busier as a second ship for the Navy appears in the wages book in the first week of work on the *Medea* in September 1777, listed simply as 'New Frigate'. By the week ending 27 September she is listed with the name 'New Frigate *Crescent*', and her presence on his books shows the Navy's confidence in him even before the *Medea* was properly under way. In addition to these two vessels, Hilhouse was building a 'new ship for Mr Chilcott' and had a steady stream of work for his other merchant clients.

Stern view of HMS *Medea* model. This model was made by Hilhouse himself.

Figurehead of HMS *Medea* model.

Below: whole side view of HMS *Medea* model.

© Bristol's Museums, Galleries & Archives.

With this volume of turnover he clearly needed another senior shipwright to lead a team, and in week seven of work on the *Medea* the name 'Harrison' appears for the first time in the wages book, below Pinnington but on the same rate of pay as him. Both men spent time working on the *Medea* and a little time on the *Crescent* as well as John Chilcott's new merchant ship, but by 15 November Hilhouse had sufficient faith in Harrison's abilities to promote him to full-time leading shipwright on the *Medea*, with a large team under him. Hilhouse kept Pinnington working on the Chilcott ship, and from time to time on the *Crescent*.

The main effort of the yard, however, was clearly directed at completing the *Medea*, with a dedicated team of shipwrights working exclusively on her, their names tending to be grouped together in the wages book; this might indicate that they were taken on at the same time, maybe recruited from the same place. Pintestock, James, Davis, David and Hughes – Welsh names aplenty, there – were regulars in the team, and while Pintestock's name appears at different points in the total list of shipwrights, it settles about half way down, and always first in his group of five. On average, 20 shipwrights worked on the *Medea* each week through the winter of 1777-78 but in the mid-April, with the Navy's launch date looming, there was a concentrated effort to reach the target and more were poured in. The average number of them working on the frigate for weeks 28 to 30 was 36, a large proportion of the total on his books. The teams delegated to each of the Naval ships rarely worked together, ensuring that the men in them were focused and familiar with the job, knew one another well and formed a competent, efficient unit. Over and above this, it would have been in Hilhouse's interests to encourage a little professional rivalry between the two groups.

With work on the *Medea* progressing well and the *Crescent* under construction, Hilhouse was shrewd enough to realise the danger of concentrating too fully on his Navy contracts; his commercial clients, after all, would be the source of work he would rely on if the Navy contracts ran out or the Admiralty was slow to pay. In the week ending 10 January 1778, for example, work in the yard was also being carried out on the ships *Constantine*, the famous privateer in which his father and grandfather had had interests, *Marlborough*, *Chard*, *Ann* and *Polly*, all trading to the West Indies, as well as that 'new ship for Mr Chilcott'. The *Medea* team was not involved in any of this merchant work, and when extra men were needed for it Hilhouse took them off the *Crescent*, which had a more leisurely timetable.

By 19 January 1778, after four months' intensive effort, the *Medea* was all but complete and Hilhouse needed instructions for her delivery to a Naval dockyard for the final stages of being rigged and fitted out for service. Surprisingly, in view of the early instructions issued by the Navy Board to Plymouth, this took time to arrange, and the bureaucratic delays and difficulties in communication were frustrating for Hilhouse and highlight one of the reasons the Navy had reservations about building in Bristol. Much of the problem lay in the fact that all communications between Bristol and Plymouth had to go via London, and at this point the Navy Board told the Admiralty

> *Medea* building at Bristol cannot be finished with masts there, they humbly propose to bring her to Plymouth with jury mast and be finished for sea at that port. If that meets with approbation will order masts there for her.[78]

This surely must have been the plan from the start, but three weeks later little progress had been made.

On 6 February 1778 the overseer at Hotwells wrote to the board asking whether the boats for the *Medea* were to be built by Hilhouse or in Plymouth. Hilhouse had a specialist team of mainly Welsh boat builders led by I James, whom he paid at the high rate of 18s a week; by the week beginning 7 March Hilhouse was growing impatient and urgently needed to know whether he should set them to work on the *Medea* project. It seems that the answer was positive, as for the three weeks beginning 11 April, several of the team were boat-building. The overseer also asked whether the jury masts for the transfer journey to Plymouth were to be provided by Bristol or sent up from Devon. It seems that by this time the Navy Board was running out of patience and considering entrusting most of the fitting out to Hilhouse of Bristol. 'Write to Mr Hilhouse to hasten the building of the *Medea* that we may know the shortest time she may be launched,'[79] was its terse minute of 10 March 1778.

By this time the *Medea* was preoccupying a large number of the men at Hotwells Dock, all well aware of how vitally important it was to meet the Navy's deadline, and on 17 April the Navy Board noted with obvious relief that it expected the frigate to be launched at the time proposed, and that the Admiralty should be informed how long after that it will take 'to compleat her'. The big day was 28 April, and two contemporary reports highlight how significant an event it was seen to be in Bristol: 'A frigate of 32 guns, the *Medea*, was launched from Hilhouse's Dock on 28 April. Ship building for the Navy had been so long suspended in Bristol that the Journal very erroneously asserted that this was the first King's frigate ever built in this Port. Four other frigates were then building in Local yards.'[80] In fact there must have been strict security measures preventing the press and others observing what was happening, since William Dyer in his diary for 28 April 1778 was guilty of the same error: 'A King's Frigate was launched at Champion's Dock built by Hilhouse. This was a novelty being the first instance of a King's ship built at Bristol.' Through all the muddle, what we can deduce is that at the time the launch of the *Medea* was regarded in Bristol as a most unusual and celebrated event, and it must have been a proud moment for Hilhouse and his workforce when they saw her slip into the water for the first time. The publicity and local acclaim did much to enhance his growing reputation as Bristol's leading shipbuilder, and he would soon become nationally recognised.

After the celebration of 28 April came the next stage of the frigate's story. Hilhouse had negotiated special arrangements for access to the floating dock adjacent to his Hotwells Dock and after her 'delivery to the King' the *Medea* was moved there for her fitting out, before being sent on to Plymouth for her copper plates to be painted with white lead. The work in Bristol was carried out by Hilhouse's men under the supervision of Captain (later Admiral) Cornwallis, but it is unclear how Bristol was granted this work, after all the signs had been that the completion of the *Medea* would follow the usual course, and she would be fitted out at Plymouth, the nearest Naval dockyard. Not surprisingly, there are many gaps in the records of correspondence passing between Bristol, London and Plymouth. Clearly the overseer at Bristol had confidence in Hilhouse. Whatever the fine detail of the decision, to be entrusted with the major part of this important and prestigious work was a further major coup for Hilhouse.

As for Captain Cornwallis, we read that:

> In April of this year he was on leave but in the following month he was ordered to fit out the *Medea*, a new ship just launched at Bristol where he remained some three months. The following August, Sandwich, who was still First Lord, gave him command of the *Lion*, a 64 gun ship.[81]

The months of May and June saw a high level of work on the *Medea,* but it seems her fitting out did not go altogether smoothly. Letters went to and fro' between Bristol and the Navy Board concerning the apparently pressingly important matter of the appointment of a ship's cook; then her foremast, held for her in Plymouth, was supplied to HMS *Milford* instead and a replacement had to be found, further contributing to the frustrating delays; and the dispatch of stores, the arrival of a surveyor and the type of boats to be built for the *Medea* were all the subject of further urgent correspondence.

Progress was made despite the red tape, however, and Plymouth dockyard finally sent the awaited supplies and stores on the transport ship *Providence*, which arrived on 27 June. Disappointingly, the presentment documents[82] give no details of what she was carrying, but it would appear that she brought what Hilhouse and his men had been waiting for, as the wages book records that some of the work was able to be charged 'to the King' in that month. In fact after week 35 all the work on the *Medea* was charged to the Crown, and it was finally completed in week 39, ending on 11 July 1778. Hilhouse's foresight in negotiating a lease that gave him rights to use the floating harbour by day and night had paid off handsomely and would continue to do so in the future. Not only had the contract been successfully completed, but work that had been expected to go to Plymouth had stayed in Bristol, to Hilhouse's great profit. The *Medea* sailed off down the Avon under Captain Cornwallis's command, and as Hilhouse and his men watched her depart they knew that, unlike most of the ships they built, they would not see her again. She docked at Plymouth on 17 August and such was the thorough job the Hotwells team had done on her, she was ready for service nine days later.

What happened to her after that? Captain James Montague was appointed to command her, and on 27 September, having taken on her stores and complement of crew, she left Plymouth Sound to begin her active service some five months after her launch. In time of war and with winter approaching this must have been a frustrating delay, but she was soon in action. On 20 October she was cruising off Cape Finisterre with the frigate *Jupiter* when they encountered and attacked the larger 64-gun French ship *Triton*. Two hours' hectic action followed, and though the *Triton* drew off with 13 men killed, about 50 wounded and with some 50 shots in her hull, it was not without cost to the British, since the *Medea* was struck below the waterline, had one man killed and three wounded.[83] Though her first engagement proved her fighting abilities, her logs do not record any further action in home waters under Captain Montague. What they do tell us of, however, is a harsh regime, with many instances of punishment being administered, usually a dozen lashes; on 6 September 1780 two hands were punished for desertion with a brutal three dozen lashes, creating the impression that the captain was a hard disciplinarian.

It seems the life of the *Medea*'s crew improved almost instantly, however, as a month later, on 3 October, Captain Henry Duncan took over her command. A detailed journal he kept of his time aboard has survived and been published by his descendants, and it gives a fascinating insight into the life of his ship.[84] On first taking over he had his wife and daughter on board as they sailed along the South Coast, but unhappily it was not all relaxation for them; they encountered rough weather and had to take shelter from strong gales before he put them ashore at Dartmouth and the *Medea* set sail for America. It was a swift and largely uneventful voyage; Henry Duncan recorded little: on 17 November the day's highlights were that they killed a dolphin and a foot-long flying fish landed on the deck. When his ship arrived at Sandy Hook, the Navy's base near New York, Duncan writes that he was greeted flatteringly by Admiral Mariot Arbuthnot and given orders to sail for Charleston, Carolina, alongside HMS *Charon*. He was pleased to do so, as the weather had been persistently foggy at Sandy Hook – but this was clearly no pleasure trip, and it was now that the *Medea* really began to fulfil her role as a frigate.

Duncan's journal entry for 13 January 1781 records that he saw a sail at 8 a.m. and gave chase:

> By 6 p.m. we appeared to have come up with her; at this time night came on and we lost sight of her ahead. Continued the course; half after nine the moon having got up, discovered her with my glass from the quarter gallery far aft upon the starboard quarter; crowded after her again... 14th January, Sunday. At half past 2 a.m. we appeared to be pretty well up with her, then upon a wind, and she a little upon the weather bow; at this time she bore away about three points and set her studding sails, and for some time after this she seemed to draw from us. Having set our studding sails and the wind freshening with now and then a jerk of a sea

so as to endanger our top masts, but carrying all we got within a gun shot of her at half past five; fired one gun and she struck. She proved to be the *Morning Star*, American privateer ship of 18 four-pounders, ten ports of a side, 190 tons and 90-odd men, belonging to Philadelphia. She now had only 79, having sent some away in a prize and a vessel they had retaken, a prize to the *Hyaena*; found two midshipmen and eight men belonging to that ship on board the privateer. Shifted the prisoners and put Mr Stevenson on board to take charge of the prize, with Mr Arno and about 25 or 30 men. The ship was just off the stocks and had been but three weeks at sea; she sailed fast; the prize she had taken was a small sloop from Charleston bound to Providence. *The Morning Star* cost the amazing sum of 400,000, paper currency.

Two days later the *Medea* took a second prize, the schooner *Blossom*, sailing with cargo from Cape Fear to St Eustatius. Duncan also records that they gave protection to a Bristol ship, *Torbay*, and took the opportunity to press five men from her crew before sailing with his two prizes into Charleston. On 21 February, with the frigates *Roebuck* and *Raleigh*, the *Medea* took two further prizes which were sent in to New York, and on 1 March took another, a Bermudan-built sloop, only to learn that the notorious American privateer John Paul Jones[85] had arrived on the coast in the *Ariel*. A week later Duncan records that the *Medea* took another vessel carrying 550 barrels of flour; he then boarded a ship carrying sugar and rum from Jamaica to New York, and learned that war with France had been declared, since the French fleet, several ships of which were close by, was actively supporting the Americans. The *Medea* soon became involved, and she was present at the Battle of Cape Henry on 16 March, though not active in this inconclusive encounter. Two days later Captain Duncan received orders to engage a French frigate, but was recalled by the Admiral twice and so returned to the fleet.

The *Medea*'s next mission was a posting to the James River, where the British force besieged in Jamestown was in urgent need of support, and on the way she took a French pilot boat which Duncan sent back to the Admiral. During April many of his men were ill with scurvy, a common danger when a ship ran out of fresh supplies of fruit and vegetables, and they were put in tents on Governor's Island while repairs and caulking were carried out to their ship. Captain Duncan records taking many more prizes, all American and most of them privateers. Some were of considerable size – for example, the Massachussetts State ship *Protector*,[86] with 198 men and 26 guns – and the *Belisarius*, with 150 men and 20 guns. Admiral Thomas Graves, the newly appointed fleet commander in America, also gave him several missions to gather intelligence about the movements of the French fleet, but on the eve of battle on 14 September 1781 he sent the *Medea* back to England with his dispatch, thus depriving her of a part in the ensuing engagement. The defeat of the British fleet at the Battle of Chesapeake meant that vital supplies could not be brought to the beleaguered General Cornwallis and his troops in Yorktown and led to their fateful surrender on 19 October.

The *Medea*'s voyage home was not uneventful and on 9 October she took the *Black Princess* from Boulogne, 26 guns, commanded by an Irishman named McCarthy. She reached Weymouth on October 18 and Duncan set off immediately to London, where he delivered Graves's dispatch to the Admiralty at nine o'clock that night. At this point we cease to have the benefit of the captain's informative journal, since Captain Erasmus Gower took over command on 10 November and the *Medea* was sent to Plymouth for repairs and refitting. An entry in the log during this time, on 18 January 1782, records the firing of a 21-gun salute for the Queen's birthday, and fresh beef being served to the crew in celebration – all very pleasant for them but something of a mystery, since Queen Charlotte was born on May 19, 1744. It may have been the birthday of one of her 15 children.

As if to remind us of Britain's far-reaching power and ambitions, the *Medea* was next ordered to sail for India by the western passage to play another significant part in what had by this stage become a global war. Having passed the Lizard on 11 February, she put in to Madiera, St Vincent and Trinidad to reach Rio de Janiero on 23 March, when shore leave was obviously a welcome diversion. Maybe a little too welcome for some, since an entry in the log for 2 April records: 'Seven punished for selling their clothes in Rio market, 12 lashes.' This was not uncommon behaviour, in fact, as visiting sailors had little apart from their clothes to sell to finance a night on the town. On 21 May 1782 the *Medea* was at the Cape of Good Hope with a prize ship, *Concorde*, in tow, but it was not until the August that she was mooring in Madras Roads to join Admiral Sir Edward Hughes's campaign against the French Comte Pierre André de Suffren – a war of attrition in which the two fought one another to a standstill but the eventual triumph of Hughes played a key part in saving British interests in India.

The *Medea*, continuing in her role of operating independently of the main fleet, captured the French 20-gun *Chasseur*, carrying important dispatches, and on 30 January took the Dutch ship *Vryheid*. Unfortunately for the prize-money hopes of the *Medea*'s crew, this valuable 50-gun prize was wrecked soon after in Madras Roads – and by summer the Indian adventure was all over. There was one last twist, however: The *Medea* was on the fringes of the battle of Cuddalore, the fifth and final bloody clash between Hughes and Suffren, and on 29 June she was the British vessel ordered to sail under a truce flag to take news to the French admiral of a preliminary peace agreement between the two nations. After this, her work done, she was recalled to England where her crew was discharged.

We can see, then, that over the five years since her commissioning, the *Medea* had been active in a variety of theatres of war, and her service history during this time, compiled from her lieutenants' logs and Duncan's journal, shows a feisty contribution by a relatively small ship. Her record after 1784 has not yet been fully traced but we know Captain Bligh of the *Bounty* was briefly in command of her in the Caribbean, researching the islands' potential resources. She went aground at Charleston in 1801, ended her Naval career as a hospital ship off Portsmouth, and was sold out of the Navy in 1805 after some 27 years of service. She had proved to be very good value for the Navy's money and had performed well – resilient and speedy, capturer of numerous prizes and a ship well equipped to carry out covert scouting assignments in a number of campaigns.

She did not do too badly for Hilhouse, either – to put it mildly. His total wages bill for the *Medea* was £686 17s, with just over half that amount paid to the shipwrights. To this must be added the cost of materials, of which oak timber was by far the most expensive item. No records survive of Hilhouse's expenditure, but there are well recognised ways of calculating the timber required to build a ship and the cost of oak bought at that time from the Forest of Dean, just across the Severn. A 'load' of timber was the amount that could be hauled by one horse, and was approximately a ton in weight. It cost £1 18s, and it is generally accepted that two loads were needed for each ton of a Navy warship. The *Medea* was classed as sixth rate, of 605 tons, so it would have taken a little over 1,200 loads of timber to build her. The cost of transporting the timber down the Severn and up the Avon was not a major issue for Hilhouse, so an estimate of £2,500 would be reasonable. He had contracted to build the hull for £6,300, so adding that to his labour costs, it seems probable that he made a profit of 50 per cent, or about £3,000 on the initial *Medea* contract – to which must be added the unscheduled fitting-out work, which we can safely assume he did not perform at a loss, to say the very least.

Yes, Hilhouse's first Navy contract had gone well and been very profitable, as he had hoped – but of course, it did not end there. The Navy Board was content with his work on the *Medea* contract and had quickly placed an order for a second frigate, the *Crescent*. There was by now a war on, and while the Navy was still placing orders with merchant yards, Hilhouse intended to take every opportunity to be one of them, preferably building larger and even more profitable ships. Nevertheless, he was equally determined to continue to serve his Bristol merchant friends and neighbours – and was quick to recognise that to do all this work successfully, he needed to expand with another dockyard in a better location than Hotwells, somewhere that would enable him to launch ships of twice the tonnage of the *Medea*, or even more. His success with that project gave him confidence and an added sense of urgency in seeking a second dockyard. He was determined to capitalise on his opportunity – and the clock was ticking.

CHAPTER SIX

೦೩৪০

New Yard at 'the Red Clift'

THE FIRST FOUR YEARS OF HILHOUSE'S SHIPBUILDING VENTURE HAD PROVED AS SUCCESSFUL AS HE could have hoped. He had swiftly built up a clientele among the merchants of the city and fulfilled his aim of attracting contracts from the Navy. His order book was full and he had more than enough work to keep his large workforce fully occupied – but there was no room for complacency. With his inside knowledge of the Navy's thinking and working methods he was perfectly aware that, despite his good relations with it, any work for it would not last forever and he needed to make the most of the opportunity while it lasted: he was sure the contracts would most probably dry up if and when the war came to an end, but in the meantime the country had a pressing need for more and larger ships, and he wanted to play his full part in meeting that demand. Any new yard had to be close to the floating dock, for fitting out the ships once they were launched and, ideally, close to his Hotwells Dock, so that it could share the facilities there and he could switch his labour force easily from one to the other. Perhaps we should not be surprised that with his know-how and contacts, he did not have to look around for long.

Hilhouse's father-in-law George Bush lived at Clift House, on the opposite bank of the Avon from Hotwells, and his river frontage included the ideal site for a new dockyard. Locating the exact site of Clift House, and thus the Redclift Dock, proved more difficult than expected, but we were succesful in the end. There were tantalising clues: Hilhouse called this second site Redclift Yard in his wages book, and contemporary records such as William Dyer's diary and *Felix Farley's Journal* refer to launchings of Hilhouse ships at 'his new yards at the Redclift' and at 'Vauxhall Yard'. No maps of the time show either yard's exact site, however, and there is only limited value in the fact that we are told that Redclift yard was 'half a mile down the river on the Somerset side. This was usually called Red Clift Yard since it was close to and more or less below Clift House, later the seat of the Dowager Lady Smyth'.[87] Investigations at Bristol Central Library led to a historical note made by George Weare Braikenridge (1775-1856) the Bristol antiquarian who commissioned mainly local artists to draw the streets, buildings and busy quaysides of the city and thus create a unique pre-photography record that is still of immense value today. He bought for his collection a scene from about 1825 by Samuel Jackson, the Bristol watercolourist, showing Clift House and the inlet next to it where a smaller river joins the Avon, a painting titled *Clift House near Cumberland Basin*. The house is in the middle of the picture, a large, imposing white stucco four-storey building standing alone on the bank of

Eighteenth-century engraving showing Mr Warren's glasshouse, with the Hot Wells across the river.

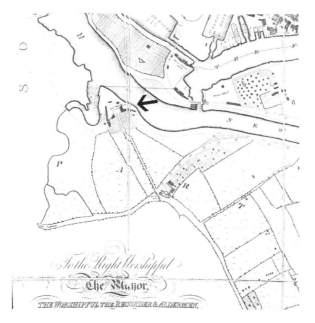

Ashmead's map, showing the position of Clift House and the Colliter Brook.
Courtesy Bristol Record Office.

the river and facing it, backed by woods and surrounded on either side by level open grassland running down to the bank. Downstream is the all-important junction of a stream and the river, creating a wide inlet which creates the space necessary to launch large ships. It is in his catalogue note on the picture that Braikenridge gives a vivid account of George Bush's habitual hospitality at Clift House:

> A long and wide Tea Room was erected close to the water's edge so that a conversation might be kept up with any person on the deck of the Vessels, and whilst Bristol sent out so many superb West India Ships, it was Mr Bush's polite custom to invite persons who had an interest in such vessels to come to the Clift that they might enjoy the pleasure of seeing them come up the River on returning from a long and perhaps dangerous voyage.[88]

We also know that Bush had built his house on the site of 'Mr Warren's Glass Houses' at some time in the latter part of the 18th century, after they had been demolished. The exact date is uncertain, but Bristol's hitherto very successful glass-making industry, in which Warren was a leading light, declined suddenly and rapidly in the 1760s, causing several bankruptcies. In March 1767 it was announced: 'Died suddenly Richard Warren Esq, at the Red Clift and Captain of the Gloucestershire Militia', and there is every reason to believe George Bush bought the site and built Clift House shortly after this. The glass houses are shown on Roque's 1746 map of Bristol, and Barrett has an interesting engraving of them in his History of Bristol written in 1789;[89] even then, of course, this was a historical rather than a contemporary illustration, but they had obviously been a well-known landmark. The Roque map helps identify the site of Clift House and shows the stream that enters the Avon at its side. Unfortunately, there are no maps of this part of the Avon and Clift House in the last quarter of the 18th century and nothing that shows the short-lived dockyard from which Bristol's largest ships were launched. It seemed extraordinary that all trace had already disappeared of the yard in which Hilhouse, Bristol's most successful shipbuilder, produced the largest Naval vessels ever built in the city.

To identify the site became an intriguing challenge, but clues to its whereabouts did exist. There are several contemporary references to the dockyard being close to Clift House, the first an account of the launch of HMS *Diomede* in William Dyer's diary entry for 18 October 1781: 'A Frigate to carry 52 guns was this morning launched from the yard at the Red Clift (formerly Mr Warren's Glass House). This was another frigate built by Mr James Martin Hilhouse.'[90] Dyer adds further information when he records the launch of the *Nassau* on 20 September 1785: 'The *Nassau* ship of War, 64 guns was launched from the yard adjoining Mr George Bush's at Redclift built by Mr James Martin Hilhouse.' The family nature of the arrangement between Bush and Hilhouse probably explains the lack any surviving leases or other agreements. Hilhouse's wages book tells us that work on 'slips at Redclyft Dock' had begun as early as February 1777 – but while St Mary Redcliffe Church records include information in a lease showing that land at Clift House had at some time before 1796 been used as a shipyard for building, at the time of the lease that use had ceased and 'the herbage was restored to its ancient state'.[91] This confirms that shipbuilding on the site by Hilhouse had ceased well before 1796, after which the land was restored to pasture or, in Braikenridge's words, 'leveled again thrown into the fields as before'. This, of course, is how Jackson shows it in his 1825 painting.

Maps are helpful in establishing the location of Clift House and the Colliter Brook, as the stream called 'the Pill' by Braikenridge came to be known, the best being Benning and Ashmead's of 1829. While not depicting the slips built by Hilhouse and used by him from 1778 to 1786, it shows clearly the small peninsula on which Clift House stood, and the mouth of the stream. It must be remembered, however, that this map was drawn after the

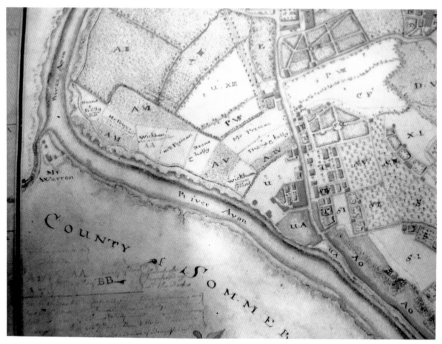

Roque's map of 1746, showing Mr Warren's glass houses and the junction of the Colliter Brook with the Avon. Courtesy Bristol Record Office.

Clift House near Cumberland Basin c.1825, Samuel Jackson. The additional width of the river caused by the inflow of the Colliter Brook is clearly depicted.
© Bristol's Museums, Galleries & Archives.

The Colliter Brook where it meets the Avon today.

creation of the New Cut, which significantly altered the shape of the river. In 1804 the Bristol Dock Company was negotiating with Robert, George Bush's son for the purchase of five acres of his land at Clift House. Robert maintained that there were two slips for building ships on this piece of land which could be unearthed 'for a trifling amount' and were of much greater value than those that the company had recently purchased from Mr Teast. It is recorded in the minutes that Robert had been advised of this fact by James Martin Hilhouse himself. On hearing this, The Dock Company forthwith upped their valuation and agreed the price asked. Hilhouse's word was enough to benefit Robert and this was some small repayment for the cooperation of his father-in-law some 30 years earlier and a clear example of the continuing close relationship. [Later Robert's son married Hilhouse's daughter and George, Hilhouse's son was his executor when he died in 1826] And what can we see of all this today? Absolutely nothing. Other shipbuilders briefly used the site after Hilhouse had left, and in the years since then a railway, warehouses and roads have been built over it. All traces of Clift House and the Navy dockyard have long disappeared, and the Colliter Brook now runs through a culvert, visible only from the opposite bank as its water emerges on to the muddy bank of the Avon. The B Bond Warehouse that contains the Bristol Record Office is on the bank level with, and opposite, the culvert.

Hilhouse specifically wanted the Redclift site for his Navy work and that is where he built all his larger ships for the King. It is not clear whether he also built merchant ships there, since his later wages books do not record the names of vessels being worked on in the way the early ones did. Neither do they indicate whether the work was carried out at his Hotwells, Redclift or, indeed, Vauxhall or Limekiln yards. That having been said, the importance of the Redclift dockyard to Hilhouse cannot be overstated. This second site, 'being so well suited to effect a launch', enabled him to take full advantage of the boom in merchant shipbuilding for the Navy during the American War of Independence. It was work he was ambitious for, it was the making of his reputation and the foundation upon which the future success of his company was built.

His achievements are all the more outstanding because of the Navy's continued reservations about trusting private shipbuilders with the vital work of helping defend the nation. The supreme importance of the Navy to Britain as a sea-trading island, vulnerable to harassment, raids and ultimately invasion, was recognised by the whole country, and the need for the efficient management of the massive expense this entailed was a national preoccupation. George III himself was closely involved, along with the Admiralty, in major policy matters, and he and they were rigorously held to account by Parliament for the funding they were voted. The Navy Board in turn was the professional body that had to make it all work.

The King and the Admiralty decided what ships were required and the Navy Board designed them and oversaw their building in the royal docks, or with merchants in time of war. In peacetime, the Navy markedly preferred to build its own ships, and this was when the merchant yards attracted naval shipwrights to them, with a reputation, which we have found to be open to dispute, for paying higher wages than they received working for the Crown. Above all, the Navy was sceptical about the merchants' capability to build warships to its standards, and concerned about how their profit motive might lead to their cutting corners. The Navy had its reasons: 'The *Temple* was of great moment for Hull ship building: she sank. The *Ardent* was found to be rotten. London builders grasped this wonderful opportunity to denigrate their Northern rivals, and in 1776 Hull's members of Parliament had to plead for further contracts to be given to the Town by a reluctant Admiralty.'[92] It is for such reasons that the Navy Board employed some of its most experienced shipwrights to act as overseers in merchant yards, and why the practice of fitting-out privately-built ships in royal docks was of comfort to seafaring officers and their men.[93]

Contrary to all this, there are sound reasons to believe that Hilhouse was regarded by the Navy Board as special and competent to a high degree. Not only did it buy the *Termagant* off the stocks from him when she had not been built under the supervision of an overseer, it ordered from him three other ships in a class that had not previously been built in a royal dockyard; the famous *Arethusa*, built by Hilhouse in 1778, was another first in her class. In all three cases the design had been in the hands of Hilhouse's old acquaintance Edward Hunt, and by giving the commissions to Bristol before they had been tried out in its own yards, the Navy showed its high regard for his abilities and reliability. Its usual practice in such a case was to give contracts only to yards on the Thames, where work could be supervised closely.

Most significantly, perhaps, Hilhouse was one of four of the best-known and respected merchant shipbuilders selected to answer a range of questions based on their experience by Middleton's 1792 Commission. He was regarded by the authorities as having been Navy trained, and he was able, hard-working and from a social position they felt comfortable

Clift House in 1890. The photograph is courtesy of Thomas Ware and Sons Ltd. It still hangs in their Clift House tannery office.

with; in brief, he was different from other merchant builders, and they trusted him. Among the Admiralty and Navy Board records there are letters from many merchants seeking orders. There are none from Hilhouse, although we know he made offers. The inference is that his relationship was such that they liked to do business face-to-face. It is true that he did not get everything he wanted, but he does not seem to have been subjected to any rigorous competitive tendering process.

As far as costing was concerned, the merchants' prices per ton increased gradually over the period but remained very similar one to another. Hilhouse charged at the lower end of the range, which might have been another reason why the Navy continued to use him. Eventually a standard rate emerged and the Navy Board records that John Fisher at Liverpool agreed to build a 32-gun ship at £11 15s per ton. The correspondence was endorsed '£11 15s was the price we agreed last week with Mr Hilhouse of Bristol',[94] so he was setting the norm. The relationship had to be good, because the Navy Board was of the firm view that there were costs involved in building at Bristol and Liverpool that were not incurred elsewhere. In a letter to the Admiralty regarding Hilhouse's request to build a 74-gun ship, the Navy Board added some further significant comments:

> ...as this Port is by point of expence at least 40s per ton (more) than any other that we build at excepting Liverpool and in point of time at least six months longer in getting them round to a Kings Port to be fitted we cannot recommend it as a port to be used in this way save in cases of greatest necessity...[95]

'Ships built at a great distance from the Dockyards occasion vast delays and expense in getting their stores to them,' Lord Sandwich went on to explain in his evidence to a 1782 inquiry, during which he had to fend off accusations that insufficient use had been made of merchant yards.

Another major factor in awarding merchant contracts was the supply of good timber, and here Hilhouse had an advantage. As previously discussed, in earlier wars the Navy Board had paid a substantial part of the purchase price of a ship on signing the contract, to enable merchant builder to buy the necessary oak and allow it to stand to season. This practice was discontinued, and we have seen that without the down payment the ensuing cash-flow difficulties were such that the biggest merchant shipbuilder for the Navy, Barnard of Ipswich and Harwich, was among those to go bankrupt. Hilhouse had no difficulty in negotiating a steady supply of timber from the Forest of Dean, via the briefest of voyages down the rivers Wye and Severn into the Avon. The growing shortage of oak, however, had long been a national problem, as highlighted by Roger Fisher, a long-established Liverpool shipbuilder who competed with Hilhouse for Navy orders. In 1763 he wrote sensationally on the subject in his 'alarmist' book *Heart of Oak: a British Bulwark*. Some generations earlier, Francis Baylie of Bristol, building for the Navy as part of Pepys's 'thirty-ship programme' in the late 17th century, was beset by problems in finding suitable timber, and a Navy Board report on his ship the *Oxford* criticised him for using bad plank and trenails. This allegation might not have been well-founded, but Baylie's defence was that he was not able to oversee work personally, and had had to leave the responsibility to his supervisor for months at a time, while he was travelling the country in search of timber. In 1740 the shipwright Teast was given the opportunity to build the *Kinsale* at Bristol, but was unable to source suitable timber and the Navy Board agreed to release him from his obligation if he repaid the £1,150 instalment he had received, and reimbursed the overseer's expenses. Forty years later, after Hilhouse had re-established Bristol in the Navy's eyes, the firm of Teast, Toombs and Blannin pleaded shortage of timber as a reason they could not achieve the launch date for the *Druid*; the Navy Board imposed a penalty for late delivery.

Hilhouse set about overcoming these problems. He had yards for storing large quantities of timber, and the provision of cranes to unload it had been one of his main stipulations when he took on the Hotwells lease from the Merchant Venturers. His timber yard at Hotwells was behind the dockyard on the far side of the road into Bristol, and transferring the timber across it caused some damage to the carriageway. On 10 September 1782 the surveyor of roads in Clifton complained: 'The road from Hotwells is greatly injured by the hawling of timber to Mr Hilhouse's Dock particularly from his yard on the other side of the road.' Hilhouse took heed and supplied gravel for the repairs. He also stored timber at Redclift, as Felix Farley tells us in his *Journal*, reporting on a fossilised bird found inside a tree there: 'The following curiosity occurred at Mr Hilhouse's timber yard at the Redclift a little time ago.'

Timber from the Forest of Dean was a vital resource for the Navy yards as well as for Hilhouse, brought down the Severn in trows and on to Hungroad, the great bend of the

Model of HMS *Cleopatra.*
Courtesy Science Museum,
London.

Avon that lies between the Crockarn Pill and Saint Katherine's Pill, now Chapel Pill, where
it was loaded into supply ships and taken in convoy to the royal dockyards. Between 1783
and 1787 a staggering 2,025 shiploads sailed to Plymouth and 2,783 to Deptford and
Woolwich,[96] while timber intended for Bristol was loaded into lighters or rafts at Hungroad
and towed up the Avon. As we have noted, the price was £1 18s a cartload or per ton,
excluding delivery,[97] and the 64-gun ship built by Hilhouse, the *Nassau*, required 2,000
loads of oak timber. There is no record of Hilhouse being delayed by lack of suitable timber
on any of his Navy ships, but the Navy Board had reason to be concerned that he might.
Benjamin Slade, surveyor at Deptford, was sent to the Forest of Dean to investigate the
supply situation and wrote a dramatic report to the Navy Board on 28 February 1780
beginning with an ominous: I should think myself very remiss in my Duty...' He told of the
use of timber from the Forest in shipbuilding, as well as the malpractices and corruption
taking place there:

> Trees were stolen in the night and cut into coopers' ware. Other trees were shipped to Bristol
> every spring tide; on one day at Gatcombe on Severn there were five or six teams (of horses)
> with timber plank and knees, among which were several useful pieces for ships of 50 and 64
> guns. Unless some method was found to prevent this depredation in a few years the whole
> Forest must be destroyed.[98]

Despite all these possible difficulties, having acquired the Redclift site and carried out the
work there to equip it as a shipyard, Hilhouse entered into a new period of impressively
intensive shipbuilding for the Navy.[99] When he launched the *Medea* in April 1778 he was
already working on the *Crescent*, and in the following month he offered to build another
28- or 32-gun ship. By 18 July, however, he was asking for a six-week gap before starting
the next Navy ship, probably because he wanted to begin building it at Redclift, which was
not quite ready. This confidence bordered on arrogance but it met with only a mild rebuke
from the Navy, saying it would discuss further projects 'when the ship he has got is
finished'. In fact he was already working on another (so far unnamed) frigate, and on 18

June 1778 the Admiralty wrote: 'The 32-gun ship building at Bristol is to be registered under the name of *Cleopatra*.'[100] She was larger than the previous two at 678 tons, carrying 220 men and 32 guns, in the Thetis/Amazon class. The *Cleopatra* was copper-bottomed at Bristol and on 1 March 1780 the Navy Board ordered Plymouth to survey her on arrival and 'see if copper properly put on'. It apparently was, as the board paid a rare compliment to the makers, and instructed the overseer to 'acquaint them that we are glad the works on the *Cleopatra* so well performed'.[101]

After these first three frigates were completed, the *Arethusa*, probably the most famous of all Hilhouse's Navy vessels, is likely to have been the first King's ship to be built at Redclift. With 38 guns she was considerably larger than the three Hilhouse had built at Hotwells, and he must have felt well justified in his decision to expand across the river. The *Arethusa*'s launch on 3 June 1780, was greeted with great acclaim in Bristol, and Nicholas Pocock, with whom Hilhouse was to collaborate a few years later on a series of naval paintings, produced a picture of her which was so popular it was engraved and sold many prints. It helped ensure that her colourful career was closely followed by many Bristolians.

1780 was a spectacularly successful year for Hilhouse, in fact, for not only did he launch his first Navy ship from Redclift, he concluded another gratifying deal in building on a speculative basis the *Termagant*, which the Admiralty bought 'on the stocks'. He had built her as a privateer for a crew of 160 men and carrying 28 guns, but her fine lines proved attractive to the Navy and she was classed as a Corvette sixth rate. Buying *Termagant* in this way was clearly an affirmation of the board's confidence in Hilhouse; after all, she was not built under the supervision of an overseer, and the decision was also a mark of official approval of the new facilities at Redclift. In fact it just got better for Hilhouse, as having launched two ships from there in the previous month, he achieved his goal on 13 July 1780, when he received no fewer than three orders for the larger ships he wished to build, two of 44 guns and one of 52.

Less than two years later, on 25 April 1782, it was with supreme confidence that he offered to build two more ships of 74 and 64 guns. Not for the first time, however, the authorities were proving to be anything but a pushover, and after the Admiralty consulted the Navy Board it replied at some length and in no uncertain terms:

> The proposal to build ships of the Line at Bristol has been before us more than once and on the most mature consideration postponed until we have acquired more experience of the safety of conducting ships of a smaller class down this river. The navigation of the Avon is so intricate and hazardous from the rapidity of the tides and the narrowness of the channel that ships of war (that) will take the ground in some parts of it with a falling tide must not only run the hazard of being ruined but also stop the navigation of the river till she could be removed. For these reasons we have proceeded with great caution in building at the Port of Bristol and begun with a frigate only. We have now ventured as far as a ship of 50 guns and

Engraving of HMS *Arethusa* scudding under foresail in a storm off Plymouth.

Engraving after Pocock of HMS *Arethusa*, built by Hilhouse in 1781. She was a favourite among the Bristol populace, who followed her exploits.

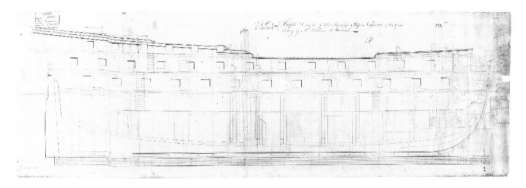

Draught of HMS *Nassau*, 1785, Hilhouse's largest ship for the Navy. The profile draught is of 'His Majesty's Ship Nassau of 64 guns building by Mr Hilhouse at Bristol' and is initialled E H by Hunt, Chief Surveyor for the Navy and Hilhouse's valuable contact. © National Maritime Museum, Greenwich, London.

> should she be got down to King Road without difficulty we shall not object to trying a ship of
> 64 guns but could not proceed further until we have more experience of the River...[102]

As before, however, it seems that Hilhouse's confidence carried the day, and on 20 September 1785 the 64-gun *Nassau* was successfully launched and conducted down the river. We have already touched upon William Dyer's diary entry for that day, and *Felix Farley's Journal* reported:

> The Nassau frigate pierced for 64 guns, one of the largest vessels ever built on the Avon, was
> launched from Mr Hilhouse's yard on 20 September 1785. Amongst the crowds gathered to
> witness the ceremony were great numbers of Peasants with red cloaks, then very popular in
> rural districts. Three Irish Bishops, visitors at the Hot Well, were also present at the launch.[103]

A fascinating glimpse of the occasion.

In all, Hilhouse built 12 ships for the Navy, and his success in fulfilling his contracts apparently allayed the Navy Board's misgivings about Bristol and opened the way for other shipbuilders in the city. On 7 January 1780 the board wrote: 'Acquaint Messrs Teast Tombs and Blannin that as soon as their slips are made safe and proper for the purpose of building a Frigate of 32 guns we shall contract with them on the same terms as Mr Hilhouse has built the *Cleopatra*.'[104] On 16 March Rundle, the overseer at Bristol, reported that 'Teast's slips suffice for building Frigates', and the contract was confirmed. Unlike Hilhouse, whose contracts all went smoothly, Teast, Toombs and Blannin had less success with their Navy ventures, lacking their neighbour's organisational skills. The launch date for their first ship, the frigate *Druid*, was missed due to 'want of men and materials', according to Rundle, and the Admiralty applied the full penalty in the contract. She was finally commissioned at Bristol in June 1783. In fact their other ship, the *Hermione*, was launched before the *Druid* on 9 September 1782, but her name was to become notorious not only within the Navy but in the country at large. In 1797 she fell to an infamous mutiny in which her crew killed their captain and – the ultimate disgrace and unforgivable offence – delivered her to the Spanish enemy. She was retaken in 1799 and retribution meted out to those mutineers captured, and in fairness, she continued in service until 1805, with her name significantly changed to *Retaliation* and finally *Retribution*.

Before moving on to the next stage in Hilhouse's career, it is interesting to look at the history of his Navy ships after they left his yards, and see how they compared with others in their classes built elsewhere. Of course, the fortunes of war and weather play a crucial part in this, as we have seen with his first two ships, the *Medea* and *Crescent*, both in the Enterprise class of small 28-gun frigates, of which a total of 26 were built. We know the *Medea* gave good value, active in wartime and then, after being hulked in 1801, serving as a hospital ship until being sold out of the Navy 27 years after her launch. The *Crescent* fared less happily, unfortunate in being captured by the French two years after her commissioning but giving a further five years after that, albeit in enemy service. Other merchant-built ships in the Enterprise class included some very long-serving ones; many of them were hulked at the end of the Revolutionary War but continued in service to an average of 41 years. The three ships in the class built in royal dockyards averaged 26 years.

Hilhouse's third ship, the *Cleopatra*, a 32-gun frigate in the Thetis class, gave 32 years' service before being broken up in 1814. She was involved in the battle of Dogger Bank on 5 August 1781 and saw much action in the Napoleonic Wars, in particular the capture of Martinique in 1809. This seems a long time, but the average length of service for this class of 18 ships, none of which was built in a royal dockyard, was 30 years. There is a model of the *Cleopatra* in the Science Museum.[105]

The *Termagant* was the next Hilhouse ship; she was the one built speculatively as a privateer but bought on the stocks by the Navy. Built for a crew of 160 and carrying 28 guns, she was initially classed as a corvette sixth rate but was modified to an 18-gun sloop two years later. This was not a success, and in 1795 she was used to form part of a boom across the Thames at Gravesend, and sold out of the Navy the next year. She gave 15 years' service with no other comparisons possible, as she was a one-off.

The *Arethusa*, launched on 10 April 1781, was unusual in a merchant-built ship as she was the first in her class to be built, and therefore had a class named after her. She was a fifth rate of 928 tons, had a crew of 270 men, and had been designed by Hilhouse's colleague at Woolwich, Edward Hunt. As we have noted, Hilhouse was asked to build the first of several of Hunt's designs, highlighting the good understanding between them. As a 38-gun frigate, the largest so far built by Hilhouse, she is said to have been particularly popular among Bristolians – and of all his ships she certainly achieved the greatest fame, as the many models, half-models, paintings and engravings of her testify.[106] She enjoyed an action-packed career under some outstanding captains. Her first, Sir Richard Pearson,

Original Hilhouse half models:

HMS *Arethusa*, 1781. 5th Rate.

Albion 1782, a West Indiaman of 350 tons for Philip Protheroe.

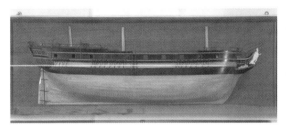

The *Lord William Bentinck* 1828, an East Indiaman of 564 tons.

© Bristol's Museums, Galleries and Archives.

did much to persuade the Navy of the advantages of the new invention in fire power, the carronade,[107] and in 1781 she was in action attacking a French convoy off Ushant.

In the next war against France she was under the command of Sir Edward Pellew, later Viscount Exmouth, who played a fringe role as the captain of the *Indefatigable* in some of CS Forester's Horatio Hornblower novels (and a rather more prominent part in the television series based on them). Along with four other British frigates she took out a squadron of four French frigates, and four months later she drove two more French frigates ashore, taking many prisoners. From then on she was regularly in action in the Caribbean; in 1806, with the *Anson*, she inflicted major damage on the Spanish at Havana and under Captain James Brisbane in 1807 she took the West Indian island of Curacao. In this, probably *Arethusa*'s most glorious action, the flamboyant Brisbane took her into the harbour until her jib projected over the town wall, and then wrote his summons to the garrison to surrender on the ship's capstan. This demand was defiantly refused, and at 6.15 a.m. the *Arethusa* opened fire. By noon the island had submitted, and honours were given to all involved on the British side for such a glorious victory. It was the highlight of the vessel's proud career of 33 years. The other two ships in her class also did well, with the *Phaeton*, built in Liverpool, giving 45 years of service and the Woolwich-built *Minerva* a solid 23.

Hilhouse's next three Naval ships were all in the larger Roebuck class of 44-gun frigates, which had been designed to fill a special need during the American War of Independence,

where vessels with a heavier armament were especially useful against the Americans' privateers along the eastern seaboard. The *Roebuck* herself features frequently in the *Medea's*
log of engagements off the American coast. Fifth rate two-deckers designed by Sir Thomas
Slade, 879 tons, 140 feet long and carrying 300 men, they were larger ships than any
Hilhouse had built before. The Roebuck was a big and successful class; 20 in all were built
and as the eponymous ship was built at Chatham while Hilhouse was finishing his apprenticeship there, he was well familiar with the design.

His first, the *Diomede*, was launched in 1781 with great ceremony: 'An incredible
concourse of people assembled on the occasion and it proved a noble launch.' This report
placed the event at the Vauxhall yard; Hilhouse refers to it simply as the Redclift yard in
his wages books but the press gave the name to the part of Redclift nearest to the old
Vauxhall Gardens. *Diomede* went into action under Captain Thomas Frederick on 20
December 1782 and took the 40-gun *South Carolina* off the Delaware in company with
the *Quebec*. In 1794 she was in action off Mauritius and a year later was raiding Dutch
settlements in Ceylon. It was her last serious action: on 2 August 1795 she struck an
uncharted rock and sank near Trincomalee, wrecked on active duty after 14 years' service.

Hilhouse's second ship in the Roebuck class, 'launched from the Hilhouse Yard at
Redcliff', was the second *Seraphis*, the first having been captured by the feared American
privateer John Paul Jones. She served in many ways until being sold in Jamaica for £500
in 1826 after 44 years' service, so she certainly did not owe the Navy very much. The third
ship, the *Charon*, served for 22 years, which surpassed the average of 19 years achieved by
the 18 merchant-built ships in the class, only two of which were 'lost'. In comparison, the
two Roebucks built at Chatham were exemplary, each serving for 37 years before being
broken up; in this class, at least, Naval yard ships appear to have out-performed their
merchant-built sisters.

After the *Seraphis*, the next two ships built by Hilhouse for the Navy were joint initia-
tives with Edward Hunt. The *Trusty* and the *Melampus* were both 'firsts', but were not
followed by others to the same design, despite proving they were good value. *Trusty* was
a fourth rate 50-gun two-decker of 1,080 tons carrying 350 men, unusual in that Hunt
adapted her design from his earlier Grampus class design, extending her length and giving
her several specific features, probably to enable her to act as a flagship. It was perhaps for
this reason that she was given to Hilhouse to build instead of going to Navy yards. She was
launched on 9 October 1782, taking no part in the American War but ready for the outbreak
of the Revolutionary war in 1793, when she became the admiral's flagship and took part in
the capture of Tobago. Since the war against the French demanded larger ships, 50-gunners
were gradually phased out, and in 1801 the *Trusty* was kept busy transporting troops for
the war in Egypt before being converted into a prison hospital ship. She gave 17 years' active
service a further 17 years as a troopship and prison ship before being broken up.

Melampus was also a fifth rate, but carrying 260 men and mounting 36 guns. She gave

Model of HMS *Melampus* 1785. © Bristol's Museums, Galleries & Archives.

30 years' service before being sold to the Dutch Navy. Launched in 1785, it was not until 1794 that she had the chance of active service when under Captain Thomas Wells she joined the *Arethusa* in action against the French admiral Descargaux. Life hotted up considerably after that, and in the following year she and three frigates destroyed a French convoy in Carteret Bay. On 12 October 1798 she took part in the capture of the French flagship *Hoche* and three frigates, while years later, on 14 September 1806 under the Bristol captain Stephen Poyntz,[108] she and two 74-gun ships opened fire on the French 74-gunner *Impetueux*, which then ran on shore and was burned. The *Melampus* was sold in 1815, again to the Dutch government, but there is a model of her in Bristol City Museum.

The *Nassau*, launched on 20 September 1785, was in the Ardent class – not a happy pedigree, since the *Ardent*'s name had been tarnished by the failure of the builders Blaydes of Hull, providing the Navy with further evidence of the fragility of merchant shipwrights, especially in the North East. The royal dockyard at Chatham had built the second ship in *Raisonable*, which as we have noted became the first ship Nelson served on. She was launched in 1768, a year after Hilhouse had arrived there as an apprentice, so again he would have been familiar with her design and given confidence in his bid to build the *Nassau*. She was the first 64-gun ship the Navy was prepared to try at Bristol; third class, 160 feet long, 1,376 tons and carrying 500 men, it is no wonder she was the largest ship to be launched on the Avon. The *Nassau* was wrecked off Holland in 1799 after 14 years' service, but the other five merchant-built ships in the class gave longer service and the *Raisonable* an impressive 47 years before she was broken up. Hilhouse's last Naval vessel in this period, the *Severn*, a fifth rate 44-gun ship launched in 1786, was a two-decker in the Adventure class, again designed by Hunt. Built at Redclift and launched in April 1786, she took the *Republique Triumphante* in the West Indies in 1797 in company with the *Pelican* but was wrecked at Grenville Bay, Jersey, in 1804 having given 18 years' service.

Of all Hilhouse's ships for the Navy, three – the *Nassau*, the *Diomede* and the *Severn* – were wrecked and lost. All the others gave an above-average length of service and good value to the Crown, compared with others in their classes. So we might now ask what went wrong, since despite this track record, the *Severn* turned out to be the last ship Hilhouse built for the Navy, with the exception of the *Albacore*, a 16-gun sloop ordered from him much later, in 1804. One of the most perplexing mysteries of his career is why, when war against France broke out again in 1793 and preoccupied the nation for decades, the Navy Board found almost no further use for him. The year 1786 saw the end of his golden age, and heralded a supremely testing time for Hilhouse and his business.

CHAPTER SEVEN

ℭℜ℀℈

Life Away from the Dockyard

WITH THE EXCITEMENT OF THE EXPANSION INTO THE REDCLIFT DOCKYARD AND THE PRESSURE OF HIS Navy contracts during this most hectic period of his life, it might have been understandable if Hilhouse had neglected other aspects of it. It is testimony to his energy and well-balanced personality that the truth was very different, for family affairs claimed much of his attention.

At the start of his time at Hotwells he had taken the sensible decision not to take on the large Dock House on site, and he and his new wife saw no reason to change that decision on their marriage. They needed to be close to the Hotwells Dock, however, to provide the board – 'good and sufficient meat and drink' – and lodging for the increasing number of apprentices they were taking on. Besides, Hilhouse was spending long hours in the two dockyards as his new shipbuilding and repairing business expanded, so that was another reason why they needed to live near by. At this time, in the fourth quarter of the 18th century, Hotwells was an exciting place in which to live. It was developing fast, both as a spa and as a dockyard centre, at a small but significant distance downriver from the city of Bristol itself. The city council watched this development enviously, and in 1776 managed to secure the transfer of the area from the county of Gloucestershire to the city of Bristol.

The Society of Merchant Venturers was also interested in getting a profitable return on its investments in Hotwells, which would be increased were the area to become a part of the city, and this was the speculative atmosphere in which the Hilhouses found themselves living. In the records of the Hotwells Dockyard two small tenements are mentioned, suitable for occupation by a foreman, perhaps, but not for the owner and his family, so it is probable that after their marriage the couple at first rented a house close to the dockyard, knowing that if all worked out well they would be able to take over the Dock House at a later date. At this early stage, when he was still working towards the Navy contracts he so wanted, the cautious Hilhouse did not wish to over-extend himself financially and knew he needed to concentrate above all on building up his business.

Their first child, George, was born on 6 April 1778 and soon after baptised at St Andrew's Church, Clifton,[109] the parish church the Hilhouses continued to attend after they moved in to the Dock House, and in which their other children were later christened. As they celebrated the birth of this first child, however, James Martin and Mary also mourned a death: that of Hilhouse's uncle William, who had guided his late brother's son through the start of his shipbuilding enterprise, and seen him marry the daughter of one of his old acquaintances and start his own family. William was only 51; like his brother he had served in public office and his wife Rachel was voted a pension of £40 a year by the Common Council of the City as 'the widow of the late Sword Bearer who died in office'.

Apart from the sadness and sense of loss his death caused to his family, William's death had a further consequence: the sale of number 12, St James Square, the house he and his family had lived in for so long, and into which Hilhouse and his mother Mary had moved after James Hilhouse's death, and where she had stayed ever since. Rachel moved to Frenchay[110] and Mary, then aged 50, made the bold decision to live in Bath; her niece, William's eldest daughter Mary, aged 24, chose to go there with her as her companion. Hilhouse's grandfather, James senior, had bought a lease on a property in Walcot Street in the city in the year before his death, probably as an investment, and while Bath's feverishly fashionable years were on the wane, property there was still at a premium. He had left the house to William in his will, and it had been let, but on his death it passed to James Martin, and opened the way for the change of scene his mother had decided upon.

It was by then called Cornwell House, as it had a well in its grounds. Bath City Corporation had originally acquired it from the Hospital of St John the Baptist next door, and James senior had bought the lease for a period of 99 years or three lives. In the lease the land on which the house stood was called St Michael's Yard, described as an orchard which ran down to the river Avon. During the years the Hilhouses owned the lease they made several changes and extensions to the house so that by the time the two Marys moved in it was a comfortable and pleasant place to live. Hilhouse's mother lived there until she died in 1796 at the age of 83, while his cousin Mary, who had married the Revd Francis Randolph, continued living there as the named tenant – and indeed was still living there as a widow aged 83 in 1836. After her death a chapel was built on the courtyard facing Walcot Street.

After the upheavals following his uncles' death, Hilhouse did not let family concerns divert him from his business objectives. In fact the early death of both his father and uncle might well have acted as a spur to him to achieve his own ambitions in as short a time as possible; his business was flourishing just as he had hoped and believed it would. At the same time, his family was also expanding: Mary Ann, the couple's first daughter, was born on 28 July 1779 and a second daughter, Caroline, was baptised at St Andrew's on 18 April 1781. The move to the Dock House was becoming more and more irresistible, and so it was that on 30 August of that year Hilhouse felt confident to sign a lease on it, and the family finally moved in. The Society of Merchant Venturers, his landlord, was generous over the necessary repairs and improvements to the house and the term of the lease was 'for as long as he shall come to the Dock'.

The accommodation was extensive and is best described in the auction particulars drawn up when Hilhouse gave notice to quit seven years later. It comprised:

A Hall, 4 Parlours, China and Pantry, Kitchen, Back Kitchen, Larder and Pantries on the

The Avon Gorge and Bristol Hotwell, by JMW Turner. This watercolour dates from his visit in 1792. He had in mind a series of engraved views of the Avon in the manner of Pocock.

ground floor and the same number of rooms on the first and second stories with boarding Garretts. It has a good cellar and plenty of both sorts of water. The house is very convenient and has lately been fitted up at considerable expence.[111]

It is said in the society's records that all Hilhouse's 'long family' were born there. This is not quite true, as George, Mary Anne and Caroline had been born before they moved in; but at least six children were indeed born in the Dock House, which would seem 'long' enough for most families. The Hilhouses stayed there until 1820, when they moved up to Princes Buildings and the Dock House was occupied by the secretary of the Merchant Venturers for a further 30 years until it was demolished in 1850. The materials from it sold for a mere £250, a sad end for a house which was insured for £1,000 when it was occupied by Hilhouse, and provided him with a busy and happy family home as well as an excellent venue for the parties to mark the launch of his various ships.

The period between 1781 and 1786 was eventful and demanding for Hilhouse and his wife. Three sons were born to them: Martin in 1783, Robert in 1784 and Abraham in 1786, in which year Hilhouse was churchwarden at St Andrew's.[112] During the same five years his yards built and successfully launched eight large Navy ships; this was the time that saw the fulfilment of his business ambition, but was also a period of continuous and intense work as he juggled the all-important Navy contracts with the needs of his merchant customers and ran his two yards efficiently and profitably. In his thirties he found himself the owner of the best-equipped and most successful shipbuilding yard in Bristol, highly regarded by his peers and the Navy Board, an involved member of the influential Society of Merchant Venturers, the father of a growing 'long family', and on the death of his uncle, the head of his extended family.

It is perhaps surprising, then, to find that during this hectic period, Hilhouse was also at his most active in pursuing his passion for drawing and painting. He was already gaining a national reputation as a shipbuilder who was also an accomplished draughtsman of the fine points of ships' lines. He had undoubted artistic ability, as his surviving paintings, drawings and draughts demonstrate, not to mention his ships' models, and his talents were very attractive to other local artists who were trying to represent ships, especially Navy ships, as accurately as possible. At this period when the exploits of the British Navy were eagerly followed and their victories widely celebrated by the public, there was a great demand for maritime paintings. Hilhouse met and became friendly with the most talented artists working in Bristol and made acquaintance with another artistic group of people, involved in the theatre. This went beyond Bristol, where the Theatre Royal had opened not long before, to London, at a time when the stage was enjoying great popularity and owners and impresarios such as David Garrick were pioneering adventurous developments in design, scenery and special effects.

It was a truly revolutionary period in the arts and Hotwells, named after its warm water springs, was at the height of its ambition to out-do Bath as a watering place. It was keen to attract fashionable visitors from London as well as tempting members of Bristol society to enjoy its spa facilities. Bristol might no longer have been the second city in the land commercially, but it was still clinging on to its 'golden age' and the Hot Wells, with their famous curative waters, assembly rooms, concerts, promenades, public breakfasts, excursions across the river to the village of Ashton and carriage drives on Durdham Down, was enjoying a reputation as a fashionable resort. Hilhouse, with his shipbuilding yard at Hotwells and his big, newly-furbished Dock House, was at the heart of it all. It was not only members of the fashionable world in search of amusement and those seeking cures for their various ailments who came to take the waters at Hotwells; writers such as Tobias Smollett and Daniel Defoe had earlier in the century visited the spa and described its attractions, and artists including JMW Turner, who sketched the spa buildings at Hotwells, were attracted there by the grandeur of the Gorge with its river traffic, the open countryside of Durdham Downs above the river and the charms of the village of Clifton.

Among the artists working in Bristol at this time, the man with whom Hilhouse forged the closest friendship and working partnership was Nicholas Pocock. It was no surprise that the two should form a close relationship, since they shared a similar background. Before he took to a career in painting, Pocock had for many years been a ship's captain in Bristol. First apprenticed to his namesake father Nicholas in 1757,[113] he was then employed by William Champion, who was later a partner with Noble and Farr at their Hotwells dock. Pocock commanded ships trading for him with Charleston, and later to the West Indies. While on these voyages he kept a lively and detailed log book, meticulously recording the essential information but also depicting in watercolours the islands' topography and events at sea. Like Hilhouse, he had a prodigious artistic talent which was at first sight perhaps at odds with his everyday work, but in the 1770s, while still at sea, he began to specialise in maritime paintings and proceeded to built up a growing reputation in Bristol.

At a time when Britain's Navy was engaged in yet another life-or-death struggle against her enemies on the high seas, paintings of naval engagements were much in vogue, and Pocock gained some lucrative commissions. While he was able to draw on his own experience as a ship's captain and was familiar with much of his subject matter, in his friend Hilhouse he recognised a man with an obvious talent for meticulous, detailed and exact depictions of ships' lines and dispositions under sail, and one with whose collaboration he could add further authenticity to his work. Hilhouse's career in shipbuilding was in this respect of great value to them both; not only did he have wide practical experience, but his fascination for ship design had caused him to collect and study the draughts of a wide range of ships. In this respect he had no doubt been encouraged by Edward Hunt, the influential man he had met at Woolwich early in his apprenticeship; in any event, he had somehow obtained the plans of many of the Navy's great ships of war dating back to the 1740s, as well as those being built or worked upon during his early career. His ambition to build large ships for the Navy meant that he had researched and studied these diligently, and kept them to refer to and compare with his own endeavours.

The high point of Hilhouse's public artistic career was his collaboration with Pocock in a series of paintings on the Battle of the Saintes, one of which now hangs in the Bristol Museum and Art Gallery. The battle, on 12 April 1782, was especially crucial to the merchants of Bristol as Lord Rodney's defeat of Admiral Grasse ensured that their vitally important colonial investments in the West Indies had been saved from invasion and annexation by the French. When news of Rodney's victory arrived in the city there were ecstatic public celebrations. He was granted the Freedom of the City and the Merchants Hall and there was another outburst of jubilation in Bristol when he came to receive these awards. There is even a monument alluding to this victory in Tortworth Church in

Series of Hilhouse drawings depicting English and French ships at the Battle of the Saintes, 1782, made in preparation for the subsequent paintings. © Bristol's Museums, Galleries & Archives.

Opening of the Battle or Breaking the Line, signed JM Hilhouse. Courtesy of Sotheby's. Painting in private collection.

South Gloucestershire, erected by the Ducie family. A popular ballad gives a flavour of the national rejoicing, and it was no doubt sung heartily by Hilhouse and his Bristol Catch Club, of which more later:

> True Britons all of each degree
> Rejoice around the nation
> Full bumpers drink and merry be
> Upon this just occasion
> Let mirth on every brow appear
> Rodney victorious is we hear
> For he had drubbed haughty Monsieur
> Success to gallant Rodney.

In the battle, off the Iles des Saintes south of Guadeloupe in the West Indies, the French were outnumbered by Rodney's force and five of their ships of the line were captured, including Admiral Grasse and his flagship. Rodney, in his flagship the *Formidable*, adopted a controversial and revolutionary tactic by mounting a vigorous head-on attack on the enemy line in order to break it, rather than the conventional sailing parallel to the opposing

The Close of the Battle of the Saintes. The painting is a collaboration between the Bristol shipbuilder and draughtsman JM Hilhouse and the Marine artist Pocock.
© Bristol's Museums, Galleries & Archive.

fleet. This surprise manoeuvre won the day, and his comprehensive victory not only ensured the safety of Britain's West Indian possessions but restored national pride in the Navy. Lord Rodney became a hero overnight, and when he dined with the Merchant Venturers as guest of honour in their hall in King Street, it was reported that:

> Several hundred of citizens met and formed a magnificent cavalcade consisting of equestrians and carriages forming a long line interspersed with bands of music embosomed in laurels in boats placed upon wheeled carriages. Also three persons in characters and costumes of Mars, Britannia and Minerva seated upon thrones likewise upon wheeled carriages with their attendants at their feet. In the cavalcade was a vessel of about 40 tons burthen also on a wheeled carriage drawn by horses, having swivels on board that were fired occasionally...[114]

It was obviously a night to remember.

On 28 October 1783 the Merchant Venturers voted the sum of 20 guineas for a commemorative painting of the victory to be painted by Nicholas Pocock; there was no discussion of any other painter, since although there were other candidates, he was the unanimous choice. Pocock was in his last days as a sea captain in the early 1780s, having married Ann Evans in 1780. Such was the acclaim with which his entries to the Royal

Academy were greeted that in 1781 he was elected a member, a quickly-gained accolade which ensured his national as well as local reputation. In 1783, the year of the Merchant Venturers' commission, he was appointed the Navy's official painter, and later accompanied the fleet to record its exploits, notably at the Battle of Aboukir. Happily, his marriage proved equally fruitful, and he and Ann went on to have eight children.

The Merchant Venturers' commission was Pocock's most important to date, and was completed after paintings on the same subject in which he collaborated with Hilhouse, at least two years after the battle had taken place. The painting hangs to this day in a prominent position in the Merchants' Hall. Although Pocock was some eight years older than Hilhouse and a Quaker, Hilhouse came from a Dissenter background and they had many family connections. Pocock had been apprenticed to his father in Bristol as a merchant seaman and knew James Hilhouse, the sugar trader and privateer. More relevantly, in 1773 Hilhouse was the new young shipbuilder who took over from the Merchant Venturers the dock originally built by Pocock's Quaker friend and employer, William Champion; and most important of all, Hilhouse was the one person in Bristol who could give the painter clear and definitive descriptions of the ships involved in the battle. Both Rodney's flagship the *Formidable* and his second-in-command Admiral Hood's ship, the *Barfleur* had been built at Chatham during Hilhouse's time there, and he knew them well.

In the Bristol Museum archive is a series of drawings by Hilhouse of French and British ships which were used to co-ordinate the collaboration between the pair in producing two notable paintings of the Battle of the Saintes at different stages.[115] A comparison of Hilhouse's pencil and ink sketches reveals that they form the exact basis for details in the finished works; some of them are quick outlines, others show just a section of a ship in detail, others are meticulous studies of the whole structure from the perspective in which they appear in the final version. In these, details of spars, rigging, pattern and the shape of the sails as they conform to the prevailing wind and the manoeuvre of the ship at the moment it is depicted are proof that Hilhouse drew on his knowledge of design and sailing qualities to give the paintings authentic and convincing immediacy, and they are potent testimony to his artistic talent. The painting showing the start of the engagement is signed JM Hilhouse, the other, unsigned, showing Grasse's surrender, is the one that hangs in the City Museum and Art Gallery. Hilhouse owned both these paintings and they were in the possession of the Charles Hill family, the successors to the firm started by Hilhouse, until they were sold at auction in 1981. A further version of the close of the battle, signed with Hilhouse's initials, remains in the Hill family.

The catalogue produced by Osmond Tricks for the auction on 5 March 1981 contains photographs and descriptions of both pictures, and the catalogue notes: 'John (sic) Martin Hilhouse was a renowned Naval Architect, building many Naval vessels for the Admiralty. He was a marine artist and a friend of Philip James de Loutherbourg RA'. That Hilhouse knew and worked with Pocock is a matter of record, but how did he come to be associated with de Loutherbourg? In many ways this quite probable association sheds a fascinatingly different light on the wealthy young man enjoying unprecedented success as a ship builder. PJ de Loutherbourg was a celebrated painter who specialised in dramatic depictions of Naval actions. One of his most famous works, *The Cutting out of the French Corvette La Chevrette*, was engraved and much reproduced as a print at the time.[116] He was a flamboyant character, born in Strasbourg in 1740. His family planned for him to enter the Lutheran church, but that was never his style and after moving to Paris to pursue his artistic dream, he became an immediate success and was the youngest person ever to be elected to the French Royal Academy.

Leaving his wife and family behind after little more than a year, he moved to London, finding equal success there and becoming a member of the Royal Academy, where he exhibited regularly, in 1781. His paintings were collected by the Prince of Wales, the future George IV, and many of his fashionable friends, while de Loutherbourg counted among his circle Joshua Reynolds and Thomas Gainsborough, the most popular and highly-paid artists of their day. As well as success with his paintings, de Loutherbourg found lucrative work in the theatre, with David Garrick hiring him at a very generous £500 a year to paint the scenery and devise the stage effects for the extravaganzas he was putting on at his Drury Lane Theatre. He made several visits to Bristol, on one occasion spending some considerable time there, producing paintings of scenes around Hotwells, the Avon Gorge and Clifton. Garrick also had links with the city as a result of his interest in the Theatre Royal in King Street; in 1776 he came to Bristol to see the newly erected theatre for himself, and was so impressed that he wrote the prologue and epilogue for its opening night.

With this background it is becoming clear how James Martin Hilhouse could find a place in this exotic painter's work, but the connection went well beyond that of visiting artist and wealthy provincial patron of the arts. Garrick was well known for putting on amazingly intricate productions at Drury Lane, often including naval scenes, and de Loutherbourg found Hilhouse's detailed knowledge and artistic ability invaluable in this work, and their common interest in ships and painting also drew them together. As an aside, Garrick was not disinterested in his appreciation of sound shipbuilding, for one of his Huguenot ancestors survived a shipwreck in the Channel while fleeing to England to escape religious persecution. His poem *Hearts of Oak* reflects his trust in shipwrights, and with William Boyce's music, it is still the official march of the Royal Navy.

It might well have been the opening of Bristol Theatre Royal that first brought Hilhouse and de Loutherbourg together. The former's hospitable father-in-law, George Bush of Clift House, had a company that was a member of the Coopers' Hall in King Street, next door to the theatre, and might well have got to know the artist and Garrick himself at this time and introduced them to his daughter's successful husband. In fact Bush's own father-in-law, Henry Bright, had been a keen supporter of the Theatre Royal project, one of the 50 who put up money to become proprietors before its opening.

Battle of the Saintes. Nicholas Pocock. Courtesy Society of Merchant Venturers.

Once Hilhouse had made contact, however, opportunities for meeting de Loutherbourg were not limited to Bristol. At this time he was in discussions with the Navy Board about building more and larger ships, and the lack of correspondence that exists in the archives at Kew suggests that he was regularly in London for talks; a considerable number of letters from his competitors in Liverpool, London and Buckler's Hard survive on file, but there are none at all from Hilhouse. We already know he was not averse to the delights of London life and no stranger to the Hum Mums club in Covent Garden, so it is easy to imagine him popping just around the corner to Garrick's Theatre Royal in Drury Lane, to cast his eye over de Loutherbourg's work.

Not that the Frenchman found lasting success in this country. It seems he had a penchant for the more lurid characters on the fringes of society, and in 1786 he met the magician and Freemason 'Count' Cagliostro and was instructed by him in occult sciences. The following year Cagliostro went to Europe and de Loutherbourg followed him but there was a falling-out and the latter returned to London, apparently after challenging his mentor to a duel. Cagliostro then found himself embroiled in allegations over the theft of Marie Antoinette's jewels, but after being sentenced to death he was reprieved and released. Meanwhile, de Loutherbourg and his English wife found another hero in the mesmerist and magnetiser Dr Mainauduc, who arrived in Bristol in 1788 from France and gave an

Third painting of the Battle of the Saintes, initialled by Hilhouse. Awaiting restoration. By kind permission of the owners.

extraordinarily wildly acclaimed series of public lectures in the city. People of 'rank and fortune' hastened west from London to be magnetised or to place themselves under Mainauduc's tuition.

Magnetism had become discredited and disreputable in France, where societies had been formed for curing disease by the process. 'Some of these societies were a scandal to morality, being joined by profligate men of depraved appetites, who took a disgusting delight in witnessing young girls in convulsions,' it was reported. 'Many of the pretended magnetisers were asserted at the time to be notorious libertines who took that opportunity of gratifying their passions.'[117] Those hastening to Bristol appear to have been of a different type, however, and it was recorded by a Dr Winter: 'They amounted to one hundred and twenty seven, among whom there were one duke, one duchess, one marchioness, two countesses, one earl, one baron, three baronesses, one bishop, five right honorable gentlemen and ladies, two baronets, seven members of parliament, one clergyman, two physicians, seven surgeons besides ninety-two gentlemen and ladies of respectability.'[118]

Philip de Loutherbourg and his wife were in great demand in Bristol, where tickets to witness their strange manipulations sold at quite extraordinary prices of one to three guineas.[119] The Vauxhall Garden was on the banks of the Avon beside Hilhouse's Redclift shipyard and opposite the Hot Wells, and when the proprietors there were seeking to attract the best clientele away from Bath they were frequently annoyed by boisterous crowds on the Vauxhall side disrupting their spa's dignity. It is certain from a collection of drawings by de Loutherbourg at the Tate Gallery that he was sketching scenes at Hotwells, in the Gorge and on the Downs in about 1786, on a tour which included copper smelting works in South Wales and several Bristol Channel ports from where Hilhouse recruited his shipwrights. Despite his wild excesses, he had many topics of mutual interest to discuss with the hard-working ship builder, and when he travelled on from South Wales to Ironbridge it is a reminder that both men were fascinated by the dawn of the Industrial Revolution. Already, Hilhouse, at this early stage, was planning to build the first steam-powered vessels at Bristol.

What brought the two together was their interest in painting and depicting ships accurately, and the rest was presumably just fun, and Hilhouse's sense of fun and taste for the theatrical are very apparent from his membership of the Bristol Catch Club. Catches were originally a round for three or more voices, with the words carefully selected and arranged so that they had a comical and often vulgar effect. Singing and listening to them was an exclusively male pastime popular in the 17th century which enjoyed a revival in 1762 when the Noblemen and Gentlemen's Catch Club was formed in London. Bristol formed a similar club in 1774 and Hilhouse joined soon afterwards. The early membership was recorded by a prime mover, Richard Smith, a surgeon at the infirmary: there were four clerics, two attorneys-at-law, a merchant, a silk mercer, Colonel Andrews of the Somerset Militia, the organist, director, composer and publisher Robert Broderip and the cathedral organist Rice Wasborough. A few years later Richard Smith's namesake son recorded that they had been joined by 'other members of the Wasborough family and also a Customs Officer; James Hilhouse Esq, a shipbuilder; a doctor; an Attorney-at-law; Dunbar, a private gentleman; and Applewaite, a West Indian'.

Robert Broderip was a musician of repute and an important member who in 1795 published a book of catches and glees and respectfully dedicated it to 'the members of the Bristol Catch Club and the Cecilian Society'. He also noted some instructions, saying that catches should be sung by 'persons accustomed to singing together and should be supported with humour, and appropriate actions should be used when the style of the catch requires it'. He concluded his dedication wishing that the club would 'long continue to enjoy that harmony and conviviality which has ever distinguished their meetings'.

The club met every Friday evening at the Bush Tavern in Corn Street, where the landlord was well known for good food and hospitality – an essential ingredient for a society with a social side at least as important as its musical accomplishments. For the meticulous Hilhouse, the discipline and precision called for in singing in harmony and interjecting at the right time would have been an added attraction to the fun and camaraderie of the evening. The participants were skilled and well educated, standards were high and their achievements were recognised beyond the Bush Tavern. A newspaper advertised that on 6 June 1786 there would be an evening of entertainment at the Old Trout Tavern in Cherry Lane, off Stokes Croft, where 'Comus Court will be held... and the Gentlemen of the original Catch Club have generously offered their assistance for that night only'. Hilhouse would not have had time to indulge in this sort of evening too frequently, but in 1793 he no doubt gave his patriotic best when singing the glee inspired by the news that the revolutionary enemy had executed the French king and his family:

Fame let thy trumpet sound
Tell all the World around
Great George is King!

It would have amused Garrick and friends in 1795 to read that Hilhouse and the Catch Club was providing a programme of music at the Theatre Royal between performances of *King Lear* and a farce, *The Positive Man* in a bid to appeal to a broader audience. It is not known when the club ceased, but there are no newspaper reports of it after an advertisement for a 'Ladies Night Concert' in 1810. Catches had for many years been gradually censored and replaced by glees to widen their appeal, and such a concert is proof that the Bristol club had followed this trend, and in doing so it might well have lost some of the old attraction of bawdy fun associated with times past. In the event, the musical scene in Bristol moved on to greater heights with the formation of the Bristol Madrigal Society, in which Richard Smith junior played some part. Looking back at the Club in 1842 he wrote: 'James Hilhouse shipbuilder at Hotwells died in 1822... Rice Wasborough, brazier of Narrow Wine Street, brother to John Wasborough the only one yet alive except the Writer'. So it was over, but the club had enjoyed much conviviality for a good number of years and provided Hilhouse with a chance to associate with different people with wide interests – and have some fun. What *would* his father have said?

What all this involvement in the artistic life of his time shows about Hilhouse is that his was a many-faceted character. At the time when he was at the height of his powers – building ships of new design for the Navy, running two dockyards, successfully sourcing his supplies, meeting challenging deadlines, keeping his local merchant customers happy, moving into a new house, buying the latest in sanitary technology, raising a young family and caring for his extended family in the wake of his uncle's death – he still made time for what was obviously to him an important part of his life. He considered his paintings so central to his being that in his will he gave specific instructions about their distribution. These went beyond his own output, since he had clearly been a keen buyer of other artists' work, and in this respect he was not alone. His acquaintance Lowbridge Bright, for example, the wealthy Jamaica merchant, Whig supporter and political activist, also amassed a large collection of paintings, in his case mostly Old Masters. Some of these were auctioned after his death while others, like Hilhouse's, passed down through his family.

Philip de Loutherbourg, *The Battle of the First of June, 1794.*
© National Maritime Museum, Greenwich, London. BHC0470.

What emerges is a picture of a man of exceptional talents in several spheres, with clear commercial instincts yet a creative artistic nature as well. This balance was to prove of great value to Hilhouse in the difficult years that lay ahead, and singing in the Bush Tavern with good friends gave him the opportunity to relax. His father and his sons were involved in local politics and issues, but while he also was concerned, he did not seek any civic or parliamentary office. He saw that there were problems at the port to be overcome and new opportunities with the advent of iron and steam that needed to be thought about and discussed; we can be sure that how best he and his family could address these matters would never have been too far from his mind on these Friday nights at the Bush Tavern.

CHAPTER EIGHT

ᏣᏁ

The French Revolution and Public Duties

On 29 April 1786 Hilhouse launched the *Severn* from the Redclift Dock and had no more Navy ships to build. The American War had ended ingloriously for Britain two years previously, and with it the immediate need for merchant-built Naval ships. It was all over. He had always feared that this might happen, and had always kept his merchant work going for that very reason. His company records show that through 1786 he was building two new merchant ships and a new 'Packett', and working on five other private vessels, so the situation was not immediately desperate. By the following year, however, he had far less work in hand and could afford to employ only 20 shipwrights in his yard. Suddenly his business was in crisis.

Hilhouse had always been a prudent businessman and cautious about over-extending himself, but he now realised decisive action was needed to save his company and stay solvent. He had the sobering example of his competitor Barnard of Ipswich in his mind: despite his national reputation as a skilled shipbuilder, he had been unable to solve his cashflow problems and gone bankrupt. Hilhouse was determined he would not follow him, and with his customary decisiveness he took immediate action: on 28 January 1787 he made what must have been the hardest decision of his life and gave notice to quit the Hotwells Dock, his proudest possession. In all probability he had already begun to dismantle his dockyard across the river at Redclift, which he had set up specifically for his Navy work, and in anticipation of having to leave Hotwells he had taken the precaution of acquiring some facilities for shipbuilding and repairing at the Lime Kiln Dock, near by.

When he informed his landlords of his decision to quit, the Society of Merchant Venturers decided to advertise the leases of the dockyard and Great Dock House separately, so Hilhouse could theoretically have given up the Hotwells Dock, remained in the Dock House and operated his business from Lime Kiln; but in typical fashion he did not compromise with half measures and gave notice to quit the Dock House, too – his family's home since 1781, occupied on a tenancy for as long as he wished to have it. The prospect of leaving the dockyard was a bitter pill to swallow for a proud man like Hilhouse, but it was based on the realities of his business situation. Giving up the Dock House was an equally hard decision, as he had carried out substantial improvements and repairs to it to provide suitably comfortable accommodation for him, his wife Mary, their growing family and various servants and apprentices. Moreover, he had no clear idea of where they would go, though he and Mary must have discussed the options, and she supported him in the decision.

Between September 1781 and February 1782, when business was flourishing, he had spent freely on the house, paying £756 14s 9d on building and decoration works including the hefty sum of £19 11s (about £1,700 in today's money) for an indulgence of his fascination with the latest technology – a very state-of-the-art water closet supplied by one Jos Bramal, who submitted a heavily-headed invoice in respect of it, complete with imposing red seal. Invoices for all these works were characteristically preserved with care by Hilhouse, so that he could reclaim money spent from the Merchant Venturers; he never had any qualms about recouping what he saw as legitimate expenses.

Hilhouse's bill seems to have come as a surprise to the society, which examined it with possibly more than due diligence. It quibbled over the details – Mr Bramal's invoice must have caused some pursed lips – but in the end most of the bill was accepted, though with how much good grace is not known. This cooling in relations between Hilhouse and the Merchant Venturers is perhaps a little surprising after his early days at Hotwells, when the society was falling over itself to provide the facilities he asked for and at the same time secure his assistance with the Floating Dock. It might be that it felt he was taking undue advantage of the terms of his lease, which were, in all fairness, generous to him. Strictly speaking, Hilhouse was quite within his rights in putting in his claim for reimbursement for the improvements to the Dock House – but times were hard, and not just for Hilhouse. Everyone engaged in commerce in Bristol was worried about money, even the Society of Merchant Venturers, which was finding itself faced with unexpected and unwelcome expenses in relation to its ownership of the Hot Wells.

For much of the century the spa had proved an excellent investment for the society, and the popularity of the fashionable wells and their amenities had grown to boost its profits. By the 1770s the Hot Wells were at their height – but then came a sudden and dramatic change, and the society realised the spa needed radical improvements if it were to continue to attract its lucrative clientele. It meant that when, in 1784, it advertised for a tenant to take on the wells, it stipulated that the newcomer would have to carry out various improvements: a wall at the river bank fronting the pump room, which would cost more than £1,000; moves costing £500 to ensure the purity of the spring water, which was liable to being polluted by mud in the tidal river; and the refurbishment of the pump room.[120] To the society's disappointment, though perhaps not entirely to its surprise, it failed to find anyone prepared to take on the lease on these terms, and was reluctantly forced to spend its own money on the improvements. It was during this time that Hilhouse presented his bill, so it is not difficult to see why the society was less than delighted by his extra demands on their resources.

It was hard for Hilhouse to confront all these upheavals and uncertainties in his personal as well as his business life, but he and the Merchant Venturers were not alone in having their problems. Following Britain's ignominious defeat by the American colonies

Hilhouse's notice to the Society of Merchant Venturers in February 1787 to quit when his business was in difficulties. Courtesy Bristol Record Office.

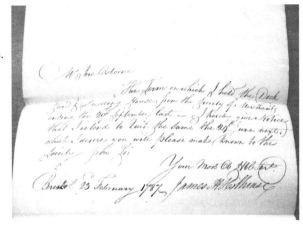

Mr Bramal's invoice for the expensive water closet, ordered by Hilhouse in more affluent days. Courtesy Bristol Record Office.

and the end of the war in 1783, the country had entered an uneasy peace which should have heralded a new period of prosperity and security for Bristol's commercial life. In many respects, this did happen: the sugar trade with the West Indies, in particular, increased dramatically once the war was over, and the threat to trading ships and plantations alike was removed. At the same time, however, even as one war ended, the country watched with growing concern events across the Channel, and with the seeming inevitability of another war with France already looming, the Navy and the country were bracing themselves to be less ill-prepared next time around.

Whatever the underlying reasons, once peace was declared, the hoped-for return of normal pre-war trading levels across the board took longer than expected to be established. As we have seen, the West Indian sugar trade was buoyant, with the volume imported into Bristol rising year-on-year throughout the 1780s; but generally speaking, the loss of the American War, and with it Britain's colonies, had a damaging effect on the economy of the city and port, so much of whose trade had been with America. In the war's immediate aftermath, with the continued disruption in trade with mainland America, trade into

Bristol from these markets was in steep decline. It meant that several of Hilhouse's merchant clients, on whom his business now depended, were finding life difficult as money was short, credit hard to come by and their trade falling. They had to pull in their horns, and orders for new ships virtually came to a standstill, with only repair and refitting work to keep the shipyard in operation. For Hilhouse and the other shipbuilders of Bristol, however, as well as for the city's merchants, there was an additional problem: as ships grew larger, the navigational difficulties of the Avon became ever more evident. The disadvantages of Bristol's tidal harbour were increasingly exposed by comparison with its main west coast rival, Liverpool, whose modern and convenient facilities were both faster and far cheaper to use than Bristol's, for ship-owners and merchants alike.

The year 1787, the low point in Hilhouse's career, was also marked in Bristol by another event which turned out to have deep significance not only for the city, but nationwide. Disquiet over the slave trade had been growing in the country for many years, and by the 1780s the movement for abolition had achieved a powerful momentum. In 1787 Thomas Clarkson[121] came to Bristol, long known as a leading port in the trade, to gather evidence of the abuses increasingly recognised in the trafficking of humans. The publication of his graphic report on what he discovered in the city caused a public outcry, and did much to swell the growing feeling in favour of reform. Most damaging to Bristol was the thoroughly adverse light in which he portrayed the city's merchants and sailors engaged in the African trade. He obtained first-hand accounts of their lives from the crews of the slave ships in Bristol, particularly the *Brothers*, the *Alfred* and the *Thomas*. The treatment of the sailors on these ships was not much better than that of the slaves: they were subject to cruelty and inhumane conditions and the death rate, among the seamen as well as their human cargo, was extremely high. Not surprisingly, they were prepared to give details that their employers were keen to suppress, though to do so entailed risk to themselves and their jobs. Because of their understandable caution in talking, Clarkson needed local help in tracing them to the drinking dens of Marsh Street in order to collect their evidence.

The effect of his report in Bristol was immediate and divisive. Like their counterparts in London and Liverpool, the two other ports most involved in slaving, the Bristol merchants trading to Africa for slaves and transporting them to the West Indian for sale to the plantations quickly organised to oppose any bill, realising their livelihoods were at risk should it be passed. In Bristol a powerful committee was formed to defend a traffic 'on which the welfare of the West India Islands and the commerce and revenue of the kingdom so essentially depend'.[122] It first met in April 1789 and its president William Miles, a plantation owner with a vested interest, was one of Hilhouse's most important customers. Among other members were many aldermen and other influential merchants, including Hilhouse's early supporters in his shipbuilding business, John and William Gordon and Richard and Lowbridge Bright, but the anti-abolitionist views of these men were shared by people far closer to home for Hilhouse. His wife's brother, Robert Bush, was a member of the committee along with his uncle, Henry; but though he had many close contacts with the anti-abolition movement, he also valued close connections with the other camp. Particularly strong among these were the Champion family and other Quakers who as a group were fiercely anti-slavery, as well as Samuel Munckley and other Dissenters from Lewin's Mead. Sir Charles Middleton, the Controller of the Navy, was also known to be firmly against slavery, so Hilhouse was having to walk a tightrope.

The passing of a bill in 1788 to regulate the trade in slaves did little to cool the debate in Bristol, and feelings ran high among Hilhouse's friends, family and business customers, only adding to the general atmosphere of uncertainty and lack of confidence within the city's merchant community. The notorious Calabar incident further fuelled the national condemnation of Bristol's traders. In 1791 it was reported that three of the city's ships, the *Thomas*, the *Wasp* and the *Recovery*, opened fire on the village of Calabar because they considered the price being asked there for slaves was too high. The three ships maintained a bombardment for several hours before the village surrendered and agreed to reduce its prices, and back at Westminster, the abolitionist William Wilberforce seized on this disgraceful incident and declared that 20 negroes had been killed and many more seriously injured, 'so that merchants in Bristol and Liverpool might make several hundred pounds' additional profit'. The resulting public scandal did nothing to enhance Bristol's reputation,[123] and further damage was done when it was known that far from reprimanding the captains of the three ships, their owners had rewarded them with further appointments. In this turbulent climate it is hardly surprising that Hilhouse found his business suffering.

Hilhouse's family life was also at a particularly demanding stage in 1787. By this time, 11 years into their marriage, he and Mary had a growing family of six children: their eldest son, George, was aged ten, Mary Ann was nine, Caroline was eight, Martin was five, Robert was four and little Abraham was a mere six months old. Later Mary was to have three more daughters of whom only one, Sarah, survived, to complete their 'long family'. Having given notice to quit, however, the Hilhouses would have to move out of the Dock House if the auction produced another tenant. The Merchant Venturers duly arranged for the auction of the dock and Dock House on 3 May 1787, but despite extensive advertising in Bristol, London and nationally, there were no bidders for either lot. This is yet another indication of the difficult state of the economy and a general view that if the hitherto successful Mr Hilhouse was in difficulties, what chance did any other shipbuilder stand of making a success of the Hotwells Dock? The result was that the notice to quit was quietly ignored and Hilhouse remained in occupation of both the dock and the Dock House, hoping that business would return to an even keel.

The immediate prospects did not look good, and at first conditions only got worse. At one time in that gloomy year of 1787 Hilhouse had only six shipwrights employed in the yard, and in the July even the name of the faithful Pinnington disappeared from the wages book. He had been Hilhouse's number two shipwright from the start of the Navy period, and the day Hilhouse had to pay him off was a hard one for them both. It was a stark illustration of just how perilous a situation he felt his business was in, but the final disaster of bankruptcy, which would have spelled the end of all Hilhouse's hopes, was somehow averted. A trickle of new work came in despite the pervading uncertainty and the company continued building at Hotwells, though on a much reduced scale. In 1787 Hilhouse built the *Pilgrim* for his cousin Richard Bright; the ship repairing work held up, and the start of the new decade saw an upturn. Important shipbuilding orders, for the *Jamaica* and the *Lord North*, came in from two of Hilhouse's long-term customers, and were completed in 1791. In fact they were the only ones he received in this dark period, but they underpinned the yard's recovery from the dark days of 1787, along with steady repairing and maintenance work for the loyal merchant customers still busy in the West Indies sugar trade. Thomas Daniel and the Protheroes were still active in the Barbadoes and Jamaica respectively and continued to give their shipbuilding and repair work to Hilhouse. More local routes, especially with Ireland, held up even while parts of the transatlantic trade slowed, and by 1791, the last year for which there are any surviving 18th-century records for Hilhouse's company, there were definite signs of recovery. The number of shipwrights employed in the yard rose to 53 and Hilhouse's average weekly wage bill went up to £95. This was not as high as it had been during the hectic Navy shipbuilding days of 1778, but then again, it had slumped as low as £30 a week in 1788. Hilhouse had somehow weathered the storm, kept his business afloat and was hopefully sailing into calmer waters.

The true light at the end of a dark tunnel came at the start of the new decade. Hilhouse received an invitation to be one of only four merchant builders nationwide to give evidence to the Middleton Commission for the Admiralty, whose report was published in February 1792. The French Revolution had erupted in 1789 and the subsequent Reign of Terror, which saw the execution of the Louis XVI and Marie Antoinette, sent shudders through the British establishment and the country at large, adding to the urgency to prepare the Navy for what was now being seen even more clearly as an inescapable war with France. The Middleton Commission was part of this evaluation of the Navy, and Hilhouse much appreciated being called to participate in it, seeing it as a mark of the regard in which he was held by the Navy Board and of his recognition as a shipbuilder of national eminence. It was now, of course, several years since he had stopped building for the Navy, but his abilities were obviously still remembered and his views respected. His building of several large merchantmen after his Navy days was also of relevance to the commission, whose leader Charles Middleton had just retired as Controller of the Navy Board, a post in which he was universally held to have excelled. He went on to be First Lord of the Admiralty at the time of Trafalgar and was clearly a man whose opinion mattered, so his high regard for Hilhouse can be seen as a great compliment. The commission's report was wide-ranging and thorough and reviewed the position since the more superficial report in 1771. Its objective was to advise the king and government on how to best to equip the Navy in defence of the country against invasion by superior ground forces. Over and above this, the need for the Navy to protect its merchants' operations and trading routes was increasingly recognised.

The shipbuilders called to contribute to the report, apart from Hilhouse, were Wells of Deptford, Barnard of East Anglia and Nowlan of Northam and Burlesdon. No-one was selected from Liverpool or Hull. The questions they were to consider were formulated by the first assistant to the Surveyor of the Navy, and one of them related to whether the 'Expence to the Public of building a Ship in the Royal Dockyards (was) greater or less that purchasing a Ship of equal Rate and Tonnage built in Private Dock Yards'.[124] Replies were: Barnard: 'Double the expence'; Wells: "Very considerably higher'; Hilhouse: 'The expence is greater than in Private Yards', and he added that there was more waste and 'nor do the workmen labour so hard' in the royal dockyards. Nowlam talked of the greater consumption of timber in royal yards.

A further question asked about the difference in durability of ships of war built in the royal dockyards or purchased, and the answers again reinforced the benefits of using seasoned timber, stressed the length of time taken to build in royal yards and explained the delay in beginning to build Hilhouse's first Navy ship, the *Medea*. Hilhouse said royal docks vessels were better for durability 'as seven is to six'. Asked how ships could be made more durable, he replied: 'I can suggest no greater improvement by which the duration of ships would be prolonged than falling the timber in winter instead of the summer'. A short response, but he was not alone in favouring winter felling. Indeed, some believed the trees should be stripped of bark for twelve months before felling. As for substitutes for British oak, Hilhouse had seen Spanish chestnut used for knees but considered it 'scarce worth the labour of faying and bolting'. A shortage of timber, particularly oak, was to remain a matter of national concern until the age of iron ships. With his self-esteem enjoying a welcome boost through this recognition, Hilhouse contributed to the commission's deliberations with his customary confident authority and plain speaking. However, his participation in it, while showing the Navy Board's continued regard for his professional expertise, did not result in any further contracts to build warships when the expected war broke out two years later.

His work with the commission took him to London, a welcome escape from the day-to-day pressures of running his business during this uncertain time, but Hilhouse maintained a close involvement in civic matters in Bristol, mainly through the Society of Merchant Venturers, to which he remained close despite his financial demands over the Dock House. Yet another confirmation of his continued good standing among his peers came on 10 November 1793, when he was elected master of the Society in succession to his close friend and cousin, Richard Bright; it was a mark not only of the respect his fellow Merchants held him in for what he had achieved in shipbuilding at Bristol, but a sign of their continued confidence in his abilities. The war against France declared in that year

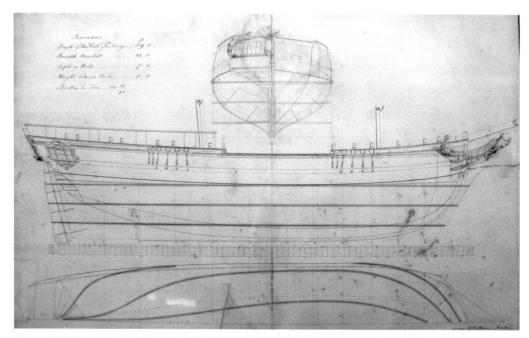

James M Hilhouse, design for a trading vessel, pen and ink on paper, signed and dated 1787. This was by way of advertisement that Hilhouse was concentrating on the needs of merchant traders. Courtesy of the Bristol Savages.

Portrait of Admiral Sir Charles Middleton, Controller of the Navy 1778-1790. After Isaac Pocock, son of Nicholas, a friend of Hilhouse. Early 19th century, oil on canvas.
© National Maritime Museum, Greenwich, London.

Nicholas Pocock. *Bristol Harbour with Cathedral and Quay*, 1785. The ship in the foreground is a typical West Indiaman as built by Hilhouse. © Bristol's Museums, Galleries & Archives M4358.

would continue with only a short break for more than 20 years, but this future could not be foreseen and Hilhouse's year in office was busy with the usual business. It began with a service at St Stephen's Church, where the preacher, the Revd Edward Colston Greville, was thanked by Hilhouse for his 'excellent sermon'. A few exceptional matters arose during his year, but none of the highly political petitions concerning trade with Ireland and the Africa Company that had marked previous years with controversy. His fierce determination to defend the country and her trade in the face of the renewed threat from France was demonstrated when he voted a sum of £200 towards a fund to form a new 'Loyal Bristol Regiment'.

Apart from this, there is little in the society's records to suggest that the war impinged to any extent on its affairs during Hilhouse's year in office. They show that he brought to the post the same clear-headed determination he had always displayed in his business dealings, and he was stern in his handling of a disciplinary matter involving a pilot named Lockier who had been complained about for being rude and aggressive, with the underlying allegation that he was drunk at the time. Captain John Shaw, the former privateer, was by then the haven master, and he told the hearing that Lockier was not 'habituated to liquor'. Hilhouse was not persuaded and insisted that the pilot should remain suspended until he produced a certificate to the society's hall asserting that he had been 'of good conduct and sober'. This he duly did and was restored to his post, since Hilhouse, though brusque, was a just man. Despite the stern attitude he showed in dealing with Lockier, he was not himself averse to drinking and he proved this by voting a pipe of wine to the Member of Parliament for Bristol and a hogshead to the treasurer of the Society of Merchant Venturers.

His year at the helm came at an opportune moment: it was a fortunate coincidence that in about 1793 both he and his fellow 'conspirator' in the acquisition of the Hotwells Dock 20 years earlier both held the highest offices in the city, Hilhouse as the master of the Merchant Venturers and John Noble, his uncle, adviser and ally who had organised his return to Bristol in 1773 to begin his shipbuilding business, as the bold and colourful mayor the previous year. With those two at the helm, seafaring trade at Bristol should have been well set to get into shape to meet the changes and challenges it faced, in particular the tidal and navigational difficulties of the port which were in a large part the causes of its eventual decline. Hilhouse took office with the Merchant Venturers with one clear priority: to make concrete progress on the problems of navigation on the Avon and the various 'dockisation' schemes, as they were known, that were being produced during the last decade of the century.[125] The improvement of the port and its navigation had long been a preoccupation of his, from his first introduction into the society soon after his return to Bristol. He had been made aware from his dealings with the Navy that the difficulties of access to and departure were likely to have an adverse effect on Bristol's ability to compete for business, and now he hoped to be in a position to do something about the situation.

Problems of navigation in the Avon Gorge had always been the Navy Board's concern when considering the award of contracts to Hilhouse, expressed forcefully in a letter of 25 April 1782 already extensively quoted: 'Navigation of the Avon is so intricate and hazardous from the rapidity of tides and the narrowness of the channel...' When inbound, ships could experience long delays at King Road at the mouth of the river before the tide and depth of water were suitable for the tow up-river, and there were dangers and difficulties which highlighted the importance of pilots in bringing ships safely into port. The main concern of the Navy, however, was the safe outbound passage of a new ship, which would have to be towed from the Floating Dock into the river just as the tide began to ebb, a manoeuvre fraught with hazard. The river channel was deep and narrow with steeply sloping mud banks, caused by the scouring effect of huge volumes of water flowing with each tide. If timed wrongly, a launch could result in the ship being dangerously stuck on the mud. Hilhouse was only too aware of the problems, and had established his second yard across the river at Redclift specifically because it offered a wider width for launching.

The Society of Merchant Venturers, in charge of Bristol's Port, had also long been conscious of the difficulties, the implications of which for Bristol's trade and competitiveness grew steadily more urgent as ships increased in size. In July 1787, six years before Hilhouse's mastership, the haven master reported to the society some of the problems for outbound ships. He referred to a point just below Rownham Point that the pilots called 'Devil's Road', where the ebb tide could carry ships on to the rocks. Chains and a capstan

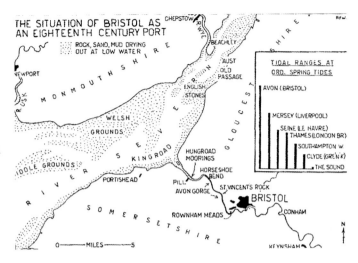

Situation of Bristol as an eighteenth century port. This map appears in *Bristol Port Plans and Improvement Schemes of the Eighteenth Century* by Alan F Williams. Courtesy Bristol and Gloucestershire Archaeological Society.

had been placed there to help in emergencies, and an account of the passage down the Avon of the *Success* on 30 July, 1789, records the assistance required to get her safely out into the Bristol Channel: Bristol to Kingroad. 6 boates and 59 men for which he charged £6 16s in total (almost £600 now). To each man a pint of ale for making a dotage (waiting period) 7 4s 1d.'[126] These unwelcome but necessary charges only added to the expenses of ships using the port, making it less attractive to potential customers than its rivals.

The river flowed swiftly and because of the narrowness of the channel there was no margin for error:

> Any sailing vessel, however, which prematurely grounded as it travelled with the tide was inevitably swung broadside in moments; the rapid fall in water level (as much as 5ft (1.5m) in one hour) gave no time to free the ship, which would begin to list down the steep underwater bank within minutes. Hobblers in rowing boats or the crew could do nothing under these conditions to haul or warp the vessel free... some might capsize or be broken in half, their remains blocking the approach to the Port for weeks.[127]

Unless some radical solution could be found, Hilhouse was aware that Bristol's future prosperity was in grave danger. As far back as the 1770s he had collaborated with Richard Bright on a report on the condition of the Somerset bank of the Avon, while through the 1780s a succession of reports and plans were presented to the society. Hilhouse's involvement in the early planning of the improvements was to assess the feasibility of various schemes that were put forward by engineers consulted by the society. His knowledge of navigation on the river, together with his experience in helping the Merchant Venturers in the construction and improvement of the former Champion's Dock at Hotwells gave him a special insight into the proposed schemes, as did the work he

The Avon Gorge at Sunset, c.1785, Pocock, showing a merchantman being towed downstream by five yawls. With the difficulties of navigation of the Avon, a not inconsiderable expense.
© Bristol's Museums, Galleries & Archives.

undertook on his own dock at Redclift. During the three years before Hilhouse became its master, the society had at last become engaged in forwarding a scheme for improving the port. Richard Bright commissioned a diary to be kept between 24 March 1792 and 14 March 1793 of movements out of the port, and its contents made the situation all too clear. It revealed that outgoing ships could not leave Bristol on 241 or 68 per cent of the days. This was mainly due to neap tides, but sometimes the prevailing south-westerly wind up the gorge made it 'improper' to leave.

The society's indecisiveness in dealing with the problem with the urgency it required gave rise to the accusation that its members acted with 'the spirit of unambitious caution'.[128] By now concern over the state of the port had become universal in the city, and the Society of Merchant Venturers recognised that it had to co-operate with the corporation if a solution was to be found. All these issues were debated by the common council of the city and the society in December 1791, and a joint committee was formed to consider their implications in detail. While these deliberations were in progress further plans were put forward, including one drawn up by Richard Toombs in 1792 which, while not adopted, is now of historical interest. Toombs's plan found its way into Hilhouse's possession,

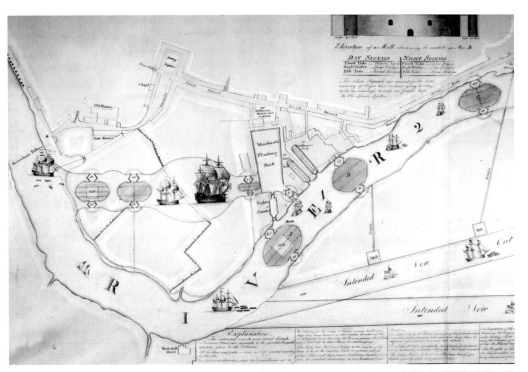

Detail from Toombs's map showing 'Mr Hilhouse's garden' and dock with, right, the complete map.
© Bristol's Museums, Galleries & Archives.

probably because they were friends and fellow shipwrights, and Hilhouse later acquired Toombs's shipyard; the Toombs family, like the Hilhouses, had been members of the Society of Protestant Dissenters at Lewins Mead. This splendid plan was later displayed at the offices of Charles Hill and Sons, as Hilhouse's company became, and was recently donated to the City Museum and Art Gallery.

Meanwhile, the joint committee was conscientiously attended by Hilhouse, present at practically all its two-weekly meetings. By September 1793, the year he became its master, the society, proposed that an 'Act for the Improvement of the Port' should be promoted in the next session of Parliament. It also agreed 'to contribute to so desireable an object to the utmost of its ability should the corporation be inclined to cooperate'. It meant that two months before Hilhouse took over as master, the society was at last taking a determined stand, and when he became master, the problems of navigation on the Avon and the various solutions proposed were the hot topics he felt he had to deal with, against the inherent inertia in the society. It is reasonable to believe that but for the outbreak of the French Revolutionary War in 1793, the Floating Harbour would have been built under the leadership and direction of Hilhouse more than a decade earlier than it eventually was. Sadly for Hilhouse's ambition to be the man finally to set 'dockisation' under way, 1793 was not the right time. As trade in Bristol suffered a temporary downturn, the need for improvements did not seem so pressing and the position of objectors to the scheme, of whom there were many, grew stronger. Just how distracted from dockisation people had become was made clear at a meeting of the joint committee on 23 February 1794, when the minutes record that despite Hilhouse's robust championing of the scheme, at this meeting there were 'insufficient members to make a Committee'. Clearly, Hilhouse's hopes of seeing his long-cherished ambition to improve Bristol's dock facilities were not to be realised yet, but in his time of greatest influence among the Merchant Venturers, great strides were made in deciding upon a scheme that would eventually be progressed when the climate was right. When this eventually came about, at the beginning of the next century, Hilhouse and his son George would both be involved closely and determinedly.

While no doubt gratified to be asked to take part in the Middleton Commission, enjoying his year as master of the Society of Merchant Venturers, involved in plans for the Floating Harbour and watching his three older sons grow into young men who like himself at the same age wanted variously to build and design ships and who might eventually join him in doing so, Hilhouse still needed to run his business and somehow make a success of it through challenging times. He had also to keep an eye on his mother, Mary, who was by now elderly and still living in the house in Walcot Street, Bath, where he visited her regularly. As we have noted her companion, his cousin Mary Hilhouse, had accepted a proposal of marriage from the Revd Francis Randolph, vicar of Corston, and when they married he too had moved into Cornwell House. Hilhouse's mother made her will in 1792, leaving all her estate to her son, and when she died in 1796 he renegotiated the lease of her house with Bath Corporation to ensure its continued occupation by his cousin and her husband (who incidentally officiated at Hilhouse's daughter's wedding almost 20 years later). That he managed to run his business successfully in spite of all this is testimony to the balance he always maintained between his business and personal lives, his careful management of resources, a steely determination to avoid unnecessary risks while grasping every opportunity, his adaptability and full use of his extensive contacts.

Conditions in shipbuilding continued to be difficult. The disruption to trade in Bristol caused by the French war over the decade following its outbreak in 1793 proved very serious indeed. The country had recovered from the previous war and the economy was again thriving, but the renewed outbreak of hostilities at first plunged it back into recession. By this time, in the years leading up to the abolition of the slave trade in 1807, Bristol merchants had almost entirely abandoned Africa, concentrating instead on the sugar trade with the West Indies, which was now of paramount importance. Some figures for the import of sugar clearly demonstrate the catastrophic affect of the war on this vital trade. In the first five years of wartime, from 1793 to 1797, only 16,515 hogsheads of sugar were imported to Bristol, while the total for the two years before the war was 18,098 and in 1785 the total for that one year had been 22,811 hogsheads. This disastrous decline affected not only the sugar merchants. Trade with the West Indies was in two directions, involving the export of a wide diversity of manufactured goods upon which the local economy of Bristol and its hinterland depended. In 1788, for example, goods exported to the West Indies from Bristol were valued at between £250,000 and £300,000.[129] With the disruption caused by French naval activity in the West Indies and on the Atlantic trade routes, this commerce suffered badly, and Hilhouse's business with it. Since Hilhouse's meticulous wages books do not survive after October 1791, it is not known precisely what he was doing in the way of building and repairing ships after this date. It appears, however, that only one merchant ship of 400 tons was launched from the Hotwells Dock until he launched his aptly-named *Hope*, 429 tons, in 1801. Indeed the only two ships registered as built by J M Hilhouse during the entire 1790s were the *Albion* and the *Hercules*.

Happily, by the turn of the century, output was starting to improve. The short-lived peace following the Treaty of Amiens gave a welcome spur to Bristol's trade, and even after the resumption of hostilities the successful blockades of the French fleet in their home ports meant that threats to British merchant ships lessened significantly. Two further ships were registered as built by J M Hilhouse in 1801, the *Fame*, 527 tons, built for Calvert and Company for the Africa trade and the *Concord*, 319 tons, built for Gibbs and Company, trading to Barbados.[130] Once more Hilhouse was able to look ahead and plan the next step for his company.

CHAPTER NINE

༦ இ

1803–1822: Hilhouse, Sons and Company

AT THE TURN OF THE NINETEENTH CENTURY, THANKS TO THE PRUDENT MEASURES HE HAD BEEN prepared to take in the difficult days of the late 1780s and the careful manner in which he had managed his business to weather the uncertainties of the 1790s and the recession caused by the French Revolutionary War, Hilhouse and his company were in good shape. At the back of his mind he always had the memory of his father's early death and the fact that his uncle William had died in his fifties, and in 1800 he himself was 52. It was a period in which his thoughts turned increasingly to the future and the need to provide security for his business and his family. He decided that it was time to put the business on a new footing to face the challenges ahead, and to involve his sons in running it, and in 1803 he put these plans into action.

His sons were growing up and though ten years separated the oldest, George, and the youngest, Abraham, they were all showing signs of the talents and characteristics they would display in later life. George, by now 25 and several years older than Hilhouse had been when he started his business at Hotwells, was working with his father; he had been apprenticed to him and in May 1800 he had been elected to the Society of Merchant Venturers and was well established there. In 1804 he married Harriet Brown of Winter-bourne, the first of his three wives. A knowledgeable shipwright with talents as a draughtsman, he was proving a sensible and hard-working manager in the business, with a strong sense of civic pride and responsibility. Hilhouse's second son, Martin, had also joined the family business, but was not showing anything like the same aptitude for it. Indeed, he was already displaying the lack of dependability and fecklessness that would mark his later life, and he was only to stay for a few years before leaving both the business and Bristol for what his father and family hoped would be opportunities overseas, in the East Indies. In view of the mistrust shown by both his father and later his eldest sister Mary Ann in his suitability to be trusted with large sums of disposable money, it is likely that his family decided that the best course in the early 1800s was to use their connections to ship the young man out to India. When he returned to Bristol a decade later it was as the husband of Mary Wallace, the daughter of a Captain Wallace of the East India Company, and their daughter Emma, who had been born in the East Indies. There was no part for him to play in Hilhouse, Sons and Company, but the family did not abandon him; he was adventurous and had charm and they hoped his marriage and young daughter would make him more responsible. When the new Floating Harbour was at last completed

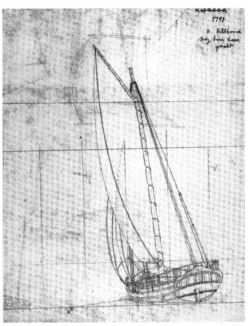

Drawing of yacht *Rebecca* by Robert Hilhouse. This shows the skills in draughtsmanship he inherited from his father.

Below, *Ferret* of Fowey drawn by Robert Hilhouse. She became a smuggler.

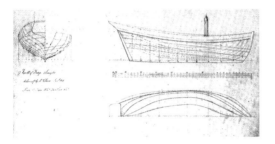

his brother George was master of the Society of Merchant Venturers and used his influence to get Martin the respectable job of harbourmaster, a post he held for 20 or so years until his retirement and departure again from Bristol, this time in his fifties. Like all his brothers he was duly elected to the Society of Merchant Venturers, but not until 1819.

Hilhouse's third son Robert was also in the business, and from his sketches and those of his ships' drawings that still exist, it is apparent that he was a very able draughtsman who had more than any of the brothers inherited his father's ability in this field, as well as his passion for new technologies. While George managed the administrative side of the business, Robert's qualities suited him for organising the practical work of the dockyard as well as the design element in shipbuilding. He was also to go on to have a somewhat unorthodox personal life, as publicly acknowledged in his father's will, though surprisingly, his behaviour did not lose him the affection or respect of his family. What the precocious youngest son Abraham had in mind was less clear, but he was already a large, forceful youth, and Hilhouse had no doubts that he, too, would make a success of his career, though it was unlikely to be in the business with his brothers. Indeed, Abraham never joined the company, but he fulfilled his early promise by growing into a tall and imposing young man who rapidly made his mark in Bristol's commercial life, being elected a Merchant Venturer as early as 1807, at the age of 21, at the same time as his brother Robert. He went on to be a colourful and influential leader of Bristol society, becoming a stockbroker, magistrate and a 'gentleman' and was mayor in 1821.

With all this in mind, in 1803 Hilhouse decided the time was right to change the name

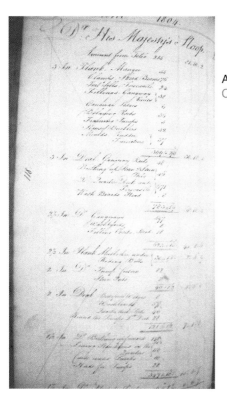

A page in the Hilhouse accounts for HMS *Albacore* 1804
Courtesy Bristol Record Office.

and the shape of his business, by taking George and Robert, who was 19 at the time, into partnership with him, trading under the new name of Hilhouse, Sons and Company. Hilhouse would remain as the head of the company; George, already proving to be a very capable partner in the business, was to run the office and Hilhouse was confident enough in Robert to put him in charge of the dockyard department. Together they were planning the way forward into the new age that was beginning to open up, and the infusion of new blood and fresh ideas soon made its mark. Sharing his father's fascination with new technology, Robert ensured Hilhouse, Sons and Co became the earliest builder of steam vessels in Bristol, and in this and other ways, the new company showed all the ambition and flair that had marked Hilhouse's early years at Hotwells.

Two landmark events took place in 1804, the first being the unexpected but very welcome order from the Navy, following the brief period of peace after the Treaty of Amiens in 1803, to build a 16-gun sloop, the first Navy ship Hilhouse had built since HMS *Severn* back in 1786. HMS *Albacore* was a Merlin class sloop of 365 tons with a crew of 121,[131] and although much smaller than any ship Hilhouse had built for the Navy in the heady days of 20 years earlier, her successful building and launch in July 1804 was a boost to morale for all. Only some three months later, in the October, she delighted Bristol when under Captain Major Jacob Henniker she engaged the enemy and destroyed five of their gunships off Cap Grisnez.[132] In fact she served throughout the Napoleonic War, being sold out of the Navy

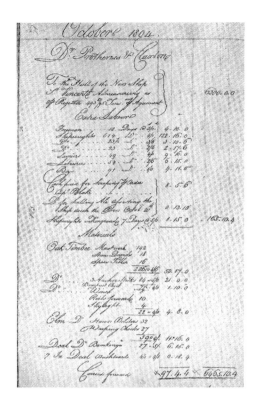

A page from the *St Vincent* accounts for the Protheroes. Courtesy Bristol Record Office.

only at its end in 1815.

The second event to put the new company in the public spotlight was the successful launch of the largest merchant ship ever built at Bristol up to that time. She was the *St Vincent*, 493 tons and three decks, especially designed by Hilhouse for the West Indies trade for Messrs Protheroe and Claxton at a cost of £7,300. She was launched to great acclaim from Hotwells Dock by Mrs Butler Claxton and Hilhouse, eager to publicise this conspicuous success, held a big party at the Great Dock House, reminiscent of the famous celebrations of earlier Naval ships. The company was fortunate in having many good and loyal customers like the Protheroes. Philip John Miles, in his turn, became a regular customer, as had been his father William.[133] He ordered two ships that year, also for the West Indies trade: the first, the *Nelson*, was to be even bigger than the *St Vincent* at 580 tons, and cost a very considerable £10,600. The second, also ordered in 1804 and of almost the same design as the *Nelson*, was named the *William Miles*. They and some other Westin-diamen the company built were termed 'armed running ships'. Large and well-armed, they were able to make their trading voyages fast and alone, rather than in a convoy under Naval protection, which necessarily travelled at the speed of the slowest ship. In these armed running ships Hilhouse drew on his experience in building warships for the Navy to the benefit of his commercial customers.

Meanwhile, the dockisation scheme which Hilhouse had so signally failed to bring to fruition in 1793 had been resurrected, and both he and George were assiduous supporters of it. A joint committee of the city corporation and the Merchant Venturers was again formed, and both men served on it throughout its negotiations over the next seven years. By early 1802 the committee was able to look at a scheme prepared by William Jessop which had an estimated cost of £200,000 (equivalent to £6 million now). It soon found, however, that the cost of any improvement scheme had grown so great that it was unable to finance the project, and that an incorporated company needed to be formed under Act of Parliament to raise the finance and carry the risks. This was agreed and set up by 1803, when a revised estimate increased the cost to £212,470, which notably included an estimate for 'iron pipe for draining Mr Hilhouse's Docks £2,200'. This would have been his Lime Kiln dock, as the Hotwells dock was not affected by the scheme. On 6 April 1803 a meeting of subscribers to the Plan to Improve the Port was held at Merchants' Hall. Hilhouse attended as a leading subscriber, and is recorded as seconding a motion on a small but important point of detail. Edward Protheroe proposed a clause that no subscriber could transfer his subscription until the whole of the subscription was paid, and the motion was passed by a majority.

Records of what Hilhouse said at meetings are rare, and the fact that he spoke up for this motion is another significant indication of his concern for financial prudence and attention to detail. The Bill received assent in Parliament and the first general meeting of the company was held on 8 September 1803, when William Jessop was appointed engineer and his son, who possibly did most of the work from this point onwards, was to be his deputy at £500 a year (£65,000 today). Despite the renewal of war with France, an increased threat of invasion and the resultant rise in prices and sense of crisis in the country at large, the company held firm and work started on the 'greatest undertaking' Bristol had ever known. The scheme progressed through the following years despite escalating costs and unforeseen problems, including an expensive accident at the Hilhouse dry dock in the Cumberland Basin – for which he claimed compensation, of course.

Throughout the years of disruption through building work on the dockisation scheme, Hilhouse and Sons continued to build at both Hotwells and Lime Kiln. The Miles ship the *Nelson*, ordered in 1804, was launched in early 1807, and the *Bristol Mercury* records that:

> The largest vessel ever built at this port was launched at Hilhouse's Dock. She went off the stocks amidst the cheers of an immense concourse of spectators, more numerous perhaps than was ever before assembled on any similar occasion here. She was named the Nelson in honour of the immortal hero, whose valour was at once the safeguard of our commerce and the terror of our enemies.

The second Miles ship, the *William Miles*, was launched the following year. Then, by 1809, sufficient of the work had been completed on the dockisation plan to enable the dock to

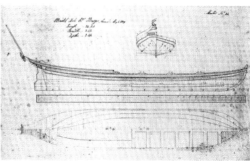

Directors' Pleasure Barge, built by Hilhouse for the directors of the Stroudwater canal for its grand opening in July 1779. His bill was paid late and not in full. The barge may be a copy of that built for Frederick Louis and now in the National Maritime Museum, Greenwich.

Directors' Inspection Barge 1809. Built by Hilhouse for Bristol Dock Company for inspection of the new Floating Harbour.

be opened, five years since it began. It seemed appropriate that the first ship to load cargo outwards from the new Floating Harbour was the *Lady Carrington*, a vessel of 471 tons that had recently been built by Hilhouse. On leaving the basin, her captain ordered her guns to be fired as a salute to the Dock Company and its achievement in building 'a safe harbour for ships to lie within the City of Bristol'.[134]

While pleased to see the improvements he had so long desired and worked for finally in place, Hilhouse did not allow the general atmosphere of satisfaction to deter him from clawing back what he was owed from the Dock Company. In this instance he claimed that one fifth of his business had been affected by work on the dockisation scheme, and in respect of the Lime Kiln Dock he was paid £4,200, a very large sum indeed. One small bonus to come out of the final success of the project was that Hilhouse and Sons received an order to build the barge from which the directors would inspect the new Floating Harbour on its inauguration. Also, because of his company's involvement with the new dock as well as its expertise, Hilhouse won orders for a gunship to defend the port, and several pilot cutters.

With business going so well, in 1810 Hilhouse made what was to turn out to be a very significant decision for the future of his company. He took on a young man by the name of Charles Hill, who had been working unhappily in a solicitors' office. The change to Hilhouse and Sons apparently suited him very well, and the knowledge he had acquired in the legal world meant he quickly made a success of his new career. He first worked with George in the office, where his administrative skills were invaluable, and within a short time he was an integral part of the team, proving a reliable and sensible manager. This was just as well, because within half a dozen years of his arrival, the younger Hilhouses' sense of civic responsibility and public duty was being called upon, and George in particular was finding his attention increasingly being taken away from the business. The post of Sheriff of Bristol was an old and honourable one which leading members of the business community had always filled. By 1812, however, it was becoming increasingly difficult to find candidates prepared to take on the office, which Hilhouse's father had filled but he himself, interestingly, had always avoided. With no-one willing to fill the post, George and the precocious Abraham stepped forward and held the office jointly. In 1817 the same situation arose and again the brothers answered the call. Further, as Hilhouse gradually handed over responsibility to his sons, Charles Hill began to fill the space he left. Without the family being aware of it, he was becoming indispensable to the company.

When Charles Hill joined, the company was securely established and the order book reassuringly full. The Miles family's business in the West Indies was prospering and in 1810 they ordered two more large vessels, the *Sarah*, 500 tons and the *Charlotte*, 427 tons. The long-running war against France, in which America had joined on the side of the French, meant that American privateers were causing losses for West India merchants' ships and in 1813 the Miles's Hilhouse-built *Nelson* was captured by the American privateer *Saratoga* and taken to New Orleans as a prize after the crew and passengers had been courteously landed at Port Royal. The *Bristol Mirror* printed a letter from Captain W Thomas of the *Nelson* on 24 April 1813:

> Fell in with the privateer *Saratoga* of New York, Captain W C Wooster, mounting 16 guns and 130 men, which took possession of the ship. The 6th February he gave us the boat and we got on shore on the Grand Caymanas, 17 in number, where we hired a schooner on 14th and arrived safe at Lucea.

Carrying passengers was a new and profitable part of the business of merchant trading ships, and it is not surprising that the courteous Captain Wooster wrote a letter to the passengers of the *Nelson*:

> I sincerely lament, that passengers on board the *Nelson*, should feel a moment's uneasiness; the fortune of war has made them prisoners, and my first care shall be to render them as comfortable as possible. They shall enjoy the same privileges as when with their former commander.

In the same year the *William Miles*, also Hilhouse-built, was almost lost, though in entirely different circumstances. She had come up the Avon to Bristol with a full cargo of sugar and rum and was about to enter the lock into the Floating Harbour when she was boarded by an officer commanding a press gang all ready to press the crew into service in the Navy. The *William Miles*'s crew decided to abandon ship immediately and escape to safety, but in their haste to leave they left the vessel undocked. She entered the lock when the tide was ebbing and being a burthensome ship with a remarkable convexity in her hold, upon the reflux of the tide she was suspended between the sides of the lock, the bottom of which forms the sides of a circle and from the weight of her cargo she immediately bilged.

This account appears in *Felix Farley's Journal* for 1 September 1813 and it goes on to record that the press gang from the *Enchantress*, the receiving ship in the port, had acted contrary to the orders of their commander in boarding the *William Miles*, which was later rescued by 'the scientific and judicious arrangement of Mr J M Hilhouse'[135] and safely taken to the Hilhouse dry dock at Hotwells for repair. After surviving the hazards of two Atlantic crossings it was a bitter homecoming for the West Indiaman, but thanks to Hilhouse, all ended well.

A significant technological development took place that same year, showing just how far shipbuilding had moved since Hilhouse started out in the business forty years earlier. In 1813 the company built Bristol's first steam-driven ships, once again leading the way over its local competitors. James Watt had successfully developed his steam engine and the race had been on to see how it could be incorporated to provide power afloat. The Scots were at the forefront of this, and the first steam-propelled ship was produced by John Wood in 1811 with his *Comet*, built in his yard at the port in Glasgow, with which Hilhouse's family had long-standing links. Four more steam-driven ships were built up there in the next two years, during which time Hilhouse and Sons successfully produced their two in Bristol. The *Charlotte* and the *Hope* were confined to river use, as their design was still at an experimental stage. The *Charlotte* was built to the order of Theodore Lawrence, a Bristol attorney, and ran on the Avon between Bristol and Bath; she must have been a fascinating sight for those who saw her passing by, belching her plume of smoke, and she brought acclaim to Hilhouse and Sons as her trail-blazing builders. The wealthy Lawrence, who obviously shared Hilhouse's and Robert's enthusiasm for this new mode of transport, probably recognized in them a couple of kindred spirits, and also ordered the sister ship *Hope* from them. She ran successfully on the Severn before being sold in 1814 to a group of businessmen in London for service on the Thames. However, despite her undoubted novelty, the *Hope* was not universally admired. She was said by some who sailed on her to be 'too slow to be agreeable and too crank to feel safe'.

Steamship design was still in its infancy, and although these two craft were reasonably successful, it was to be another nine years before steam-driven ships built at Bristol progressed beyond the experimental stage. Hilhouse and Robert were right up with the leaders in this field, however, which must have given them much satisfaction. Nevertheless, the advent of steam was a development that was to change shipbuilding in ways that they could not have foreseen. The centre of the industry began inexorably to migrate from the south of the country to the north, where an abundance of coal favoured industrialisation. At first the boats into which the steam engines were fitted were of traditional wooden

The Limekiln Dockyard. Hilhouse took on this yard in order to have facilities to build when he gave notice to quit the Hotwells Dock in 1787 and for disruption to which during the dockisation scheme he got compensation.

construction and their activity was confined to estuaries and rivers. The first sea-going steamships were not built until 1822 and the first in Bristol, in 1826, was built not by Hilhouse and Sons but by a Scot from Greenock, William Scott. The revolution in shipbuilding in Bristol was complete several years later when the first iron steamship was built in 1839. Nevertheless, Hilhouse had been in the vanguard of this new era.

The year 1815 heralded the period of peace following the long Napoleonic Wars. Hilhouse and Sons had prospered throughout the latter stages of the conflict, and civic life in Bristol had also not stood still. Hilhouse's status as the foremost shipbuilder in the city brought him further recognition in this year of celebration as president of the Commercial Rooms. In fact he was the third president of the rooms, which began building in 1811, and it was a sure sign that shipbuilding was central to the commercial life of the city. He had enjoyed a major role in Merchant Venturers, and now he was recognised in the wider business community.

With the end of the war there was a gradual increase in shipbuilding in Bristol as merchants cautiously explored the possibilities of expanding their areas of commerce. Looking at the records of ships registered in the city in these years does not give the full

Wapping, c.1760, Nicholas Pocock. This shows the yard on the Somerset bank of the Avon within the city of Bristol, owned by the firm of Teast, Toombs and Blannin, with ships in various stages of construction over a decade before Hilhouse started his yard at Hotwells. Hilhouse later took over the yard and Toombs's apprentices which is how the Toombs's map came into his possession.
© Bristol's Museums, Galleries & Archives.

picture of what was actually built, as some produced for owners elsewhere were registered in other ports, but it does give an indication of what was happening during this final period of Hilhouse's shipbuilding career. The trend for the company was towards building larger ships. In 1815 seven were registered as built by Hilhouse and Sons, of which two were over 400 tons,[136] and the same number was recorded for 1816.[137] In 1817 only five ships were registered, but three were of over 400 tons.[138] In 1818 and 1819 again only five Hilhouse-built ships were registered each year, two of which were 400 tons-plus.[139] In 1820 the company built three substantial ships, one over 400 tons – but we are nearing the suddenly traumatic years of 1822 and 1823,[140] when both Hilhouse and Robert died. This understandably threw the company into a state of emergency, and while it nevertheless built 13 ships, only one was more than 400 tons. This pattern of production became the norm in the years that followed, but what would certainly have given Hilhouse much satisfaction in those last years of his life, as he left the running of his company increasingly to his sons

Hilhouse's new dock (later Albion Dockyard) seen from Mardyke, 1826. T. Rowbotham. Hilhouse and Sons had been established in their new dockyard here since 1820.
© Bristol's Museums, Galleries & Archives.

and Charles Hill, was that once again his firm was the pre-eminent shipbuilder in Bristol. No other company in the port in the years between 1815 and 1822 produced a single ship of a tonnage approaching 400 tons.

While Hilhouse in his sixties might have been gradually delegating some of his responsibilities, he still maintained a close interest in the company. An event in 1817, of no great importance in itself, clearly demonstrates that he had not lost his meticulous and determined character. Some repair work had been carried out for Protheroe and Claxton – long-time customers, influential people and well known to Hilhouse – on the two vessels the company had built for them, the *St Vincent* and the *Severn*. The amount charged was challenged by Protheroe and Claxton, but Hilhouse characteristically refused to compromise over the bill and pursued his claim for payment until the dispute was referred to an arbitration committee, which emphatically found in his favour. The arbitrators were apparently impressed by the clarity and detail of the accounts that Hilhouse and Sons had rendered, so once again his precision and attention to detail had stood him in good stead.

The arbitrators also noted that the materials used in the work on the two ships were 'of the best quality that could be obtained anywhere in the world'. For whatever reason, they also added that the Hillhouses' company was the only one able to provide dry dock facilities of such a size as to be able to repair such large vessels,[141] and doubtless such glowing official endorsement would have given Hilhouse quiet gratification: he had not lost his touch, and he was still a force to be reckoned with.

In his home life, Hilhouse was equally intractable. While his four sons were all making their mark in various ways in Bristol life, his four daughters led a much less adventurous existence at home. From the meticulous provisions he made for his family in his will it is very clear that Hilhouse was a somewhat authoritarian patriarch. He and Mary had four surviving daughters in addition to their four sons and unlike the way in which he actively promoted his sons' careers and was even prepared to condone their occasional lapses from propriety, he had no intention of allowing his daughters to leave his protection to pursue independent lives. Of the four, only two were to marry, and only one of them, Caroline, in his lifetime. Quite why he was so reluctant to see his daughters established in their own homes is a mystery, as is his reason finally to agree to Caroline's marriage; but agree he did. On 16 March 1815, exactly three months before the Battle of Waterloo, Miss Caroline Hilhouse was married to the Revd Thomas Allies in the old St Andrew's Church in Clifton. She was the second daughter in the family, born three years after George, and was 34 by 1815. Her husband was the curate at Henbury, and a widower, previously married to Frances Elizabeth Fripp, the daughter of a well known Bristol merchant; sadly, she had died a week after giving birth to their only son, Thomas William, in February, 1813. Just over two years later, Caroline became the toddler's stepmother, taking 'little Tom' to her heart and loving him 'as one of her own children'.

'Little Tom' turned out to be an extraordinary child. For some time after his father's remarriage he was an only child – though it is good to know that Caroline went on to have a family of her own – and his 'musings as a boy were uttered in poetry'. Precocious and talented, he won a prize for an essay at Bristol Grammar School when he was 12 before going on to Eton at his own request in 1827; from there, when he was 14, he went on to Oxford where he excelled in classics and took Anglican orders. How much he knew about his stepmother having a grandfather who was a devout Presbyterian Dissenter we cannot know, but despite his father being a minister in the Church of England and himself being ordained into that ministry, he moved even further from his step-family's religious roots. Influenced by Cardinal Newman and the Oxford Movement he forsook the Church of England to become a prominent Catholic, devoting his life to poetry and writing while earning a living by teaching. His reputation as a Catholic philosopher was such that in 1885, towards the end of his long life, Pope Leo Xll created him a Knight Commander and conferred upon him the signal favour of the Gold Medal for merit.[142] Of course, all this was long after Hilhouse had died, but one cannot help wondering how he would have regarded

Merchantman *Severn*. Oil painting by Joseph Walter, c.1835, presented to Bristol Museum and Art Galleries by the great grandson of the captain TE Etheridge. It was built for Protheroe and Claxton, 478 tons, launched in 1807. It cost the owners £7,300.

this exotic graft on to his family tree. He must, however, have derived quiet pleasure from the decorous atmosphere of Caroline's wedding in 1815. The service was conducted by his cousin Mary's husband, the Revd Francis Randolf, and the list of witnesses shows that this was a solidly family occasion. The marriage register was signed by his daughter Eleanor and son George, Mary Ann Bush, (continuing evidence of close relations with his wife's family), Maria Allies and Harriet Hilhouse, George's wife. After the departure of Caroline, her three sisters remained living with their parents, and there were to be no more marriages for them in their father's lifetime.

Meanwhile, the Hilhouse sons were making their mark in Bristol society. In 1820 George was elected mayor and in the following year he was followed in the post by Abraham, married since 1812 to his first wife Phebe and busy forging a successful career for himself outside the family business. While George grew increasingly involved with city offices, it was reassuring to have Charles Hill so competently running the administration of the company. Martin, the acknowledged black sheep of the family, at least as far as business went, was by now long returned from the East Indies and was holding down the post of harbourmaster in the Port of Bristol, while Robert, who remained unmarried, was steering the company into the age of steam. He also became father to three sons of his own,

Robert, George and James; but although they all had solid Hilhouse family Christian names they were illegitimate, the product of a long liaison with a Mrs Poole, and it was her surname they bore. Whatever the reasons behind Robert's choice of lifestyle, this unorthodox arrangement was, surprisingly, tolerated within the family, though such a union was scarcely socially acceptable and would surely have raised eyebrows among their acquaintances. Nevertheless, regardless of public opinion and the conventions of the day, Hilhouse loved and valued his talented son, probably because, of all of them, Robert had inherited his artistic interest and abilities. He proved his regard for family ties above compliance with social acceptability by specifically naming Robert's sons in his will, and making provision for them. It is ironic that these were the only grandsons Hilhouse had who could have carried his name, with none of his other sons producing a boy to carry on the family name.

In the years immediately following the creation of Hilhouse and Sons, as business steadily increased, the company was busily building at three different locations: Hotwells, Lime Kiln and a third site it had acquired, Wapping, near Prince Street Bridge, where Teast Toombs and Blannin had built their two Navy ships. Although the company needed the capacity the three yards gave them, there were obvious inefficiencies in operating on such a widespread basis; by 1820 Hilhouse and his sons had made the major and far-sighted decision to rationalise their operations, give up all three existing yards and relocate on one new site. The site they chose was to be on the south bank of the river, across from Hotwells. Of course Hilhouse had built around here before, from 1778 to 1788, at the Redclift and Vauxhall yards, in his Navy work days, but these were only temporary operations. This new, ambitious development was undertaken with the clear plan of creating a modern, purpose-built shipyard that would place the company in the best competitive position for the foreseeable future.

George and Robert were not to know it, but their plans had consequences long beyond their lifetime, and the yard they created was to provide the base for the changing face of shipbuilding under their successor Charles Hill and Company, until the firm finally ceased trading in 1981. In 1820 Hilhouse and Sons built their new Albion dockyard on ten acres they acquired on the Redcliffe bank of the Avon, and here they created two wet docks, a dry dock and several building berths. They also provided on-site houses for their key workers and a villa for the yard manager, later to be lived in by Charles Hill and his family. This project, briskly put into practice, summed up how the two sons saw the future of their company. For their father, it was with more than a tinge of regret that he agreed to give up the Hotwells dock, and with it, the Great Dock House. The decision must have caused him much heart-searching. Hotwells was, after all, where he had first started his shipbuilding venture all those years ago, and the site he had occupied ever since – even through the hardest times, when he thought he had lost it but it had come back to him. Now it really was going, and to him it was the end of an era. It had been the scene of his early triumphs, building for the Navy; he and Mary had brought up their family in the Great Dock House, where over the years there had been lavish launch parties to celebrate his greatest successes. From Hotwells he and his sons had launched their new company, and until now his life had not really changed with the change of name. The move to the new Albion dockyard marked the true point at which he handed over the reins to his sons, and finally acknowledged that the future belonged to them. It is typical of his approach to life that at this vital point, as at so many others in the past, he did not allow sentiment to overrule sound business sense, but embraced the challenges of the future that this new start represented; and, as expected, the move proved the right one to make. As for Hilhouse, he, Mary and his three unmarried daughters had to move out of the Dock House, and for the remaining years of his life their home was at 13-15, Princes Buildings, up on the heights above the Avon Gorge, the Hotwells dock and the pump rooms, with magnificent views across to Leigh Woods. It is understandable that after so many years spent at Hotwells, he did not want to leave the view he had known for so long, and he certainly kept more than a fatherly eye on his business until the end.

In the last years of his life Hilhouse had the satisfaction of seeing the future of his business looking secure. The Albion dockyard gave the company the facilities it needed in this new age of shipbuilding, and the yard soon began to attract a variety of new business to complement the company's traditional markets. Among the most interesting orders it received was one from the War Office. In 1821 it ordered two ships of an important new type: paddle-wheel steamers. They were to be built to replace the sailing packets that carried mail and passengers between Bristol and Cork and were named the *George IV* (135 tons) and the *Viscount Palmerston* (188 tons). They transformed the reliability and speed of the service between the two countries and aroused a startling amount of interest among the Bristol public, enhanced significantly when the implications of an experiment using the *George IV* were fully appreciated. She was employed to tow a large sailing ship down the Avon, which she accomplished with ease and panache. The consequences for navigating this difficult passage, which up until that time had depended on the vagaries of wind and the muscle power of rowboats, were soon appreciated and acted upon by the port authorities. The trend towards steam was gaining an irresistible momentum.

The move to the new yard was not the only major change in the air as the 1820s approached. Besides making the brave decision to relocate to a new purpose-built site, the brothers opted for diversification and went into ship-owning. They embarked on it with vigour, investing heavily in buying a fleet of ships, and from 1817 Hilhouse and Sons vessels sailed regularly for Jamaica and other destinations in the West Indies, carrying cargoes in both directions. This part of the business continued to expand in the following years, and as he watched the early stages of all this, Hilhouse must have been struck by how very different an operation Hilhouse and Sons had become from the one he started in 1773. There is no doubt that he was proud and relieved to see how competently his two sons

Princes Buildings. Numbers 13-15 were lived in by Hilhouse.

Princes Buildings, originally 'Prince of Wales Crescent', was owned by the Society of Merchant Venturers. The architect was William Paty and the builder Samuel Powell. Work began in 1790 and it was an innovative scheme, a crescent of seven pairs of quasi semi-detached three-storey houses joined by a single storey annexe said to be the first such development. Hilhouse acquired the pair at the north end now next to the Avon Gorge Hotel and *Mathews Directory* for 1820 records him living at 14 with his son Robert and the unmentioned females in the family.

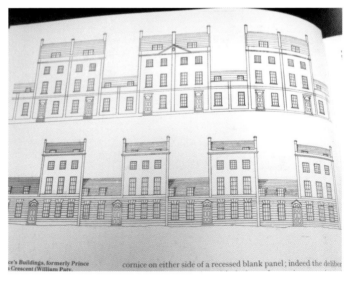

ce's Buildings, formerly Prince
Crescent (William Paty.

cornice on either side of a recessed blank panel; indeed the deliber

were managing the company, but it was not in his nature to retire and leave them to run what he still regarded as his business. He remained the titular head of the company until the day he died, and the brothers were glad of his wisdom and experience as well as his shrewd commercial acumen, from which they learned so many valuable lessons. Hilhouse was nothing if not a realist, however; he trusted his sons, having worked alongside them for almost two decades, and was still astute enough a businessman to see clearly that the direction they were mapping out with the energetic and reliable Charles Hill was just what he, as a young man, would have grasped. He could not let go entirely what had been the ruling passion of his life since the time when, as a young boy, he had decided that shipbuilding was to be the focal point of his life.

It would be pleasant to imagine Hilhouse at the end of his life, enjoying in tranquility a peaceful retirement from the exertions of his busy and active life, surrounded by his family of females in the house overlooking the river, looking back with satisfaction at his life and congratulating himself on having achieved all the ambitions he set out with as a young man so many years ago; but that was never his nature. To the end he remained immersed and involved in the direction of his company, alert to opportunities, relishing the new challenges his sons were facing and contributing his ideas and opinions. Even had he wished for a peaceful end, events conspired to make sure that his life had one last unexpected crisis for him to confront. As we have seen, in 1820 George was elected mayor of Bristol, but it was reassuring to Hilhouse that his protégé, Charles Hill, was able to run the administration of the company so competently, and of course, there was always Robert there to oversee the working of the yards.

Then disaster struck. On March 18 1822, Robert – unconventional, talented, innovative Robert – died entirely without warning at the age of 38. It is hard to imagine the turmoil his death caused both in his family and for the company. The blow must have come near to shattering all who loved him, not least his father, whose artistic and technical talents he had inherited. The cause of Robert's death remains uncertain, but its consequences for the business were immediate and profound. George was busy as master of the Merchant Venturers in 1822, following hard on his year as mayor; Hilhouse, while still involved in the business, had increasingly of late left its management to his sons and was conscious that, however much he would have liked to resume control in this critical situation, he was no longer in robust enough shape to fill the gap left by Robert. Had it not been for the excellent Charles Hill, the company would have been in serious difficulties. As it was, the three men together worked to keep it functioning and sought to restructure it to face a future without Robert's vital contribution.

Sadly, Hilhouse was unable to be of much help in this crisis. In the wake of his son's death, always the competent organiser, he remade his will to reflect the changed family circumstances; but the shock of Robert's death was the blow from which, for the first time in his life, he was unable to recover. Three months later, on 24 June 1822, James Martin Hilhouse died. He was 72 years old.

CHAPTER TEN

❧

The Hilhouse Legacy

HILHOUSE'S DEATH, COMING JUST THREE MONTHS AFTER ROBERT'S, MIGHT HAVE LED TO THE ENTIRE breakdown of his family and business, quickly unravelling all his life's work. True to his nature to the last, however, he had done all he could to arrange the future as he saw best. His death might not have been unexpected; three weeks before he had summoned his lawyer, William Bryce, and made his final will, altering it to reflect the changes necessary now that Robert was no longer alive. To the end, he clung on to his need to arrange his own and his family's affairs in meticulous order, and made sure that his will made his wishes perfectly clear. He certainly intended that his guiding hand over his family and his business would not cease to be felt when he was not there in person.

He was buried in the new St Andrew's Parish Church, Clifton, not the building he, Mary and the family had attended for many years, and in which his daughter Caroline had been married. The original St Andrew's dated from the 16th century, when Clifton had been a modest village outside the city; with its rise in importance as the home of many wealthy merchants and other well-to-do Bristolians and its rapid development as the fashionable area of the city, a larger and more impressive church was thought necessary. The site was big enough for it to be built alongside the old one, which remained in use until the new church was complete. Work started in 1816 and though the official consecration did not take place until August 1822, it was in the new St Andrew's that Hilhouse's funeral took place.

There was plenty of burial space available in the new church and his body was placed in a vault beneath the church, beside his son Robert. They were to be joined later by his wife Mary and their two unmarried daughters, Mary Ann and Sarah. A tablet was put up in the church, commemorating all these family members, but like so much of the physical evidence of Hilhouse's life in Bristol, it has disappeared. In the Second World War a bomb fell on St Andrew's Church and the damage was so great that it had to be demolished and the site levelled, leaving only the outline of the walls in the grass to show where it once stood. Fortunately, a transcript was made of all the inscriptions in the church before they disappeared; a further tablet marked the burial there of Abraham Hilhouse, along with his first wife Phebe and members of her family, and recorded the death of Martin Hilhouse and the burial of his wife Emma and her daughter.

After the burial came the reading of the will, attended by the beneficiaries, the executors and trustees, as Hilhouse had stipulated. He had drawn up a characteristically thorough

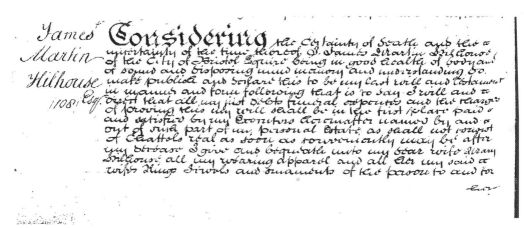

Part of Hilhouse's will made three weeks before his death.

and precise document, making very clear what his intentions were in respect of his business, his provisions for the various members of his family and the disposal of his possessions. The executors and trustees would have an arduous job: he gave unusually detailed instructions but even so, his executors would have to exercise their own judgment in carrying them out, so he chose them carefully, concerned that their decisions should be objective and fair to the various members of his family. He had no hesitation in appointing his eldest son George, utterly upright and reliable in the family business and in his public life; he would, after all, be running the business on which the future of the family depended. For the second executor he decided on the Revd John Shipton, a Doctor of Divinity from Portishead who with his wife Jane had inherited a substantial estate from the first John Noble, the father of a man Hilhouse had long known, and whose judgment he had trusted through all his working life. Finally, his choice of Josiah Gist as his third executor and trustee is not an obvious one, but is interesting and will be discussed presently. His name was suggested by George, and the fact that Hilhouse took his son's advice over the matter shows how much he had come to rely on his opinion.

Not included was any member of his wife's family, the Bushes, with whom he continued to have close and friendly connections; perhaps he considered them to be too close to be impartial, since the intimacy between the two families in the younger generation was well illustrated when Henry Bush, son of Hilhouse's wife's brother Robert, married the Hilhouses' daughter Eleanor two years after her father's death. Merchant colleagues of his would not necessarily have George's confidence and their advice, especially regarding the business, might not be welcome to him. In his choice of John Shipton, yet again, Hilhouse had relied on close personal connections. Indeed, that of his family with the Nobles and the Shiptons was to continue in the third generation when Abraham married Ann Noble Shipton as his second wife in 1853. John Shipton was a man with experience, wealth and property, and over and above that, he had moral integrity. Hilhouse felt he could trust him to exercise his judgement with fairness and compassion.

How Josiah Gist came to act as trustee to Hilhouse's will is an intriguing tale, if not of rags to riches, then at least of unexpected transformation. The Gist family had lived at Wormington Grange, near Cheltenham, for many years, and had made their very substantial fortune with plantations in the American colonies, in particular Virginia, where some of them lived for much of the time. By the early 1800s the family's plantations were in the hands of Samuel Gist and his two daughters, as were the other extensive family estates in Gloucestershire, Oxfordshire and Warwickshire; Samuel had no son and was therefore exercised about how he should leave his substantial fortune; he was also, significantly, concerned for the welfare of the slaves working on his Virginia plantations as the prospect of the abolition of slavery came ever nearer. In his will he granted them all freedom but later, considering that this might cause his daughters problems with the Virginia authorities, he revoked the request but directed in a paternalistic way that his slaves should all be kept together.

As far as succession was concerned he left all his English estates to a distant male member of the family, James Gist, as long as he could be found in seven years. If he could not, they were to go to a complete outsider, a Bristol businessman named Josiah Sellick, a man whom Gist obviously rated highly and who shared many of his views and interests. Sellick was known to Gist and favoured by him in this extraordinary way because he and his forebears had been involved in supplying indentured servants, mainly from Ireland, to work on the Virginia plantations, so the two families had business ventures in common. Sellick, like Gist, had an enlightened and humanitarian attitude towards slavery during the period of abolition, and did his best to secure his own slaves' futures. Lacking a clear heir, Samuel Gist clearly considered Josiah a worthy recipient of his large fortune, if his distant relation could not be found. The only proviso was that Sellick should change his name to Gist...

Samuel died in 1813 and the hunt for James Gist began. Meanwhile, the two Gist daughters unsurprisingly did their best to retain control of their father's estate and upset the succession to it by Josiah which, under the terms of the will could not, in any case, take place until 1820, seven years after the death. Equally unsurprisingly, Josiah Sellick duly changed his name to Gist and the resulting dispute with the daughters was heard in the notorious Chancery Division, where matters inevitably proceeded very slowly. The court did, however, appoint a receiver of rents to try to protect the interests of the inheritor, and in 1816 it was George Hilhouse who was appointed to this role. He knew Josiah Gist well, and the part he played in the long-drawn-out case cemented their mutual respect. George performed his tasks as receiver of rents conscientiously and prepared accounts which included details of his own travelling expenses and those incurred 'entertaining the tenants'. The disputes were resolved, the missing heir stayed missing, and the estates were settled upon Josiah in 1820, following which he took up residence at Wormington Grange.

From their dealings together, George had recognised the good qualities in this man which had brought about the remarkable change in his circumstances; for his part, Josiah appreciated George's competence and his high standing in the city and county, which had resulted in his appointment by the Chancery Court. Furthermore, it was no coincidence that the Revd Thomas Allies, recently married to George's sister Caroline, was the rector at Wormington during this period, giving added grounds for friendship between the families. Hilhouse, influenced by George's commendation of Josiah Gist, was happy to appoint him as his executor and Josiah, despite having so recently come into the enjoyment of his vast fortune, apparently carried out his duties conscientiously, working closely with George. He continued to live at Wormington, assisted by his son William in running the estates when his health began to fail towards 1830. He had a philanthropic bent, using his fortune to set up many charitable schemes including one for sending paupers from Britain to America to give them a chance of a better life. In 1834 he was appointed High Sheriff of Gloucestershire, but died before he could take office. All in all, Josiah Sellick/Gist was an intriguing man.

When the family and executors gathered for the reading of Hilhouse's will, it must have been a lengthy process. His solicitor, James Brice, had done a splendid job in living up to his profession's reputation for money-making. Judging by the length of the document he was surely charging his client by the word, and was determinedly repetitious and exceedingly cautious in his drafting. He succeeded in drawing the document out to a formidable 22 pages, though being charitable, it could be said in his defence that he was probably merely reflecting his client's careful attention to detail, and if a person's will, disregarding the legal verbiage, is an indication of character, then Hilhouse's is certainly revealing. Its lengthy formality makes it difficult to draw any conclusions about his state of health at the time, but it certainly speaks of his clarity of his mind. The fact that he died within three weeks of making it could indicate that a crisis in his health had occurred and he knew this was indeed his 'Last Will and Testament', with its provisions made completely clear. Robert had died without making a will, and Hilhouse had stepped forward and applied for letters of administration in respect of his son's estate, showing he felt still very much in control of his family's affairs; before the letters could be granted he himself had died, and they were granted instead to George.

Although only 72, Hilhouse had at least passed the three-score years and ten mark that his father and uncle William had both fallen short of by some considerable margin. In Hilhouse's case it seems likely that there had been a gradual decline in his health, but we do not know more than he signed up to in his will: 'Considering the certainty of death and the uncertainty of the time thereof I James Martin Hilhouse of the City of Bristol Esquire being in good health of body and of sound and disposing mind memory and understanding do make publish and declare this to be my last Will and Testament...' His first concerns were to dispose of his personal possessions. His wife Mary was left 'during her life' 'all my wearing apparel, (her own) rings jewels and ornaments, all my household goods, furniture, plate, china and Books, Rings, Jewels, watches and trinkets… all my wines and other liquors… and also all my pictures and paintings other than and except my drawings, prints, instruments, implements for drawing, models and blocks and also except my gold chain and seals.' These excepted items were all to go to George. Everything left to Mary, with the emphatic exception of the pictures and paintings, were to pass on her death to 'such one or more of my daughters as shall be single and not have been married'. (He covered every eventuality.)

Hilhouse obviously regarded his extensive collection of paintings as his most valuable possession, and its disposal was of paramount importance to him. He gave very precise directions for what he wanted to happen to them after the death of his wife, and made an interesting distinction between his own works and those of other artists he had collected. On Mary's death, George, again singled out, was to have 'any such six of my oil paintings not painted by myself as he may think proper to have for his own use'. The rest of the oils 'not painted by myself' were to be shared equally among all his surviving children, and the method he set out to do this gives a clear indication that, certainly at the end of his life, Hilhouse was almost obsessively controlling. Not content to leave his children to share the paintings out as it suited them, he stipulated a very exact procedure: 'Each of such children shall have due notice of the time and place for making such division and shall then chuse successively according to seniority of age and so on until each of them has chosen a Picture and then to proceed to a second and such future choice as may be necessary in such manner until the whole are disposed of and if any of my said children cannot conveniently attend such division then it shall be lawful for him, her or them… to nominate any other person or persons to attend and to act for him, her or them.' As for his own pictures, 'All my oil paintings and pictures painted by myself', he gave to George. It would appear from this that he valued these above all the rest.

Once he was satisfied he had made provision for his art collection, Hilhouse could turn to the more mundane matters of providing financially for his family. Again, he had very clear ideas of what he intended, and again, it was to George and his two other executors that he looked to carry out his wishes. First he needed to safeguard the future of the company. His shares in the Albion dockyard site, purchased by him, George and Robert in Bedminster, were to go to George, thus ensuring he had full control of the business. In addition, he willed that:

> any capital money in the trade of shipbuilding and repairing and in any other trade business which I… carry on in partnership with my son George Hilhouse (is) to remain with my said son on his bond to the other trustees.

This settled, he left all his other property to George: the Limekiln dock, his various land holdings leased from the City of Bristol and the Society of Merchant Venturers, including the Hotwells site, his freehold property in Bedminster, the house in Princes Buildings. In return, George and his fellow trustees were to hold in trust the rents and incomes from all the properties, as well as any interest and shares in ships, in order to fund the various provisions he made for his family. This would entail them in quite a lot of work.

The first provision was for Mary, and this was to take precedence over any other charges on the estate. The trustees were to pay her an income of £1,500 a year under the terms of her marriage settlement, to maintain herself and any unmarried daughters living with her; Hilhouse required her 'to supply them with apparel and pocket money'. In addition, each of the three unmarried daughters, Mary Ann, Eleanor and Sarah, was to have £50 a year of her own, not an overly generous amount. The house in Princes Buildings was to be held by the executors for Mary and the unmarried daughters to live in during her life, and it is quite striking how these three young women played on their father's mind. Mary Ann, the oldest, was well into her thirties and was deemed unlikely to marry. Her two younger sisters still at home, Eleanor and Sarah, might marry – as we know, Eleanor did so, two years later – but from his meticulous provision for them, Hilhouse apparently did not expect them to. At the least, he intended to make sure their future was secure. He obviously expected them to continue to live with their mother and even after her death, to stay in the family house in Princes Buildings. He was not totally authoritarian in the matter of where they would live, however: within a year of Mary's death they would be allowed to purchase the house for £2,600, or be given £2,600 each if they decided not to continue living there together. In addition, Mary Ann, as the oldest daughter, was to receive a further £30 per annum. In the event, Mary Ann lived in the house for the rest of her life, while the youngest daughter, Sarah, chose to go to live with her married sister Eleanor on her mother's death. It has to be said that in due course, Mary Ann's will showed much the same autocratic turn of mind as her father's, which may explain her sister's decision.

While perhaps not expecting them to marry, Hilhouse nonetheless had to consider the possibility that they might, so he typically made provision, with £2,000 each to be set aside by his trustees for each of them if they married in their mother's lifetime. He had a healthy distrust of any possible husband's financial motives, however, spelling out in no uncertain terms that this money was to be paid 'into her hand', and that any husband 'with whomever they intermarry' must not 'intermeddle therewith'. Not content with this stricture, he went on to specify exactly and at great length how this money should be divided on the married daughter's death, being divided equally between any 'lawful issue' she might have, or if this lawful issue should die before reaching 21, between the survivors. This management, stretching to his putative grandchildren's generation, seems excessive: he clearly meant to make his presence felt in his family well beyond the grave.

Hilhouse's bequests to the rest of his children are equally revealing. The deceased Robert might have left no 'lawful issue', but this did not mean that he was ignored. The trustees were charged with the duty to pay £100 annually for the maintenance of Robert,

George and James Poole, Robert's 'natural children', 'for as long as they think fit'. No further detail is given, but the mere fact that Hilhouse mentions these children with no explanation suggests that the arrangement their parents had was openly condoned by his family. The irony, of course, is that these were the only grandsons Hilhouse was to have by his sons, and they did not carry his name. Who Mrs Poole was is not known, but coal merchants of that name were beginning business on the wharf close to Hilhouse's Hotwells dock.

Martin, the rather unsatisfactory third son, was left an annuity, but under strict conditions: he was to be paid an annual income of £100 by the trustees 'into his hand' during the term of his natural life, but he could not assign or transfer the money to a third party during his life, the implication being that he was easily taken advantage of and his father did not trust him to deal with money sensibly. More than three close-written pages in the will were taken up with detailed provisions to prevent Martin from disposing of his inheritance, showing just how concerned Hilhouse was in this matter. While recognising his son's fecklessness, he obviously wished to provide for his wife and daughter in the case of his death, not trusting Martin to be able to do so, as he instructed his executors to continue the payments to Martin's widow as long as she remains unmarried.

This solicitude for Martin and his family points to Hilhouse's underlying care for all his children, which makes his treatment of Abraham, an upright citizen and mayor of Bristol, rather surprising: he received only the same £100 annuity as Martin, though with no strings attached. It is just possible that Hilhouse had already made some provision for him, giving him an interest in his grandmother's house in Bath, but apart from to his firstborn, Hilhouse seems not to have been notably generous to his sons. His at that point only married daughter, Caroline was the only one of his children not to receive any bequest, possibly because he had made a settlement on her at the time of her marriage seven years earlier; she was certainly included in the equal share-out of Mary's estate to her surviving children after her death.

These, then, were the terms in which Hilhouse sought to take care of his family and his business after his death. He had looked into the future as far as he could and thought of and provided for every eventuality. His prime aim was to protect the two aspects of his life he cared about most, and presumably died feeling that he had done just that. So how did his legacy work out as time went by?

The years immediately following Hilhouse's death saw several changes in his family. On 1 February 1823, nine months after his father's death, George married his second wife. It is not known what happened to his first, Harriet, who had been a witness at Caroline's wedding in 1815. George was clearly very busy with his civic duties as sheriff of Bristol in 1818, mayor in 1820 and master of the Merchant Venturers in 1822, and it was some time during those years that Harriet died. The couple had no children, and it might be that she suffered from ill health. He married his second wife Mary Walker Chapman in Bridgwater, and with his new wife and recent inheritance they moved into the big Coombe House, Westbury-on-Trym and quickly started a family. Mary Rebecca was born on 8 February 1824 and Anna Chapman two years later.

On 16 September 1824 there was another happy family event when Eleanor married at St Andrew's, Clifton, at the age of 33. Henry Bush, a big man (6 feet 4 inches and apparently the wearer of the largest shoes and gloves in Bristol),[143] was the son of Robert 'Cock and Hen' Bush, Mary Hilhouse's brother, and the grandson of George Bush of the Clift House. This wedding was of course a big affair for both families. Eleanor's brothers George and Abraham were witnesses (though significantly not Martin), as were her sisters, Mary Ann, Sarah and Caroline Allies and Phebe Hilhouse, Abraham's wife, as well as three Bushes and the groom's father, Robert, who died two years later. As both families were so delighted with the match and the bride and groom had known each other since childhood, one wonders why they waited so long, and until after Hilhouse's death, to get married.

After their marriage Henry and Eleanor lived at Litfield Place in Clifton, where he reportedly kept chickens, at first sight an unusual hobby until one recalls his father's nickname: in fact both were well known for breeding and showing poultry. Eleanor was described as 'a tall graceful amiable lady'. The couple had two sons and four daughters, 'all remarkable for height',[144] and their eldest son was named Robert Hilhouse Bush. As we have seen, the Bush children's father was a mighty man, and it would seem that his sister Mary introduced the tall genes into the Hilhouse family. Her youngest son Abraham, in particular, was also exceptionally tall, as the Bristol chronicler Latimer remarked when recounting an episode during the Bristol Riots in 1831.[145]

The next family event, not such a happy one, was the death of Hilhouse's widow Mary in 1827. As he had wanted, she had continued living at Princes Buildings, and through the terms of his father's will, George was her executor. Mary's death, of course, triggered many of the conditions in Hilhouse's will. He had left her his personal effects, which now had to be divided between her unmarried daughters. Mary Ann and Sarah also found themselves having to decide what to do about the family house; it would seem that Sarah was thankful to be offered a home with Eleanor and Henry and their growing family, and she went to live with them for the rest of her life, until she died in 1863. Mary Ann continued to live at Princes Buildings until she died in 1848. Another consequence of Mary's death was that Hilhouse's picture collection now had to be divided up under the terms set out in his will. The gathering of the seven siblings on the day specified for this solemn event can only be imagined, but it paints an intriguing picture. What became of these works of art so lovingly collected by Hilhouse is unknown; Martin probably sold his fairly soon.

So far, Hilhouse's provisions for his daughters' futures had worked well. What of his three sons? As the eldest, George had benefited most from his father's will and was able to keep the company trading in the way he and his father had envisaged. His private life did not run quite so smoothly. After a decade of happy marriage his wife Mary died, leaving him a widower for the second time, but now with two young daughters. Just as before, however, he did not stay a widower for long. He chose for his third and last wife Agatha Barclay, who came from a wealthy family and brought with her a generous marriage settlement of £15,000 and a legacy of £5,000 under her father's will. George was himself a good prospect, being a well respected figure in Bristol and living in affluent circumstances. Theirs was to be a happy marriage; Agatha, though having no children of her own, was a fond stepmother to George's daughters and later, after George's death, made generous provision for them in her will. In 1842, the younger girl, Mary Rebecca, perhaps not wishing to emulate her two aunts and wait until her thirties, married George Cappelen Sawyer at Holy Trinity, Westbury-on-Trym when she was just 18.

As for Hilhouse's beloved business, through the 1830s the shipbuilding and repairing company at the Albion yard, now known as Geo Hilhouse and Company, did well, developing the ship-owning side of the operation and expanding into the China trade as well as building some magnificent ships. There was a good level of activity and some 40 ships were registered as being built by the company in the 1830s.[146] As the decade went on, however, George took increasingly less direct interest in the business, which was being run mainly by Charles Hill. In 1840 George recognised the reality of the situation and renamed the company Hilhouse and Hill, but he nevertheless remained the owner, and before the profits were shared between him and Hill he received a rent of £500 a year for the dockyard and a further £50 in rent for the modest house on the dock occupied by Hill and his family. George's dilemma was that he wanted to retire, but had no sons or other suitable relatives to whom to give or leave his share of Hilhouse and Hill. In the end he resolved the dilemma by transferring the business outright to Charles Hill and retiring entirely. In 1845 the company officially became Charles Hill and Sons, with Charles taking his 16-year-old namesake son Charles out of school as a matter of urgency when he found himself in sole charge. So it was that less than 25 years after Hilhouse's death, the company he had started, though still prospering, no longer bore his name. Quite what he would have thought of this is hard to know. He would have appreciated the reasons behind George's decision, never having been one to duck a difficult decision himself, but this would surely have been a sad day for him.

George's first move after retirement was to sell Coombe House and move with Agatha to Caledonia Place, back in the heart of Clifton near his sister Mary Ann in Princes Buildings and not far from the Henry Bushes in Litfield House. And at this stage he also made his will. Relations with his second wife Mary Chapman's family were still very strong, and he appointed her brother Henry Chapman his executor, along with his brother Abraham, with whom he had always been very close since they shared civic office together all those years ago. The third executor was his son-in-law, George Cappelen Sawyer. The will having been made, George did not enjoy a long retirement; he died in 1848, the same year as his formidable sister Mary Ann.

Charles Hill, died 1867, the same year as Abraham, the youngest Hilhouse son.

Agatha inherited everything from George except his father's paintings. These, which he valued as his father had, he willed to Abraham, trusting that his brother would look after them as he had, and keep them together. Agatha went to live with her sister Lady Lucy Fox in Falmouth and the 1851 census records her living there, at Grove Hill, not only with her sister but three nieces, a nephew and eight servants. She transferred most of the property bequeathed to her by her father and George to Charles Barclay in 1850, but she was generous to George's family in her will, which she made in 1853. She gave legacies to her late husband's two daughters and also to the younger one's husband, George Cappelan Sawyer, who seems to have been well liked and respected in the family. It appears that Anna Chapman Hilhouse, George's older daughter, had by that time also found a husband, John de Courcey Hamilton.

Hilhouse's confidence in George had proved well founded. It would appear that his opinion of his second son, Martin, was equally justified. He managed to hold down his job as harbourmaster until 1843, but unlike his two brothers, who lived in style, he led a more hand-to-mouth existence, keeping only one servant in the house in Dowry Parade, close to his place of work, which he shared with his wife and daughter, both named Emma, and Samuel Wallace, possibly his stepson, until the elder Emma's death in 1840. Hilhouse's assessment of his character was shared by the rest of the family; they had little to do with him socially, though George and his fellow trustees ensured that he had the annuity from his father paid 'into his hand' each year. His sister Mary Ann maintained her concern for

Charles Hill Junior, 1829-1899, taken out of school in 1845 aged 16 to help run the business. Abraham Hilhouse appointed him as executor.

him and in her own very precisely detailed will left him a further annuity, but on the same strict terms: he was not to assign the money or pledge credit against it, and must be paid in instalments 'into his own hand'. By the time Mary Ann and George died, however, Martin had left Bristol. Two years after his wife's death he gave up his job and went with his daughter to live in St Helier in Jersey, where he was described as 'fundholder' – the fund presumably being his annuities. His family's support was enough for him to live on, and after his death in November 1858 they inscribed a tablet to him at St Andrew's Church.

By comparison, Abraham lived a charmed life. His father had obviously not thought he needed to provide for him in his will and the youngest son certainly appears to have done well for himself, though exactly what his line of business was is unclear; for a time he was a stockbroker specialising in company flotations.[147] From a precocious boy he had grown into a large, forceful, expansive man with a strong civic sense who enjoyed life and lived it to the full. As well as being sheriff of Bristol and master of the Merchant Venturers at a very young age, he was also at different times mayor of Bristol and an alderman, magistrate and deputy lieutenant of the county. Let us return to one minor incident from his long career, related by Latimer, who clearly appreciated his robust character. Abraham was an alderman at the time of the Bristol Riots in 1831, but together with his fellow alderman, appears not to have taken the threat too seriously at first. When warned that the rioters intended to storm the Bridewell and 'urged (of) the necessity of immediately guarding the prisons, Alderman A Hilhouse treated the warning very lightly, asserting that the wall and gates "were strong enough"'.[148] He was proved wrong, the situation deteriorated and reinforcements were hurriedly sent for from Gloucester. When their commanding officer, Major Beckwith, arrived at the Council House, 'He was received by the mayor, three or four aldermen and the town clerk. They appeared, he (later) said, bewildered and stupefied with terror. Having requested that one or two magistrates would accompany him on horseback, they individually and positively refused to do so. One of them stated it would make him unpopular; another, that it would cause his shipping to be destroyed; another, his property. They also informed me that none of them knew how to ride on horseback, except one gentleman, and they pointed to the tall alderman Hilhouse. Mr Hilhouse said he had not been on horseback for 18 years, and he would hold anybody responsible who said a second time that he could ride'.[149] The threat was apparently effective. Abraham obviously felt his civic responsibilities did not extend to personally putting down a riot.

In 1812, the year he was jointly sheriff with George at the age of 26, Abraham married Phebe Anne Perry, who was 34. Her family came from Tipperary but they married at St Mary Walcot, Bath. He and Phebe, who had no children, lived in Clifton in Sion Row, later sharing their house with two relatives of Hilhouse's executor the Revd John Shipton of Portishead, the sisters Ann and Ellen Shipton. After Phebe died in 1852 Abraham married the older sister, Ann Noble Shipton in the following year, and the three continued to live together at 23, Sion Hill. In 1858 he was still active in the affairs of the Merchant Venturers and caused a typical outcry when he stoutly maintained that with the proposed removal of Colston's Boys' School from its original site to Stapleton, its purpose should also be changed: he claimed the sons of working men were sufficiently provided for in National Schools, and that the 'great want of the day' were 'schools for the poor sons of decayed good livers, such as bankrupt merchants, bankers, traders, deceased clergy and other professional men'.[150]

It might be that he felt a personal bond with such people, as when he died at the age of 80 in 1867 his estate was under £2,000, a surprisingly small amount for such a prominent citizen. One suspects that having made provision for his widow, to whom he left all his estate, he had felt no need to leave his funds unspent at his death. He was, after all, the last of Hilhouse's children, and had no direct heirs. His will was comparatively simple in its terms, yet typically he had it drawn up not by a local solicitor but by a barrister, Joseph Coates from the Inner Temple in London. He named Charles Hill's son, Charles Hill of Avonmore, as his executor, which shows that though he had never been directly involved in the family business, he retained a close relationship with and respect for the family to whom it had passed. With him died Hilhouse's last surviving direct male descendant bearing his name, and 1867 also saw the death of the first Charles Hill, breaking the last personal link between James Martin Hilhouse and the Bristol shipbuilding company he had founded. Though his company lived on for another 120 years as Charles Hill and Sons, his part as its founder was largely forgotten.

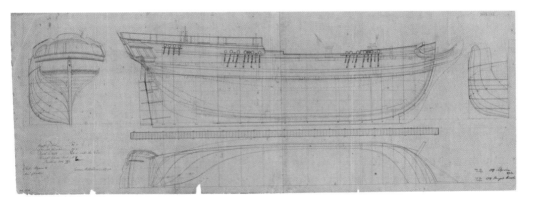

Draught of *Pilgrim* and *Marquess of Worcester.* © National Maritime Museum, Greenwich, London

So what *is* Hilhouse's lasting legacy? The Albion dockyard, which he and his sons set up and where their company traded so successfully until it closed in 1977, still exists and is at the heart of Bristol's maritime heritage as the site of the new Brunel Institute, next to the dry dock to where the SS *Great Britain*, designed by Brunel and built by Charles Hill's competitors, Pattersons, has returned and stands in restored splendour. The replica of the *Matthew*, built in Bristol to mark the anniversary of John Cabot's first voyage to North America, is now berthed in the Albion dockyard, which itself is still in use. Very recently the yard has become the site for the restoration, using traditional building methods, of another ship that represents a memorable episode in Britain's maritime history, the *Medway*. The Kent coast paddle steamer was one of the Dunkirk small boats that took part in the evacuation of British troops in 1940, ensuring the fight could continue. Over and above this, at least one of Hilhouse's own ships still exists, albeit as a wreck. His West Indiaman the *Marquis of Worcester*, launched in 1789, has been discovered lying off Fleet House on Chesil Beach. She was wrecked on 9 December 1797, returning from St Vincent to London. All hands except for one were lost, as were the passengers, 'a Mrs Marden and her two daughters, a lady, a doctor and a young man'.[151] Despite the difficulties, Bristol University maritime archaeologists hope to conduct investigations of the site.

Also surviving are Hilhouse's paintings, drawings, ships' models and plans, of which he had been so proud and which he bequeathed to George. He, in turn, left them to Abraham and he, having no direct heirs, gave them when he died to Charles Hill junior. The collection, also including several plans and draughts by his son Robert, remained with Charles Hill and Company for the next 120 years, and when it finally ceased business the directors ensured its future safe keeping. Some of the pictures and drawings were kept in the Hill family; others were given to the Bristol City Museum and Art Gallery, including the sketches Hilhouse made as preparation for the oil paintings he collaborated on with Nicholas Pocock; others are now in store for the waterside building that will succeed the Bristol Industrial Museum, where there are also his models of the *Mars, Melampus,*

Arethusa and *Medea*, which so clearly demonstrate both Hilhouse's outstanding technical ability and his eye for visual beauty. Yet other items from his collection, along with those personal papers that survived the fire that destroyed so many of the company's records, including his wages books, were donated to the National Maritime Museum at Greenwich. One of his drawings is now at the Red Lodge museum in Bristol; Pocock's *Battle of the Saintes* painting commissioned by the Merchant Venturers on which Hilhouse colaborated, still hangs in the Society's Merchants' Hall; another showing the opening of the battle, signed by Hilhouse, was sold at auction and is now in private hands. Its companion picture, showing the close of the battle, was bought by Bristol Museum and Art Gallery at the same sale. Yet another painting of the battle, initialled by Hilhouse, remains in the Hill family; and yet another, showing the opening of the battle, was sold at auction and is now in private hands. Its companion picture, showing the close of the battle, was bought by Bristol Museum and Art Gallery at the same sale.

As the city continues to interpret and celebrate its long maritime history the contribution made by Hilhouse must be seen as an important part of that story. Bristol owes so much to this one man who had talent, vision and drive, who built on the efforts of his forebears, harnessed the energy of his sons and had the wisdom to include Charles Hill in his future plans; almost single-handedly, he created the city's most successful and long-lived shipbuilding company.

The painting of the Battle of the Saintes bought by the city now hangs in the Art Gallery, an atmospheric and informed depiction of one the Georgian Navy's most famous victories. It can be viewed but should also be contemplated. This was a time when the Navy's importance had been neglected for economic reasons – but thanks to the strenuous efforts of Hilhouse and his workforce and others, it recovered its power and proved that strength at sea was vital to the nation. From that point onwards, throughout the Napoleonic Wars and the prosperity that flourished through the protection of our trade routes, this naval supremacy was relied upon, and we still have cause to be thankful for it today. This is an impressive painting, and it is a very fitting legacy to Bristol from the city's greatest builder of wooden ships, James Martin Hilhouse.

NOTES

Chapter 1

[1] The four periods of war were: Queen Ann's War 1701–1710; The War of the Quadruple Alliance 1718–1720; The War of Jenkins' Ear/The Austrian Succession 1739–1748 and the Seven Years War 1756–1763.

[2] The Burgess Books at the BRO. The more frequent misspelling is Hillhouse.

[3] *The Inhabitants of Bristol in 1696 compiled from 17 parishes and the Castle Precincts* by Elizabeth Ralph and Mary Williams at BCL.

[4] Hill, J.C.G., 1983. *Ship Shape and Bristol Fashion* Redcliffe Press Ltd Bristol. From information obtained in the Glasgow Record Office it appears that James Hilhouse's father was a member of the Brethren and Burgesses of Glasgow and may well have been a successful merchant.

[5] Glasgow Record Office. It is not known why he had the status 'gratis' but it may be because he was not a merchant in the city but had good connections there through his family and that of his new wife.

[6] Registers and Minutes of the Society of Presbyterian Dissenters at Lewins Mead Meeting House 1670–1787. BRO Collections 39461 and 6687.

[7] Ibid 39461/R/1/(a).

[8] *The Annals of John Latimer* are a frequently quoted source of information. Writing at the end of the 19th century, he researched items of interest reported in the newspapers and journals of the time and published them as Annals of the 17th, 18th and 19th centuries. They are referred to as Latimer 18thC etc. BCL has many of the original papers which were also relied upon extensively by Damer Powell in his book referenced below.

[9] *The Members of the Society of Merchant Venturers between 1701 and 1803. Politics and the Port of Bristol in the 18thC* Ed. W.E. Minchinton, Bristol Record Society 1963.

[10] The currency conversion calculator on the National Archives website is used whenever equivalents today are stated. See www.nationalarchives.gov.uk/currency. £1 in 1700 is the equivalent of £78 in 2010 and varies between £85 and £56 in that century and fell sharply in 1800.

[11] *The Trade of Bristol in the 18thC*. Ed. W. E. Minchinton, Bristol Record Society Vol XX 1957.

[12] Hall, I.V., *The Garlicks, Two Generations of a Bristol Family (1692–1781)* and a box of un-indexed papers at BRO on Bristol Sugar Trade.

[13] Abraham and Isaac Elton were successful and influential public figures at the Meeting House and helped the Hilhouses as well as the Garlicks.

[14] A Partnership of 10 Merchants at Old Market to cast 'pig or sow iron, iron pots and other cast iron wares' trading between 1728 and 1757.

[15] Bristol Record Society Probate Inventories Part III 1690–1804.

[16] Correspondence of William Miles and John Tharp 1770–1789. Ed. K Morgan Bristol Record Society Publications Vol XXXVII 1985.

[17] Pares, R. A. West, India Fortune, London 1950. A history of the Pinney Family based upon the

Collection of papers held by Bristol University. They made far more money trading in sugar from Bristol than planting on Nevis.

[18] The Bright–Meyler Papers: 'A Bristol–West India connection 1732–1837'. Ed. K. Morgan *Records of Social and Economic History* New Series 40, 2007.

[19] Capt William Snelgrave published a book in 1734 entitled *A New Account of some parts of Guinea and the Slave Trade* and the book is quoted extensively by George Francis Dow in his book *Slave Ships and Slaving*. Snelgrave recounts that in 1727 he visited the camp of the King of Dahome who had recently conquered the people of Whidaw and on our way 'saw two large stages on which were heaped a great number of dead men's heads that afforded no pleasing sight or smell.' He explains that it was the custom to make slaves of those captured in war but before they had the opportunity to sell them to white people they were often obliged to kill great multitudes – in this instance 4000.

[20] The cost of fitting out a slave ship appears to have been £3000–£4000 and to be profitable a cargo of near full capacity had to be sold. Vessels that failed to deliver more than 50% of their proposed complement of slaves produced financial losses for their owners. See *Bristol, Africa and the Eighteenth Century Slave Trade to America* Vol 1 p.XVIII.

[21] Trade at the Port of Bristol, Minchinton.

[22] HB6 23 October 1740 'Mr Corsley Roper took for a period of seven years at £162 pa the crane and dock formerly let to Mr Hilhouse'.

[23] BRO SMV 2 Archive.

[24] Latimer 18thC p.216.

[25] Letter of Marque for Constantine. See Damer P. pp.143–144 and Starkey p.133.

[26] *Southwell* letter to the captain see Damer P. appendix. Bright's letters to Meyler pp.493–497.

[27] Many authorities. See Damer P. pp.143–144 and Starkey p.133.

[28] Exeter Record Office QS/129 series contains contracts and bonds for the 1750s and 60s and Bright papers mention this partnership see p.280.

[29] N E Somerset Record Office at Bath, ref BC 152/2244, 2819 and BC153/2819/2.

[30] Latimer 18thC p.463 comments on Beavan's List of the values of the estates of local worthies who had made significant fortunes according to contemporary sources.

[31] The Seven Years War was global, involving battles between England and France and Spain in the Mediterranean, North America, West Indies, India and Africa. The opportunities for privateering were greater than ever and after London Bristol had the most commissions.

[32] Barrett records that 15 December 1768 William Hilhouse was chosen as sword bearer in place of John Wraxall deceased. The 1775 Directory has Nathanial Wraxall as a North American merchant.

[33] Cornwallis House was lived in by the Hobhouse family for 100 years, after which it became La Retraite School and is now apartments.

[34] William's sons did not join their cousin in the shipbuilding business. Correspondence held in the British Library from a William Hilhouse written from Demarara in 1826 suggests that his eldest son may have settled there. Henry Parsons Hilhouse is recorded as having granted a lease of a property in Clifton jointly with his mother in 1782 to a John Lewis. Mary married and lived in Bath

and there is no record of any children. Elizabeth may have married John Wilcox and had a son John Hilhouse Wilcox who was Mayor in 1809.

Chapter 2

[35] Woolwich DY Pay Book 1765 ADM 42/1912.

[36] Joseph Harris is named as builder of the 50-gun *Salisbury* at Chatham 1776.

[37] Apprentice Record for Hilhouse at Chatham ADM 42/213-218.

[38] The *Barfleur* and the *Formidable* are the subjects of drawings by Hilhouse based upon his knowledge of their technical construction while at Chatham. They were subsequently used in the paintings of the Battle of the Saintes.

Chapter 3

[39] William Dyer's Diary is an unpublished manuscript at BCL. He wrote a volume for each year between 1750 and 1800 but when he reflected upon them he found them too scandalous. Rashly, he burned them all except one but not before he had compiled a digest. The digest is disappointing and does not seem to be entirely accurate.

[40] BRO SMV 2/4/2/16/18. This important letter from John Noble to Hilhouse may not have been found but for the help of Pat Denny who had been the dedicated curator of this valuable archive at the Society and followed it to the BRO.

[41] Hill, J.C.G. Ibid p.3.

[42] John Noble was on a business trip to London with William Champion and was going to relax at the Hum Mums baths at Covent Garden and maybe go to the Theatre nearby in Drury Lane. Hilhouse understood this life style and it fitted in with that of de Loutherbourg and Garrick.

[43] SMV Archive ref 7/1/3/2.

[44] *The New Bristol Directory* in 1792 states, 'The Merchants Floating Dock exceeds in dimensions any at Portsmouth or Plymouth.' However as a commercial venture for the Merchant Society 'it fell short of expectations' (Minchinton,1972 p.11.) Hilhouse's negotiations secured special rights to use the fitting out facility which proved of considerable benefit not least for the *Medea* who was there for four months.

[45] BRO, SMV Archive but conveniently copied at Appendix 4F fig 15 p.104 in my dissertation at Bristol University.

[46] As above at p.106.

[47] He came from Exeter in 1738 as a fatherless boy. He was apprenticed to Richard Farr and the bond of £300 was put up by an Uncle, Sir John Duntze.

[48] Advertisement for ship *Perkins* in FFJ Hill, J.C.G. Ibid p.4.

[49] Wages Book 1775 NMM HIL/ 1.

[50] *James Sketchley's Bristol Directory* for 1775 has been reprinted with an Introduction by Bryan Little who makes a number of observations. 'Not many seem to have been foreigners, but Welshmen, in those days before the industrial rise of South Wales, were numerous in what was

still a town of ambition for young men from Glamorgan'. There are pages of Jones, Lewis, Morgan Thomas and Williams but only just over one of Smith. Total inhabitants were 35,444 as compared with Liverpool 34,107 and London 651,580.

[51] Sandwich had had to make economies in the Dockyards which resulted in bitter strikes during 1774 and a shortage of shipwrights when they were again required in 1775 there was political panic and Sandwich and Middleton were pressed to approach merchants and a greater number than ever before were built in merchant yards see *The Royal Navy's Recovery* R. J.B. Knight.

[52] It may seem surprising to see sawyers included among the most highly paid but it was of vital importance and ferociously hard work: 'This sawing often went on for days from dawn to dusk, and when in hot weather the sweat and friction rubbed the sawyers armpits raw, fullers earth was dabbed on them.' Anthony Burton quoting from Frank Booker in *The Rise and Fall of British Shipbuilding* p.29.

[53] Holland, A.J.(1971) *Ships of British Oak. The rise and decline of wooden shipbuilding in Hampshire*. p.56. David and Charles, Newton Abbot.

[54] FC/AB/1(T) 1 and see my dissertation pp.140 and 141 for his Burgess oath.

[55] Henry Adams at Bucklers Hard had been trained in the Portsmouth Dockyard and sent to supervise building for the Navy in Lord Montagu's yard. He was persuaded to take over the yard and successfully built many ships there including Nelson's *Agamemnon*.

[56] BCL. 1774 Poll Book.

[57] The auction particulars for the Dock House referred to in chapter four state that in addition to rooms on the first and second floors there were 'boarding Garretts'.

Chapter 4

[58] In January 1775 Petitions against taxes in the colonies were presented by the merchants trading with America at all chief ports but fell upon deaf ears. Within a few weeks 8,000 tons of cargo had to return unloaded because of the blockade. In Bristol the poor rates increased 150 per cent and great distress prevailed. Latimer, C18th, p.415.

[59] Clare was an 'Irish gentleman, risen to immense wealth and high position by three successive alliances to wealthy, fat and cow like widows'. Horace Walpole's *Nugentising* quoted by B. Little op.cit. p.176.

[60] Bright Meyler Papers p.470.

[61] They would go to St. James's church yard, where a special grave had been dug, and, standing on each side of the grave, they would say 'death do us part' and go their separate ways'. *Bristol Sea Port City* p.97.

[62] Damer Powell, W.J. p.275. The advertisement for the cruise by the *Mars* refers to her being built on the approved plan of the famous *Ceres*. She was built at Woolwich 1774–7, indicating that Hilhouse had access to information several years after he left the Dockyard through his contacts at the Navy Board. Unfortunately his father-in-law, George Bush, and associates invested heavily in this venture.

[63] The name *Jackal* was popular in the US Navy for small ships as was *Ferret, Fox* and *Rattlesnake*.

[64] HCA26/63. The Letter of Marque for the *Jackal* shows that Richard Toombs, shipbuilder (and author of the plan for the Floating Harbour) and George Watson, merchant (who participated in privateering ventures with James Jnr) put up the bond for £1500.

[65] Damer Powell,W.J. p.266.

[66] Damer Powell,W.J. p.268.

[67] In the spring of 1779, 'The Directors ordered a barge of pleasure from Mr Hilhouse to convey the assembled worthies down the new navigation.' Michael Handford, *The Stroudwater Canal*, p.315.

Chapter 5

[68] Pool, B., *Navy Board Contracts 1660-1832* p.13. Francis Baylie at Bristol built the 4th Rate *Oxford* in 1674 and was the only merchant to receive an order for one of Pepys's 'thirty ships', the *Northumberland*. This contract did not go well for Baylie, who died before the ship was finished.

[69] Ibid, p.64. Where ships were of a new design the Navy Board considered it 'most adviseable to have them built on the River (Thames) where our eyes would be more over them'.

[70] The discontinuance of the practice of making the first payment on signing the contract and the discounting of the Navy Bills put pressure on cash flow, which Hilhouse could meet by continuing his merchant work.

[71] ADM 106/3072. The contract is reproduced in my dissertation at p.144.

[72] Barnard, J.E. (1997) *Building Britain's Wooden Walls*. Anthony Nelson, Oswestry.

[73] ADM 106/2596.

[74] ADM 106/25960.

[75] Charles Middleton, when he retired as Controller of the Navy, was rewarded with a peerage for his excellent service. Prof. Roger Knight has edited a facsimile reproduction of this comprehensive report.

[76] ADM 106/2596.

[77] Navy Board draught for *Medea* is reproduced at p.62.

[78] ADM B194.

[79] ADM 106/2596.

[80] Latimer, J. 1893 *Annals of Bristol in the Eighteenth Century*, p.434.

[81] Cornwallis–West, (1927). *The Life and Letters of Admiral Cornwallis* p.92.

[82] These records are held at the BCL.

[83] Damer Powell, J.W. p.268.

[84] Duncan, H. (1902). *The Journals of Henry Duncan, Captain, Royal Navy 1776–1782*. The Naval Miscellany, Vol 1 pp.166– 209. Laughton.

[85] John Paul Jones, with his French ship *Bonhomme Richard*, captured the first *Seraphis* by coming along side her and boarding while his sharp shooters with their musketts cleared the decks. His ship was severely damaged in the process and so he took the *Seraphis* back to France. Her captain, Richard Pearson, received a knighthood for his brave resistance. His next ship was Hilhouse's *Arethusa*.

[86] *Protector* was a 26-gun frigate built by the State in 1779. Following her capture she was renamed *Hussar* by the Navy. H.I. Chapelle, *History of American Sailing Ships,* p.61. The *Belisarius* was built as a privateer and said to have been 'one of the fastest sailing ships that swam the Seas.' She was captured when becalmed and subsequently taken into the Navy. Ibid p.139.

Chapter 6

[87] Farr, G.E. (1977) *Shipbuilding in the Port of Bristol.* NMM, London.

[88] Braikenbridge papers at BCL.

[89] Barrett, W. (1789) *The History and Antiquities of the City of Bristol.* Alan Sutton Publishing Ltd., Gloucester.

[90] William Dyer, BCL.

[91] BRO ref 20132/200–209.

[92] Jackson, G.(1972) *Hull in the Eighteenth Century. A Study in Economic and Social History.* Oxford University Press.

[93] Knight, R.J.B. (2003) 'Devil Bolts and Deception? Wartime Naval Shipbuilding in Private Shipyards 1739–1815', *Journal for Maritime Research.* Issue: April 2003. http:www.jmr. nmm.ac.uk/server?show=conJMRArticle.

[94] ADM 1243 and Pool, B. (1966) *Navy Board Contracts 1660–1832* p.97. Longmans London.

[95] ADM/A/2774.

[96] Hart C. (1995) *The Forest of Dean: New History 1515–1818.* Alan Sutton Publishing Ltd., Stroud.

[97] Holland, A.J. (1971) *Ships of British Oak: The Rise and decline of wooden shipbuilding in Hampshire* p.31. David and Charles, Newton Abbot.

[98] Slade's Report is ADM 106/2790 and is reproduced at p.221 of my dissertation.

[99] A comparison of the Hilhouse ships with other Navy ships built in other dockyards and in Royal Dockyards, based on records in ADM series at Kew and Greenwich and research by Lyon, D. (1993) *The Sailing Navy List.* Conway Maritime Press Ltd., London and other sources, is in my dissertation.

[100] ADM A/2728.

[101] ADM 106/2602.

[102] ADM A/2774. Copy in appendix.

[103] Latimer, J. *Annals of Bristol in Eighteenth Century,* p.466.

[104] ADM A/2775.

[105] The Science Museum, London used to keep the Hilhouse collection of draughts but these have now been photographed by the NMM and can be viewed online.

[106] Hilhouse was a skilled model maker and there are four of his ship's models in the Bristol Museum.

[107] On the first trial of the carronade it is reported that the French hauled down their colours after just one broadside.

[108] This family living at Latteridge were informed that Henry Vlll would spend his honeymoon with them and built suitable accommodation for him at Acton Court, recently restored under supervision from English Heritage.

Chapter 7

[109] The earliest St Andrew's Church, Clifton, was rebuilt in 1634 and further enlarged in 1768. Clifton's prosperity and size continued to grow and a larger church was built between 1816 and 1820 next to the old church, demolished in 1822 once the new church was open. This new church was so severely damaged by bombing in 1940 that it was also demolished in 1956. Its site is now a grass lawn and is marked by a plaque.

[110] Rachel Hilhouse moved to Frenchay and a pension was granted to her by the Corporation as William was the Sword Bearer and died in office. She and her son, Robert Parsons Hilhouse, let property in Clifton in 1782 to a John Lewis.

[111] BRO, SMV archive, auction particulars, draft and printed, dated 3 May 1787. These are reproduced in my dissertation p.106.

[112] The names of the Church Warden for each year from 1717 to 1795 are listed. Thereafter there were two wardens each year and they frequently served for more than one year. Some familiar names on the list are William Hollister, Isaac Elton, John Martin, William Gordon and Richard Farr. Also there was a Samuel Poole in 1771. See *Concerning Clifton* A.J. Green-Armitage p.78.

[113] BRO Apprentice Books.

[114] Latimer, 18th C, p.453. The collection amounting to over 200 draughts was known as the Hilhouse collection. Initially the draughts were kept by the Science Museum, London but recently they have been transferred to the National Maritime Museum where they have been photographed and can be viewed online. There is a wide variety of ships, not just war ships but merchantmen, barges and specialist boats. Copies of the plans may be purchased and some are reproduced in this book.

[115] The Osmond Tricks Catalogue for the auction on 5 March 1981; states, 'John (sic) Martin Hilhouse 1750–1822. A 'very fine' late 18th century oil on canvas. Seascape depicting the start of the engagement at the battle of the Saints with the English Fleet under Admiral Rodney and the French Fleet under the Comte de Grasse with the Flag ships and many other vessel already closely engaged. 41' x 65. Signed J.M. Hilhouse. (label to verso. In gilt frame with top rail decorated military trophies.)' Lot 71 is similarly described but as 'fine' and depicting the close of the battle with no mention of any signature.

[116] De Loutherbourg's famous painting, *The Cutting out of the French Corvette La Chevrette*, was a sensation in its time, taken on display throughout the country and reproduced in engravings which sold widely. This grand painting now languishes in the vaults of Bristol's City Art Gallery. His paintings of naval and land warfare and sketches of Industrial Revolution landmarks done on his tours are many. He is particularly known for his entertainment, the Eidophusikon, and his dramatic theatre scenery and effects. See Allen R.G., *The Stage Spectacles of Philippe de Loutherbourg,* PhD Diss. Yale University 1960 and work by Iain McCalman (ANU).

[117] Mackay, C. 1814–1889. *Memoirs of Extraordinary Popular Delusions and Madness of Crowds*, ch.7.

[118] Winter, G. *History of Animal Magnetism*. There are many articles and publications on the internet about Count Cagliostro, some of which must contain a grain of truth about this unbelievable character. Mackay, C. 1814–1889. *Memoirs of Extraordinary Popular Delusions and Madness of Crowds*, ch.7.

[119] Rosamund Bayne Powell asserts that the de Loutherbourgs were not imposters and indeed did not charge for their performances but a third party issued tickets and charged two to three guineas for them. *Eighteenth Century London Life* p.262.

Chapter 8

[120] Waite,V. (1960). *The Bristol Hotwell.* The Bristol Branch of the Historical Association Local History pamphlets.

[121] Thomas Clarkson based himself in Bristol at the Seven Stars public house, which still exists. A visit is recommended as it is a thriving and enjoyable old pub with a lot of information about its past.

[122] Latimer, *Annals of C18th.* p.477.

[123] Ibid. p.477.

[124] Knight, R.J.B. (1993) *Shipbuilding Timber for the British Navy.* Scholars' Facsimiles & Reprints Delmar, New York 1993.p78.

[125] For dockisation schemes see Buchanan and Williams in the Record Society, ibid.

[126] Rich, J. (1996). *The Bristol Pilots.* Anthony Rowe Ltd.

[127] Elkins, (1988) p.28.

[128] In 1800 it was decided that the Mansion House Dinners would sacrifice the second course. (Latimer, p.532) but despite the hard times members voted themselves an increased allowance.

[129] Morgan, K. *North Atlantic Trade in 18th C.*

[130] Farr, G. *Ship Building at the Port of Bristol.*

Chapter 9

[131] Lyon, D. (1993). *The Sailing Navy List.* Some Hilhouse records relating to the contruction are at BRO and there are ship draughts drawn by Robert Hilhouse among the The Hilhouse Collection.

[132] Damer Powell.

[133] William Miles of Herefordshire had made his fortune in Jamaica as a sugar planter. He returned to Bristol and used his experience to become a most successful ship owner and merchant in this trade and a banker. His son PJ Miles lived at Naish House, Clapton in Gordano and then built Leigh Court.

[134] Williams (ibid), gives an account of the *Lady Carrington* leaving the Floating Harbour.

[135] Damer Powell, pp.316–319, describes events involving the *Nelson* and the *William Miles.*

[136] G Farr (ibid) has created a list of ships registered at Bristol in 1815.

[137] Ditto 1816.

[138] Ditto 1817.

[139] Ditto 1818, 19, 20.

[140] Ditto 1822, 23.

[141] BRO.

[142] Thomas William Allies www.newadvent.org/cathen/01323b.htm

Chapter 10

[143] Bristol Worthies at BRO and BCL.

[144] Ibid.

[145] Latimer, *Annals of the Nineteenth Century*, p.171.

[146] Farr G (ibid) lists ships registered in the port of Bristol but not those built for merchants who registered them elsewhere.

[147] BRO, Brice and Burgess Archive contains papers relating to dealings with the shares in the Bristol Dock Company in 1810 when Abraham was in partnership with Mr Palmer who was a well-known figure. The dispute was with a Mr Randall and Abraham was successful in keeping with what is known of his large and straightforward persona.

[148] Latimer, *Annals of the Nineteenth Century*, p.159.

[149] Ibid, p.171.

[150] Ibid, p.363.

[151] Richard Larne, *Shipwrecks off the Dorset Coast*.

APPENDIX

1 Grant of Probate on death of James Hilhouse Junior in 1764

2 Letter from John Noble to Hilhouse at Chatham 9 June 1772

3 The Hilhouse Wages Book pages for the week ending 11 July 1778

4 Lists of Hilhouse Apprentices 1773–1786

5 Indenture and Burges Oath of Charles Stewart

6 Letter from Navy Board to the Admiralty of 24 April 1782

Transcript of the Probate of
James Hilhouse 1 September 1764

KNOW ALL MEN by these Presents that
Mary Hilhouse widow and (Samuel Brice
deleted) John Noble and (William Hilhouse
deleted) Thomas Evans all of the City of
Bristol are held firmly bound unto the Right
Reverend Father in God Thomas by Divine
permission Lord Bishop of Bristol in the sum
of five hundred pounds of good and lawful
money of Great Britain to be paid unto the
said Reverend Father or to his attorney ....
For which payment well and truly made we
bind ourselves... Sealed with seals dated the
First day of September in the year of our
Lord Seventeen Hundred and Sixty Four.
The Condition of this Obligation is such that
if the above bounden Mary Hilhouse widow
and relic of James Hilhouse late of this City
and Diocese of Bristol merchant deceased
and natural mother and also guardian
lawfully assigned to James Martin Hilhouse
a minor and residuary legatee named in the
last Will and Testament of the said James
deceased...Do make or cause to be made a
true Inventory of all and singular the goods
chattels and hereditaments of the said
deceased and the same shall exhibit into the
Registry of the Episcopal Court of Bristol on
or before the last day of December next
ensuing and the same shall be well and faith-
fully administered according to law and the
last will...
And further shall make or cause to be made a
true account of the said administration...

Probate document for will of James Hilhouse
jnr, 1764. The crossing out of the original
executors' names shows that the alterations
were made hastily. John Noble's signature
appears boldly and clearly at the bottom.
Courtesy Bristol Record Office.

Sealed and Delivered
in the Presence of:

Wm Gundry   Mary Hilhouse
              Thos Evans
              John Noble

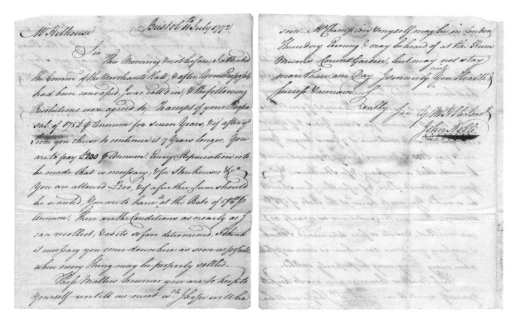

Noble's letter to Hilhouse at Chatham concerning the proposed deal to take over the Merchants Dock at Hotwells, 1772. Note also page 2 of letter has social significance.

Courtesy Bristol Record Office.

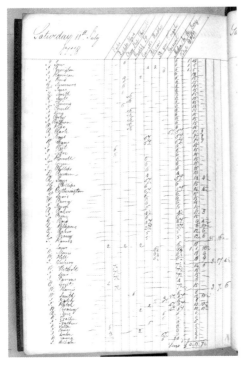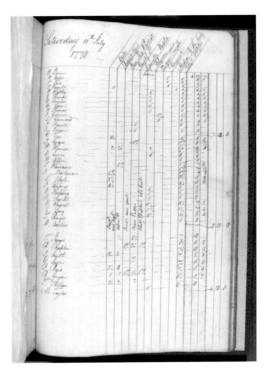

Pages from the Hilhouse wages book showing HMS *Medea* 'to the King'.
The men employed and their task are clearly listed. An explanation is below.
© National Maritime Museum, Greenwich, London.

Hilhouse Wages Book
For week ending 11 July 1788

The two pages above are from Hilhouse's wages book held at the National
Maritime Museum. It is an exceptional record. At the head of each column is the
ship or task worked on and down the side are listed the employees.

The week ending 11 July 1788 was week 29 in the construction of HMS *Medea* and
after a hectic period with much overtime she had been launched in week 27 now
she was being fitted and as this was work beyond the contract it was charged 'to
the King'. Hilhouse needed to meet his other commitments and effort was now
being concentrated upon the merchant ship Pilgrim and there was steady work on
the next two Navy ships HMS *Crescent* and the 'New Frigate' later named HMS
Cleopatra. Some work is being carried out to the docks as usual but now work is
also progressing with the new yard at Redclift.

The shipwrights are listed first from Jones down to Harris and then follow
sawyers and joiners down to Trathen, next come apprentices down to Powell
followed by a miscellaneous group including labourers. At the end is a list of
boatbuilders under I James, a different part of the business.

Apprentice shipwrights indentured to Hilhouse

The Records at the Bristol Record Office have been researched by the author in the first instance to see if a record of Hilhouse's apprenticeship could be found. There was no record and it has now been established that he was apprenticed in the Royal Dockyards at Woolwich and Chatham to Joseph Harris.

Apprentices to Hilhouse are numerous at the BRO and are indicative of a long term strategy and an economic contribution to the local community. They were relatively inexpensive to employ but they had to be fed and lodged as well as responsibly trained.

Apprentices at the time of the *Medea*

Name	Father	Occupation	Address	Date
Thomas Took	Robert Took	Gardiner	Bristol	1/2/73
John Parsons	Henry Parsons	Labourer	Bristol	1/2/73
Will Bracey	Richard Bracey	Labourer	Westbury-on-Trym	1/2/77
John Bevan	John Bevan	Shoe maker	Abbots Leigh	27/4/76
Joseph Brown	Henry Brown	Labourer	Bristol	
Will Seddon	Ralph Seddon	Gardiner	Clifton	
Joseph Cole	Jeremiah Cole	Labourer	Henbury	
William Young	James Young	Dockyard painter	Dockyard	1/5/76
George Thomas	Thomas Thomas	Labourer	?	8/8/76
Thomas Powell	Thomas Powell	Shipwright	Hilhouse Dockyard	8/8/76
John Barry	Joseph Barry	Mariner	Bristol	8/8/76
Patrick Leony	Patrick Leony	Shoe maker	Kingdom of Ireland	8/8/76
Thomas Shilling	Anthony Shilling	Shipwright	Bristol	8/8/76
Benjamin Givium	Benjamin Givium	Labourer	Abbots Leigh	8/8/76
John Dowlin	John Dowlin	Customs Officer	Portbury	8/876
William Pim	Isaac Pim	Baker	East? Somerset	8/8/76
William Hobbly	William Hobbly	Mariner	Late of Dunster	8/8/76
Stephen House	William House	Weaver	Bristol	8/8/76
Lazarus Horwood	James Horwood	Labourer	Long Ashton	8/8/76
John Aldridge	John Aldridge	Mariner	Bristol	12/8/76
Charles Hutton	Charles Hutton	Plantor	The Island of Novis	22/8/76
Wiliam Tyler	William Tyler	Confectioner	Bristol	22/8/76
Stephen Stone	Stephen Stone	Labourer	Gloucester	26/8/78
Stephen Shaw	Stephen Shaw	Labourer	Bristol St George	26/8/78

Apprentices during the Navy Ship building period 1778-1786

BRO, FC/AB/2 (s) 1

At the BRO the indexes FC/AB/2 (s) 1 and FC/AB/1 (t) 1 give lists of apprentices from 1764–1787. In the first series the following appear as apprentices to Hilhouse and his wife Mary:

Phillips 490

Parrot 493

Williams 364

Young 491

Bevan 490

Brown 360

Bracey 362

West 366

BRO, FC/AB/1 (t) 1

Aldridge	Savage 144
Allan 131	Spradd 145
Arthurs 217	Seddon 386
Brocks 196	Stephens 149
Cave 269	Pickford 237
Chambers 302	Pike 258
Davies 338	Powell 53
Dowling 54	Williams 175
Daniel 238	Hill 163
Dyer 216	Shipham 174
Merchant 318	Sellick 204
Pinnington 103	Tregaskes 197
Powell 53	Tanner 303
Price 175	Piddle 175
Phillips 218	Skenford 217
Parry 259	Tyson 217
Rice 239	Stoyer 269
Rogers 282	Smith 322
Richards 317	Stacey 374
Hillings 54	Thomas 52
Stone 58	Williams 144

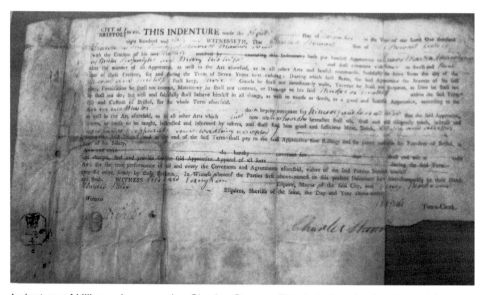

Indenture of Hilhouse's apprentice Charles Stewart. This is in the standard format for apprenticeship agreements. Courtesy Bristol Record Office.

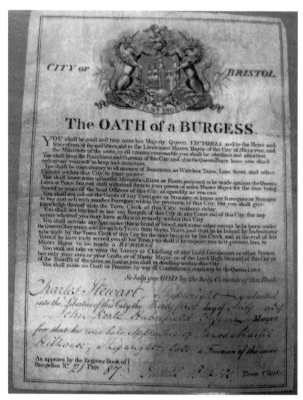

A copy of Charles Stewart's Burgess oath. He later acquired that status by reason of completion of his apprenticeship to Hilhouse.
Courtesy Bristol Record Office.

First page of Navy Board letter to the Admiralty, April 1782,
expressing strong views concerning difficulty of navigation
on the Avon. The transcript is overleaf.

© National Maritime Museum, Greenwich, London.

Transcript of letter of 24 April 1782 (see previous page)

Philip Stephens Esq
Secretary of the Navy Board
To the Admiralty.

In return to your letter of 23 instant enclosing one from JM Hillhouse (sic) offering to build for his Majesty, at Bristol. a Ship of 74 guns, and another of 64 upon the terms therein mentioned. We desire you will pleas to acquaint the Rt. HL Admiralty that the proposal of building Ships of the Line at Bristol has been before more than once and on the most mature consideration postponed until we have acquired more experience of the safety of conducting Ships of a smaller class down this river. The navigation of the Avon is so intricate and hazardous from the rapidity of the tides and the narrowness of the channel that ships of war will take the ground in some parts of it with a falling tide must not only run the hazard of being ruined but also stop the navigation of the River till she could be removed. For these reasons we have proceeded with great caution in building at the Port of Bristol and begun with a Frigate only. We have now ventured as far as a Ship of 50 guns and should she be got down to King Road without difficulty. We will not object to trying a ship of 64 guns but would not wish to proceed further until we have more experience of the River and as this Port is by way of expence is atleast in its consequence 40/- per ton dearer than any other that we build at excepting Liverpool and in point of time at least six months longer in getting them round to King's Port to bere fitted we cannot recomme4nd it as a Port to be used in this way, but in cases of greatest necessity at the beginning of a War when there is a probability of having them in service before the conclusion of it. With respect to the Ship Mr Hillhouse proposes to be built by the Draft of the Triumph, we must observe that we should not even venture to build such a Ship by Contract, in the River Thames.

We are etc..../

REFERENCES

Primary Sources

The Bristol Record Office

The SMV Archive indexed in a series of documents 1–10.

Series 2–Administration–contains the Minutes of Hall Proceedings since 1708. SMV 2/1/2/3 1733–1797.

SMV 2/4/2/18 Letter from Noble to Hilhouse, June 1772.

Series 6–Leases granted by SMV.

SMV 6/1/7/3 Abstract of title to 9 acres of land at Rownham Meade June 1763.

SMV 6/1/7/4 and 5: subsequent transactions.

SMV 6/5/2/12–Lease of Lime Kiln Dock.

SMV 6/2/2/2–Lease of Champions Dock to Hilhouse 11 July 1772 and subsequent leases and The Dock House
    30 August 1781.

Series 7–Trade.

7/1–Ports and Docks.

7/1/3–Merchants Dock. 7/1/3/1 to 16.

7/1/3/5–J. Paty's 1776 Plan of Merchants Dock.

7/1/3/8–Hilhouse Papers.

7/1/4–The Port Development Act 1776 and subsequent management.

The BRO also holds Apprenticeship Records on Microfilm: see FC / AB series and some Hihouse records, eg Timber for the Ship Jamaica (BRO 40578) other records (BRO 36075 and 36079) and the Will of James Hilhouse, father of Hilhouse, made in 1752 and some some Bristol Diocesan Probate papers (but no inventory). The Maps and Plans held there are: Roque 1746, William Champion Plan 1767 (BRLB16614), Donne 1806 (09193), Lavar New Map of Bristol and Clifton 1849.

Bristol Central Library

William Dyer's Diaries 1752–1785. (20095 and 20096)

Felix Farley's Journals 28. 1778 printed, other years on microfilm.

Bristol Mirror and other newspapers 1778–1786 sampled.

Bristol Presentament Book for 1778.

Lloyd's Registers of shipping 1772–1780.

Sketchley's Bristol Directory of 1775 with Donne's New and Correct Plan of Bristol.

Bailey's Western Midlands Directory for 1773.

Bailey's Bristol and Bath Directory for 1787.

The Bristol Directory for 1785.

The New Bristol Directory for 1792.

The New History Survey and Description of the City and Suburbs of Bristol or Complete Guide,
    William Mathews 1794.

The Braikenridge Collection–historical note on Clift House.

Various copy maps and plans Ashmead's 1828 edition and Ordnance Surveys since 1884.

M Shed (formerly a collection in Bristol Industrial Museum)

C 1778 4 foot model of HMS *Medea* hull and models of Hilhouse ships HMS *Arethusa* and HMS *Melampus*.

Manuscript notes by Commander Damer Powell relating to his research into Bristol Navy ships and Privateers.

Various maps and plans relating to dockisation schemes in the late 18th century, particularly Smeaton J. 1775.

Bristol's Museum and Art Gallery

Poole's Wharf, Hotwells Archaeological Excavation. First Draft Report by Jonathan G P Erskine BA MIMgt MIFA and Lee Prosser Ph.D Avon Archaeological Unit 1997.

Artefacts held under Accession number BRSMG 58/1996.

Hilhouse drawings and watercolours, Registered Numbers K5010 to K5025.

Oil painting: *The Close of the Battle of the Saintes*, painted jointly by Hilhouse and Nicholas Pocock. Gallery 4.

Maps: a collection includes most maps between1746 and1828 but most do show the Somerset side of the river at Clift House, exceptions are Tombs 1793, Plumley 1813 and later Ashmead 1828.

The Bristol and Gloucestershire Archaeological Society Library

Clifton Antiquarian Club, volume. v. Paper by Latimer on Roque's map given 28 November 1900.

Bristol University Library

Collection of studies of Records at the BRO under the supervision of Ralph and Minchinton, volumes 1 and 5.

MacMillan, J.G. (2003) *The port of Bristol during the latter part of the Eighteenth Century; An in depth Review of its operations and of its limitations as a Functional port.* MA Dissertation.

Hooper, J.G. (1963) *A Survey of Music in Bristol with Special Reference to the Eighteenth Century.* MA Thesis pp.200–205.

Whitefield, A.T.E. (2007) *How did James Martin Hilhouse build ships for the Navy at Bristol, 1776–1786?* MA Dissertation.

The National Archive

Admiralty In Letters: 1778 ADM 106/1243–1290 letter H.

Navy Board Out Letters: 1778ADM 106/2206–1785 ADM 2212.

Navy Board Minutes : 1777 ADM 106/2595–1786 2620.

ADM 7 Muster Books for *Medea*: 7/441–447.

ADM 106 / 3072 *Viper* ship building contract.

ADM 106 / 3615 supplies contracts.

Dockyard Pay Books in Ordinary and Extraordinary at Woolwich:
> ADM 42/1912–1914.

Dockyard Pay Books in Ordinary and Extraordinary at Chatham:
> ADM 42 / 213–218.

ADM 49 / 36 Ships in Merchant Yards 1740–1810.

ADM 49 / 94 Ship building by merchants 1784–1797.

ADM 52 / 2393 Captains' logs.

ADM 95 /4, 5, 6, 7, 36, 37, 46, 67, 83, 84, 94 shipbuilding sailing qualities.

ADM 174/ 17, 18, 116, 173 ; ADM 180/26. Navy Board correspondence with Plymouth Dockyard.

Various Hilhouse Family Wills proved at Canterbury.

The National Maritime Museum

ADM A/ 2699–2788.

ADM B/193–195.

ADM B . P . / 1, 2, 3, 4, 5,6 a, 6b.

ADM E/ 47.

ADM F/ 29.

Middleton Papers.

MID /8/1. Shipbuilding.

The Hilhouse Collection:

HIL/1 Manuscript Wages Book 1775–78.

HIL/2 Manuscript Wages Book 1779–83.

HIL/3 Manuscript Wages Book 1786.

HIL/9 1779 ship building materials and ship supplies ledger.

Ship Plans at the Brass Foundry, Woolwich.

The Science Museum, London

Model of HMS *Cleopatra*.

Hilhouse collection of draughts (now accessed through NMM)

Secondary Sources

Albion, R.G. (1926) *Forests and Sea Power. The Timber Problem of the Royal Navy 1652–1862*. Harvard University Press, Cambridge.

Baker, W.A. (1966) *Sloops and Shallops*, University of South Carolina.

Ballard, M. (1966) Bristol: *Sea–Port City*. Constable Young Books Ltd, London.

Banbury, P. (1971) *Ship builders of the Thames and Medway*. David and Charles, Newton Abbot.

Barnard, J.E. (1992) *John Barnard the Younger, Shipbuilder of Ipswich and Harwich, 1705-1784. Mariners Mirror*, Volume 78. No. 2 (May 1992) pp.155–175.

Barrett, W. (1789) *The History and Antiquities of the City of Bristol*. Alan Sutton Publishing Ltd. Gloucester.

Barnard, J.E. (1997) *Building Britain's Wooden Walls*. Anthony Nelson, Oswestry.

Baugh, D.A. (1998) *Why did Britain lose command of the Sea during the War for America? In the British Navy and the use of Naval Power in the Eighteenth Century*. Black, J. and Woodfine, P. (eds) Leicester University Press.

Bayne–Powell, R. (1937) *Eighteenth Century London Life*. John Murray, London.

Black, J. (2004) *The British Seaborne Empire*. Yale University Press, New Haven and London.

Blake, B. (1946) *British ships and Shipbuilders*. Collins, London.

Bristol and Gloucestershire Archaeological Society Volume LXXXV111 pp.184–204.

Buchanan, R.A. (1969) *Construction of the Floating Harbour in Bristol: 1804–1809*. Transactions of the

Burton, A. (1994) *The Rise and Fall of British Shipbuilding*. Constable, London.

Chappelle, H.I. (1935) *The History of American Sailing Ships*. Bonanza Books, New York.

Coad, J.G. (1989) *The Royal Dockyards 1690–1850*. Scholar Press Aldershot.

Coad, J.G. (1992) *The Development and Organisation of Plymouth Dockyard 1689–1815*, in the *New Maritime History of Devon*. Conway Maritime Press and the University of Exeter.

Cordingly, D. (1986) *Nicholas Pocock 1740–1821*. Conway Maritime Press in Association with the NMM.

Damer Powell, J.W. (1930) *Bristol Privateers and Ships of War*. J.W. Arrowsmith Ltd., Bristol.

Davies, R. (1972) *The Rise of the English Shipping Industry in the Seventeenth and Eighteenth Centuries*. David and Charles, Newton Abbot.

Doe, H. (2009) *Enterprising Women in shipping in the Nineteenth Century*. Boydell and Brewer, Woodbridge.

Dow, G.F. (2002) *Slave Ships and Slaving*, Dover Publications, Inc. New York.

Dresser, M. and Ollerenshaw, P. (1996) *The Making of Modern Bristol*. Redcliffe Press, Bristol.

Duncan, H. (1902) *The Journals of Henry Duncan, Captain, Royal Navy, 1776–1782. The Naval Miscellany*, Volume.1, p.166–209. Laughton, P (ed)

Edwards, T. (1951) *Bristol*. Batsford, London, New York.

Elkin, P. (1988) *Aspects of the recent development of the port of Bristol. In Waterfront Archaeology*, 3rd International Conference on Waterfront Archaeology, Bristol, pp.27–35.

Ehrman, J. (1966) *The Younger Pitt. [Volume 3], The Consuming Struggle*. Constable, London.

Farr, G.E. (1963) *The History of Bristol Ships 1800–1838*. The Bristol Record Society, Bristol.

Farr, G.E. (1971) *Bristol Shipbuilding in the Nineteenth Century*. Bristol Historical Association, Bristol.

Farr, G.E. (1977) *Shipbuilding in the Port of Bristol*. National Maritime Museum, London.

Farr, G.E. (1953) *Bristol Channel Pilotage: Historical Notes on Administration and Pilotage*. Mariners Mirror 39, pp.27–44.

Fellowes, J. (1974) *Shipbuilding at Sheerness: The Period 1750–1802. Mariners Mirror* 60, pp.73–85.

Frank, J. (1872) *The Diary of Sarah Fox nee Champion Bristol 1745–1802*. Bristol Record Society's Publication Volume. 55.

Gardiner, L. (1968) *The British Admiralty*. L. Gardiner.

George, E. and S. (2008) Bristol Probate Inventories, Part 3 1650–1804. Bristol Record Society, Volume 60, Bristol.

Goldenberg, J.A. (1973) *An Analysis of Shipbuilding Sites in Lloyd's Register of 1776*. Mariners Mirror 59, pp.419–435.

Goodwin, P. (1987) *The Construction and Fitting Out of the Sailing Man of War 1650–1850*. Conway Maritime Press, London.

Greenacre, F. (2005) *From Bristol to the Sea*. Redcliffe Press Ltd., Bristol.

Green-Armytage, A.J. (1922) *Concerning Clifton. A Historical narrative from Saxon times until this present day*. J. Baker & Son, Clifton.

Hall, I.F. (1961) *The Garlicks, Two Generations of a Bristol Family (1692–1781)* Transactions of the Bristol and Gloucestershire Archaeological Society pp.132–159.

Handford, M. (1979) *The Stroudwater Canal*. A. Sutton, Gloucester.

Hart, C. (1995) *The Forest of Dean. New History 1515–1818*. Alan Sutton Publishing Ltd., Stroud.

Hill, J.C.G. (1983) *Ship Shape and Bristol Fashion*. Redcliffe Press Ltd., Bristol. (2nd ed)

Hobson, J. (2010) 'Bristol and the Foundation of its Madrigal Society'; published in *A Grand City–Life, Movement and Work,* Bristol and Gloucestershire Archaeological Society, (ed) Crosseley Evans, M.J.

Holland, A.J. (1971) *Ships of British Oak. The rise and decline of wooden ship building in Hampshire.* David and Charles, Newton Abbot.

Howard, F. (1979) *Sailing Ships of War 1400–1860.* Conway Maritime Press, Greenwich.

Hunt, W. (1887) *Bristol.* Longmans, Green & Co., London.

Hutton, S. (1907) *Bristol and its Famous Associations.* Arrowsmith, Bristol.

Jackson, G. (1972) *Hull in the Eighteenth Century. A study in economic and social history.* Oxford University Press.

Jackson, G. (1983) *The History and Archaeology of Ports.* World Works Ltd.

Jones, A.G.E. (1972) *Shipbuilding in Ipswich, 1750-1800.* Mariners Mirror, Volume 58, No. 2, 1972. pp.183–194.

Jones, D. (1992) *A History of Clifton,* Phillimore and Co Ltd., Chichester.

Jones, D. (2003) *Bristol's Sugar Trade and Refining Industry.* Bristol Branch of the Historical Association. M Local History Pamphlets No 89.

Jones, P. (2007) *Satan's Kingdom: Bristol and the Transatlantic Slave Trade.* Past & Present Press, Bristol.

King, A. (2003) *The Port of Bristol.* Tempus Books.

Knight, R.J.B. (1971) *Sandwich, Middleton and Dockyard Appointments.* Mariners Mirror volume 57, pp.175–192.

Knight, R.J.B. (1973) *The Introduction of Copper Sheathing into the Royal Navy, 1779–1786. Mariners Mirror* volume 59 pp.299–309.

Knight, R.J.B. (1993) *Shipbuilding Timber for the British Navy.* Scholars' Facsimilies and Reprints, New York.

Knight, R.J.B. (1994) *The Royal Navy's Recovery after the Early Phase of the American Revolutionary War in the Aftermath of Defeat.* Yale University Press, New Haven. Andreopoulos, G.J. and Selesky, H.E. (eds)

Knight, R.J.B. (2003) 'Devil Bolts and Deception? Wartime Naval Shipbuilding in Private Shipyards 1739–1815'. *Journal for Maritime Research.* Issue: April 2003. http://www.jmr.nmm.ac.uk/server?show=conJMRArticle.

Lacey, M. (1773) *The Female Shipwright.* National Martime Museum, Grennwich. Edn 2008.

Large, D. (1984) *The Port of Bristol 1848–1884.* Bristol Record Society, Bristol.

Latimer, J. (1893) *The Annals of Bristol in the Eighteenth Century.* John Latimer, Bristol.

Latimer, J. (1887) *The Annals of Bristol in the Nineteenth Century.* W. & F. Morgan, Clare Street, Bristol.

Lavery, B. (1991) *Building the Wooden Walls. The Design and construction of the 74 Gun Valliant.* Conway Maritime Press, London.

Lavery, B. (1987) *The Arming and Fitting of English Ships of War 1600–1815.* Conway Maritime Press, London.

Lavery, B. (1983) *The Ship of the Line Volume 1. The development of the battle fleet 1650–1850.* Conway Maritime Press Ltd., London.

Little, B. (1971) *Sketchley's Bristol Directory 1775.* Kingsmead Reprints, Bath.

Little, B. (1954) *The City and County of Bristol; A Study in Atlantic Civilisation.* Werner Laurie, London.

Lloyd Phillips, I. (1978) *Lord Barham at the Admiralty, 1805–1806.* Mariners Mirror vol 64 pp.217–233.

Lyon, D. (1993) *The Sailing Navy List.* Conway Maritime Press Ltd., London.

MacInnes, C.M. (1963) *Bristol and the Slave Trade.* Bristol Branch of the Historical Association; 7, Bristol.

Malpass, P. and King, A. (2009) *Bristol's Floating Harbour: The first 200 Years.* Redcliffe Press, Bristol.

Marsh, A.J. (1992) *The Local Community and the Operation of Plymouth Dockyard, 1689–1763.* In the *New Maritime History of Devon*, Conway Maritime Press and the University of Exeter, pp.201–208.

Marcus, G.J. (1975) *Heart of Oak. A Survey of British Sea Power in the Georgian era.* Camelot Press Ltd., Southampton.

May, W.E. (1999) *The Boats of Men-of-War.* Chatham Publishing, London.

McGrath, P. (1975) *The Merchant Venturers of Bristol: A history of the Society of Merchant Venturers of the City of Bristol from its origin to the present day.* The Society of Merchant Venturers, Bristol.

McGrath, P. (1985) *Bristol Miscellany Miles Tharp correspondence.* Bristol Record Society publications vol. 37.

McGrath, P. (1972) *Bristol in the Eighteenth Century.* David and Charles, Newton Abbot.

McGrath, P. (1970) *John Whitson and the Merchant Community of Bristol.* Bristol Branch of the Historical Association, Bristol.

McGrath, P. (1950) *The Merchant Venturers and Bristol Shipping in the Early Seventeeth Century.* Society for Nautical Research, London.

Minchinton, W.E. (1962) *The Port of Bristol in the Eighteenth Century.* The Bristol Branch of the Historical Association.

Minchinton, W.E. (1963) *Politics and the Port of Bristol in the Eighteenth Century.* Bristol Record Society.

Minchinton, W.E. (1972) *The Port of Bristol in the Eighteenth Century* in McGrath, P., *Bristol in the Eighteenth Century.* David & Charles, Ltd., Newton Abbot, pp.127–161.

Minchinton, W.E. (1995) *The Trade of Bristol in the Eighteenth Century.* Bristol Record Society publications volume 20, Bristol.

Morriss, R. (1983) *The Royal Dockyards during the Revolutionary and Napoleonic Wars.* Leicester University Press, Leicester.

Morriss, R. (1992) *Industrial Relations at Plymouth Dockyard, 1770–1820.* In *The New Maritime History of Devon.* Conway Maritime Press and the University of Exeter, London, pp.209–215.

Morriss, R. (1983) *St Vincent and Reform, 1801–04.* Mariners Mirror Volume 69 pp.269–290.

Morgan, K. (1993) *Bristol and the Atlantic Trade in the Eighteenth Century.* Cambridge University Press.

Morgan, K. (2007) *The Bright–Meyler Papers: A Bristol West India Connection, 1732–1837.* O.U.P.

Morgan, K. (2000) *Slavery and Servitude in North America 1607–1800.* BAAS Paperbacks, Edinburgh University Press.

Pares, R. (1950) *A West India Fortune.* Longmans, Green, London.

Pool, B. (1966) *Navy Board Contracts 1660–1832.* Longmans, London.

Pool, B. (1963) *Some Notes on warship building by contract in the Eighteenth Century.* Mariners Mirror Volume 49 pp.105–119.

Powell, A.C. (1925) *Glass Making in Bristol.* Transactions of the Bristol and Gloucestershire Archaeological Society, Volume 67, pp.211–259.

Press, J. (1976) *The Merchant Seamen of Bristol, 1745–1789.* The Bristol Branch of the Historical Association; 38, Bristol.

Pryce, G. (1861) *A Popular History of Bristol.* W. Mack, 52 Wine Street, Bristol.

Rediker, M (1987) *Between the Devil and the Deep Blue Sea. Merchant Seamen, Pirates and the Anglo-American World, 1700–1750.* Cambridge University Press.

Reid, H. (1992) *A Chronicle of Clifton and Hotwells.* Redcliffe Press Ltd., Bristol.

Reid, W.N. and Hicks, W.E. (1934) *Leading Events in the History of the Port of Bristol.* W.C. Hemmons, Bristol.

Rich, J. (1996) *The Bristol Pilots.* Anthony Rowe Ltd. (out of print, copy at BCL.)

Richardson, D. (1986) *Bristol Africa and the Eighteenth Century Slave Trade to America, Volumes 1–4.* Bristol Record Society Publications.

Sandwich Papers, Vol IV. Naval Record Society, Vol LXX, V111

Stewart-Brown, R. (1932) *Liverpool Ships in the Eighteenth Century, including the King's Ships built therewith Notes on the Principal Shipwrights.* The University Press of Liverpool, Hodder & Staughton, London.

Stone, G.W. and Kahri, G.M. (1979) *David Garrick, A critical Biography.* Southern Illinois University Press.

Sutton, J. (1981) *Lords of the East.* Conway Maritime Press, London.

Syrett, D. (1988) *The Failure of the British Effort in America, 1777,* in Black, J. and Woodvine P. (eds)

Syrett, D. (1991) *Home, Wales or America? The Dilemma of British Naval Strategy in 1778. Mariners Mirror* 77, 1991, pp.365–377.

Thomas, E. (1983) *The Shirehampton Story,* E. Thomas.

Vanes, J. (1977) *The Port of Bristol in the Sixteenth Century.* Historical Association, Bristol.

Waite, V. (2002) *The Bristol Hotwell.* The Bristol Branch of the Historical Association, Bristol.

Webb, P.L.C. (1997) *The Rebuilding and Repair of the Fleet, 1783–1793.* In Institute of Historical Research, Volume 1. University of London.

Webb, P.L.C. (1988) *Construction, Repair and Maintenance in the Battle Fleet of the Royal Navy 1793–1815,* in Black, J. (ed), pp.207–221.

Webb, P.L.C. (1996) *The Frigate situation of the Royal Navy 1793–1815.* Mariners Mirror 82, pp.28–40.

Wells, C. (1909) *A Short History of the Port of Bristol.* Arrowsmith Ltd, Bristol.

Williams, A.F. (1962) *Bristol Port Plans and Improvement Schemes.* Transactions, Bristol and Gloucestershire Archaeological Society, volume 81, pp.138–188.

Williams, D.M. (2000) *Merchants and Mariners: Selected Maritime Writings.* International Maritime Economic History, St. John's, Newfoundland.

Winfield, R. (1997) *The Fifty-Gun Ship.* Chatham Publishing Ltd., London.

INDEX

Numbers in **bold** are illustrations